Models for Library Management, Decision-Making, and Planning

Library and Information Science

Consulting Editor: *Harold Borko*
Graduate School of Library and Information Science
University of California, Los Angeles

This list of books continues at the end of the volume.

Models for Library Management, Decision-Making, and Planning

Robert M. Hayes

ACADEMIC PRESS

A Harcourt Science and Technology Company

Academic Press
A Harcourt Science and Technology Company
525 B Street, Suite 1900, San Diego, California 92101-4495, USA
http://www.academicpress.com

Academic Press
Harcourt Place, 32 Jamestown Road, London NW1 7BY, UK
http://www.academicpress.com

Library of Congress Catalog Card Number: 2001092379

International Standard Book Number: 0-12-334151-5

Printed in the United States of America

01 02 03 04 05 06 SB 9 8 7 6 5 4 3 2 1

Contents

2

Library Decision-Making Contexts   31

3

The Library Planning Model   58

4

Library Operational Requirements   84

5

Services to Library Users   99

6

Processing of Library Materials

7

Institutional Requirements   161

8

Information Production and Distribution   187

9
Libraries Within Larger Structures   219

Preface: The Purpose, Contexts, and Structure of the Book

Purpose

The purpose of this book is to provide an overview of models that are of utility for library management, decision-making, and planning. Many of the models to be covered are quantitative in the sense that they consist of mathematical equations that embody variables that are measurable and produce results that are quantitative. Such models are similar to those that characterize the natural sciences and, in some respects at least, they can be used to test their own validity. That is, they can serve as the basis for hypotheses that can then be tested by experiment. Beyond that, just as the equations underlying models in the physical sciences can serve as means for engineers to design structures, the quantitative models for library management can be used as means to explore the effects of alternative values for variables, to determine the best choices for a management decision and to engineer the design of new library systems. Perhaps of most fundamental importance, they provide means for learning about the world of library management.

Most of the quantitative models presented in the text have been incorporated into a computer spreadsheet, the *Library Planning Model (LPM)*, that provides a structure within which the several models presented in the book can be interrelated and easily brought together for application to specific libraries and policy contexts.

However, the nature of libraries as institutions of society is that many of the issues of greatest importance in management cannot be well represented by quantitative models and may even be badly misrepresented by them. In fact, the attempt to draw parallels with the natural sciences can lead to an unwarranted belief in the efficacy of quantitative models. The facts are that, unlike the phenomena of the natural sciences, those of the social sciences are governed primarily by the goals of the participants in them. Measurable variables may simply describe what has happened, not why it has happened. Of course, sometimes quantitative models can be designed to represent those goals, and some models will be presented in the book that do so. But for most decision problems in libraries, such goal-oriented quantitative modeling is still remote.

Therefore, among the models presented are some that are essentially qualitative and descriptive. That by no means diminishes their value and utility; it simply means that they must be dealt with in ways different from quantitative models. Some of these qualitative, descriptive models have also been incorporated into *LPM,* even though only in a preliminary form, so as to provide a framework within which quantitative aspects of such models might be developed and related to the entire set of models for library management.

Contexts

In the discussions of applications of models to libraries as well as their representation in *LPM,* three management contexts are considered. The first, operational management, focuses on the day-to-day operational tasks of the library. The second, tactical management, focuses on the allocation of resources, including money, staff, and facilities; it is the context in which decision-making is likely to be of most importance. The third, strategic management, focuses on things that are external to the library and over which the library manager usually has little if any control but that vitally affect the management in every respect; it is the context in which planning is most crucial.

As will be described below, Part 2 of the book presents models for operational and tactical contexts, and Part 3 presents models for strategic contexts. Specifically, the workloads that drive library operations and that determine the allocation of resources within the library are the focus of Part 2. But they are largely, if not totally, determined by forces external to the library, and those are the focus of Part 3.

Most directly, as covered in Part 3, the institution within which the library operates determines the nature of uses to be served and the magnitude of budget to fund the operations. Decisions made in the publishing community determine what information materials will be distributed and how they will be distributed. Schematically, the following flowchart shows the relationship of these two of the strategic contexts to the elements that are specific to the library:

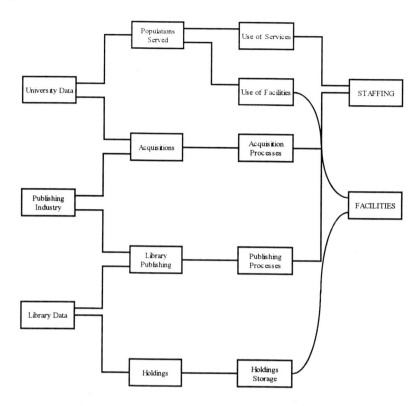

The impact of the third strategic context included in Part 3, national information policies, is perhaps less direct but still it is of such fundamental importance that it needs to be recognized in library management, decision-making, and planning. Decisions made by governments, at every level, determine the economic, political, and legal environment within which the library must operate. Of special significance are interlibrary cooperative developments, many of which are made within the framework of such international, national, regional, state, and local policies. They have direct impact on decisions that might appear to be internally determined but that actually depend upon the larger strategic contexts.

Structure

The structure of the book reflects this set of contexts, and the nine chapters of the book conceptually should be considered as grouped in three parts.

Part 1. Scientific Management and the Library Planning Model

Part 1 consists of Chapters 1 through 3. Chapter 1 discusses the nature of scientific management and the use of models to support general management, decision-making, and planning. Chapter 2 then places special emphasis on their applications to libraries and information policy issues in a range of library management decision contexts and, in doing so, sets the stage for the detailed discussions in the ensuing two parts. Chapter 3 presents an overview of *LPM*, its conceptual structure and its operational structure, as the tool for bringing together several of the models for use on the kinds of decision problems discussed in Chapter 2.

The purpose of Part 1 is to provide a general introduction to the concepts and methods of modeling as they are relevant to library management. It concludes with the overview of *LPM* to provide knowledge about this tool so that easy reference can be made to it in subsequent sections.

Part 2. Library Operational and Tactical Management Contexts

Part 2 consists of Chapters 4 through 6 and deals with operational and tactical issues in library internal management. Chapter 4 presents a framework for estimating staff, materials, facilities, and associated costs needed to handle workloads for typical services and internal operations in a library. Within that framework, Chapter 5 presents models for representing the needs of users and related library services, for estimating the associated staffing, and for determining the needs for space and facilities to serve users and staff. Chapter 6 similarly presents models for representing the acquisition of materials and the related technical processing, for estimating the associated staffing, for determining requirements for storage of materials, and for making the related decisions concerning allocation of materials to alternative means for storage and access.

Part 3. Library Strategic Management Contexts

Part 3 consists of Chapters 7 through 9 and deals with strategic issues, those that are essentially external to the library but that must be considered in library management. Specifically, Chapter 7 presents models of institutional requirements, representing the needs to be served by the library, not as determined by library acquisitions, services, and internal processes but rather as they are determined by the institution's own objectives. Chapter 8 discusses models for representing the past, present, and future status of means for information production and distribution, representing the context of information resources that are the basis for library acquisitions and services. Among the topics considered is the potential and, in some cases, actual role of libraries as publishers, and models are presented for assessing the impact of such a role on library operations. Special emphasis is given to the impact of digital libraries and of Internet access to them. Chapter 9 presents models of larger information structures, with special emphasis on the impact of information on national economics and on the role of libraries within them. It includes discussion of interlibrary cooperation as a critical example of larger information structures.

Summary

The following table summarizes the array of models presented in the book, identifying the chapters in which they are each discussed and the management issues to which they each apply.

Model	Chapter	Applications
Cooperative Game Model	1, 9	Library Cooperation
Cobb–Douglas Econometric Model	1, 5, 9	Balance Between Investment &
Staff		
Leontief Matrix Model	1, 9	Structure of Information Economy
Systems Analysis Model	1	Planning & Design
Cost Accounting Model	1–9	All Applications
Workload Factor Model	1–9	All Applications
Organization Chart Model	1	Management Structure
Operations Matrix Model	1	Management Structure
Frequency of Use Model	5	Services to Users
Population Growth Model	5	Services to Users
Queuing Model	5	Services to Users
Ratio of Level of Use to Average		
Use Model	5	Services to Users
Facility Use Factors Model	5	Services to Users
Library Location Models	5	Services to Users
Collection Growth (1)		
Exponential Model	6	Collection Management
Collection Growth (2)		
Linear Model	6	Collection Management
Collection Growth (3)		
Steady-State Model	6	Collection Management
Collection Growth (4)		
Logistic Model	6	Collection Management

(continues)

Model	Chapter	Applications
Collection Use (1)		
Zipf Law Model	6	Collection Management
Collection Use (2)		
Mixture of Poisson Model	6	Collection Management
Collection Use (3)		
Date Related Model	6	Collection Management
Allocation Decision Model	6	Storage Location Decision
Allocation Decision Model	6	Acquisition vs. Access Decision
Allocation Decision Model	6	Serial Deacquisition Decision
Inflation Distribution Model	6	Serial Deacquisition Decision
Collection Development (1)		
Clapp-Jordan Model	6	Collection Management
Collection Development (2)		
Voigt-Susskind Model	6	Collection Management
Collection Development (3)		
Budget-based Model	6	Collection Management
Collection Development (4)		
Peer Comparison Model	6	Collection Management
Governance Model	7	Information Management
Information Value (1)		
Entropy Model	8	Information Distribution
Information Value (2)		
Weighted Entropy Model	8	Information Retrieval
Information Value (3)		
Information Structure Model	8	Information Production
Information Value (4)		
Information Reduction Model	8	Information Production
Information Value (5)		
Combinatorial Model	8	Information Production
Accounting Standards for Information		
Investment Model	8	Information Production
Library Networks (1)		
Structural Model	9	Library Networks
Technology Development (1)		
Grosch's Law	7	Technology Management
Technology Development (2)		
Moore's Law	7	Technology Management
Library Networks (2)		
Communication Traffic Model	9	Library Networks
Library Networks (3)		
Response Time Model	9	Library Networks
Library Networks (4)		
User Response Model	9	Library Networks
Library Networks (5) Cost Trade-off Model	9	Library Networks
Information Economy Model	9	Libraries in the Economy

1

Scientific Management

Introduction

Scientific management, as represented by operations research or, more generally, by the use of quantitative methods in support of decision-making, should be seen as the last among five means for decision-making: (1) forces of the marketplace, (2) political negotiation, (3) fiat or personal decision, (4) social, ethical, and moral objectives, and (5) formulas or quantitative methods. It is important to note that, in the context of real organizations, the use of quantitative methods is simply a tool, a support to the processes involved in the other four. In fact, it is frequently the case that quantitative methods will be used not to make decisions but to provide support to decisions that have already been made. In that respect, a major issue in the use of quantitative methods is determining what may be needed to assure that the data used adequately reflect the decision-making priorities; frequently the choice of data to be used is itself a political process. This is in sharp contrast to the use of quantitative methods in the physical sciences and, perhaps, in the biological sciences, in which they are the crucial, even ultimate, basis for decision-making.

The bibliography at the end of this chapter includes a number of references for scientific management and the more general use of models that should provide a useful starting point for identifying the most recent literature. Included among the references are several that exemplify pitfalls in the use of models and, most specifically, the role of political, social, ethical, and moral agendas in the choice of models and variables to be included in them.

Scientific management can be defined as an attitude of mind, a belief in the use of the scientific method—with its emphasis on definition of basic assumptions, measurement, experimentation, quantified evaluation, and repeated reexamination of assumptions and results. The belief is that use of the scientific method can produce better management than blind acceptance of existing practice or the choice of alternatives by intuition. It is debatable whether the underlying belief in the power of scientific method is valid. There are just too many issues in the management of large organizations, including libraries,

1

which are not amenable to measurement or experimentation. But there is little
question about its value as an aid to management.

1.1
Models to Support Management

Louis D. Brandeis probably first made the phrase "scientific management"
publicly known when he used it in October 1910 to describe the application
of scientific methods to management issues.[1] Since then it has been a continuing theme of modern management, gaining acceptance in an ever-increasing
variety of management tasks.

Scientific management developed around the turn of the century, as the
size of industrial organizations became so great that management was no longer
able to maintain the day-to-day knowledge of operations necessary for direct,
intuitive control. It became clear that objective, quantified standards of performance were needed.

In summary, the history of the development of scientific management can
be seen as a natural evolution of techniques. They were created to solve management problems which appeared in a succession of organizational contexts—
manufacturing productivity, project management, paper work control, decision
making, and large-scale systems development—as each became large enough to
require scientific management. In each case, the new techniques developed drew
heavily on both the philosophy and the methodology of their predecessors.

1.1.1 Time and Motion Studies

Since the giant organizations of the era of transition from the nineteenth
to the twentieth centuries were manufacturing companies, it was natural that
scientific management originated with the study of the production rates to be
expected from manufacturing employees. The man generally regarded as the
father of scientific management, Frederick W. Taylor, developed the early methods of "time and motion study" for measurement of industrial production.[2]
Subsequently, other individuals (notably Frank and Lillian Gilbreth, with their
definition of a "therblig" as a component motion in manufacturing operation)

[1] Brandeis, Louis, "Economies Through Scientific Management," in *Evidence Taken by the Interstate Commerce Commission in the Matter of Proposed Advances in Freight Rates by Carriers* 8, pp. 4756–4803 (Aug.–Dec. 1910). This is a remarkable historical event. Brandeis brought together the persons who created scientific management during the decades around the beginning of the twentieth century.
[2] Taylor, Frederick W., *Principles and Methods of Scientific Management*. New York: Harper, 1911.

refined and extended Taylor's methods.[3] Today, time and motion study is an integral part of the kit of tools of the "industrial engineer" in his or her solution of specific problems in industrial management.

In Chapter 3, in which methods for determining staffing requirements will be discussed, specific attention will be given to the use of time and motion study.

1.1.2 Project Management

But time and motion studies only measure the performance of the individual worker. Methods were also needed for measurement and control of the management process itself—assignment of personnel, scheduling, cost control, for instance—and they too were developed. Henry L. Gantt, during the period from 1911 to 1919, defined the precursors of almost every modern tool for "project management."[4] His charting techniques, called Gantt charts, provide the means of relating components, personnel, and machinery in an organization with the tasks assigned to them over time. Requirements, assignments, costs, and schedules are pictured in a form easy to visualize; management performance can be easily measured by comparison of actual production or expenditures with scheduled ones; and problem areas can be readily pinpointed for management attention. Present-day refinements of Gantt's original concept include PERT (Program Evaluation and Review Technique), CPM (Critical Path Method), and LOB (Line of Balance) techniques.[5] They expand the capabilities of Gantt charts to show interrelationships among tasks (particularly time dependencies), to reflect uncertainties in schedules or costs, and to predict problem areas.

Despite their importance as a tool for scientific management, there will be no specific attention given to techniques for project management in subsequent chapters.

1.1.3 Cost Accounting

These methods of management required the development of comparable methods for accounting and reporting, so that the actual status of progress and costs could be monitored. As a tool of scientific management, accounting is

---

[3] Gilbreth, Frank Bunker, *Motion Study: A Method for Increasing the Efficiency of the Workman*. London: Routledge/Thoemmes Press, 1993.

Barnes, Ralph M., *Motion and Time Study,: Design and Measurement of Work,* 5th ed. New York: Wiley, 1963. Time and motion study, first created by the Gilbreths, is one of the central tools of scientific management. This is a relatively modern textbook for it, but doubtless there are more recent ones.

[4] Clark, Wallace, *The Gantt Chart: A Working Tool of Management.* New York: Ronald Press, 1922.

[5] Archibald, Russell, and Villoria, R.L., *Network-Based Management Systems (PERT/CPM).* New York: Wiley, 1967.

actually the most historic, dating from at least the Renaissance. It was regarded so highly at the time that "double entry bookkeeping" was a trade secret of the Florentine merchants using it.[6] As modern scientific management grew, however, it was apparent that adequate control required far more detailed cost data than existing budgetary accounting provided. This led to the development (by about 1910) of cost accounting systems which related costs to work performed. These are now an essential part of modern industrial management.

Methods of cost accounting and, more generally, managerial accounting are of fundamental importance to scientific management. They will be considered throughout the remaining chapters and are central to the structure and operation of the *Library Planning Model*.

1.1.4 Systems and Procedures

As a result of the need for accounting data, whether scientific management was involved or not, there was a concomitant increase in the amount of paperwork needed, to the point where it became a management problem in itself. In the decades after the turn of the century, developments occurred that provided the solution to that problem—the technology for information processing. The growth in the number and variety of devices for business data processing—accounting machines, punched-card equipment, computers—was a direct result of the need for systems and procedures to handle the "paperwork explosion."

Of course, there had been developments of information technology throughout the nineteenth century, from the conception of the precursor of the modern-day computer by Charles Babbage as early as the 1820s, to the invention of the cash register and other key-operated accounting machines in the 1880s, to the application of punched cards to calculation of the U.S. Census in 1890. The dramatic changes, though, came when these technological developments became the basis for companies—the National Cash Register Company and International Business Machines, Inc., in particular—that created markets for the equipment.[7] The result was that the technologies provided the basis for recording and processing the data needed to support scientific management.

---

[6] Pacioli, Luca, "Ancient Double Entry Bookkeeping," in Bursk, E. C., et al. (eds.), *The World of Business,* Vol. I. New York: Simon and Schuster, 1962, pp. 89–115. Pacioli was a mathematician and was responsible for the development of double entry bookkeeping, which is certainly part of the foundation for modern scientific management and, more specifically, managerial accounting.

[7] Rodgers, William, *Think: A Biography of the Watsons and IBM.* New York: Stein and Day, 1969.

Marcosson, Isaac, *Colonel Deeds: Industrial Builder.* New York: Dodd, Mead, 1947.

Friedman, Walter A, *The Efficient Pyramid: John A. Patterson and the Sales and Competition Strategy of the National Cash Register Company, 1884 to 1922.* Boston: Division of Research, Harvard Business School, 1998.

Johnson, Roy Wilder, *The Sales Strategy of John H. Patterson, Founder of the National Cash Register Company.* Chicago: Dartnell, 1932.

By the 1930s and 1940s the use of technology had become so widespread that a branch of scientific management—systems and procedures—was created to provide the tools for its management. The concern of systems and procedures was with analysis of the process of information flow within an organization, with design of appropriate forms and procedures for facilitating it, with management of the resulting reports and records, with measurement of the effectiveness of clerical work involved, and with design and evaluation of equipment systems for handling the clerical work.

Systems and procedures are a critical body of techniques for management of clerical operations and, especially, of the application to them of automated methods, a body of techniques that include flow-charting, functional analysis, methods analysis, standards for forms design, and computer programming software.

1.1.5 Operations Research

The most significant steps in formalizing models to support management occurred during World War II as "operations research" established a body of techniques. The need for them especially arose in managing large-scale military operations. Since then, they have become an integral part of management in a large number of industrial concerns as well as in the military. In large part, operations research simply provides mathematical formalisms by which to model the behavior of complex organizations and processes within them.

There are three quite distinct threads in operations research which, in a very real sense, correspond to the three management contexts around which this book is organized. The first thread of operations research is at the operational management level; it focuses on modeling of specific issues of concern. In industry, for example, they might include such things as inventory control in every kind of industry, machine tool replacement in manufacturing industries, and queuing and waiting times in service industries. Many of the models that will be presented in Part 2 of this book (Chapters 4, 5, and 6) for their application to library operational management are of exactly this kind.

The second thread, at the tactical level, deals with the organization as a whole and is concerned with issues of concern in planning and designing new organizational structures. In the years since operations research began, this thread has itself become an identified body of techniques, called "systems analysis," which is of such importance that we will look at it in more detail in the next section of this chapter.

The third thread, at the strategic level, deals with the problem of decision-making in various kinds of environment—competitive, cooperative, and uncertain. Again, the body of decision-making techniques has also become an identified body of techniques called "game theory," to which we now will turn.

1.2
Models for Decision-Making

The crucial reference for game theory is the classic book by John von Neumann and Oscar Morgenstern, *Theory of Games and Economic Behavior.*[8] First, we will focus on those models. After doing so, two other econometric models, independent of the game theoretic approach, will then be discussed.

1.2.1 Understanding a Decision Problem

The starting point for modeling any decision problem must be an understanding of the problem as it is seen by the decision-maker, a definition of the objectives of the decision-maker, the identification of alternative solutions to the problem, and the formulation of means for representing the objectives in a way that can be used to select among the alternative answers. All of that may sound self-evident and trite, but each of those steps is fraught with difficulty.

Most fundamentally, there are likely to be decision-making problems for the library manager that are not well understood, for which the objectives are by no means evident, and for which the alternative potential answers may not be known. The task in modeling in such cases clearly is much more complicated and requires an exploration by the library manager with whatever professional assistance, such as systems analysis, can be brought to bear.

The process of systems analysis, as will be discussed in the next section, provides an array of techniques and tools that can aid in that exploration and in characterizing the decision problem. They permit the library manager conceptually to explore the library, its purposes, its structure and organization, its functions and forms of data, and its resources in persons, facilities, and equipment. By doing so, the library manager can test intuitive knowledge, the gut feeling that something is amiss, against the result of that exploration. In that way, the problem can be clarified and the alternative solutions visualized, even if only tentatively. It is partly for this reason that the techniques and tools of systems analysis will be explored in detail in the next section of this chapter, since they are so useful as means for characterizing problems as well as means for planning and design.

Fortunately, though, many of the problems faced by the library manager are in principle well understood, as are the potential solutions of them. Some of these well-understood problems will serve as examples in most of the remaining chapters of this book. Even in such cases, though, there still are difficulties

---

[8] von Neumann, John and Morgenstern, Oscar, *Theory of Games and Economic Behavior.* Princeton: Princeton University Press, 1944.

in properly representing the objectives. To resolve those difficulties requires definition of an appropriate "utility function," to which we now turn.

1.2.2 Utility Functions

A utility function is a means for representing the objectives in a way that can be used to select among the alternative answers. To represent the objectives, two aspects must be recognized. One is the relative importance of the objectives and the second is the scale for individual assessment for each of them. In this respect, it is important to note that an unweighted mix of criteria, such as "the greatest good for the greatest number," is irrational; one cannot in general optimize two objectives simultaneously. To do so, there must be a single criterion, and if there are two or more objectives, that criterion must suitably represent their relative importance. It is that requirement that makes the utility function necessary.[9]

To illustrate, the library manager may have two objectives in mind: (1) to decrease the net cost for providing access to materials and (2) to improve the effectiveness of service in providing that access. On the surface, the two objectives are likely to be in opposition, since decreases in costs are likely to result in decreases in services, but the potential solutions may in fact include some that can to some extent meet both objectives. The utility function is the means for bringing those two objectives into a single criterion for assessing the alternatives.

This example, simple though it is, highlights the difficulties in creating a utility function. First, note that while the first objective is, in principle, quantitative, with net cost measurable in dollars, the second may be essentially qualitative and not adequately assessable in numerical form. Second, note that identifying the relative importance of the two objectives, however they may be assessed, is a near impossibility. Indeed, in any real situation it may shift as the alternative answers represent different combinations of costs and effectiveness.

Despite those difficulties, the process of modeling a decision-making problem requires that there be a utility function, and there are means for resolving the difficulties. First and, in a real sense, simplest is to translate the problem of comparison among objectives into "quantitative/qualitative" ratios. In the

---

[9] It is important to note that game theory fundamentally represents a means to reconcile or combine simultaneous objectives, as represented for example by those of the players in a game. The solution of the game is that mix of meeting the simultaneous objectives that is called "Pareto-optimum," meaning "the best that could be achieved without disadvantage for at least one objective." In other words, no objective can be bettered without reducing another objective. There is extensive research on the implications of the criterion of Pareto-optimum and alternatives for it. (See, for example, Schmid, A. Allan, *Property, Power, and Public Choice: An Inquiry Into Law and Economics,* 2nd ed. New York: Praeger, 1987. Reviewed by Kenneth Boulding in *Journal of Economic Issues* 13, 3 (Sept. 1979): pp. 781–785.)

example, that would become a "cost/effectiveness" ratio, a measure of "dollars per service provided."[10] Second is to translate, to the extent possible, the qualitative objectives into quantitative ones. In the example, this might be accomplished by translating "effectiveness" into a combination of measurable characteristics, such as "response time" and "frequency of satisfaction." Third and most fundamental is to translate the process of assessment into relative comparisons of alternative options, which might be represented by $U(A) > U(B)$, with $U(X)$ being the utility function and $U(A)$ and $U(B)$ being the respective "values" for options A and B, respectively.

The third means for resolution reflects the fact that the only requirement for the utility function is that it be "order preserving." Specifically, $U(A) > U(B)$ means that option A is preferable to option B (in the order of preferences of the decision-maker). Of course, it may be that two options are of equal preference, and that is represented by $U(A) = U(B)$. The crucial requirement for a utility function is that, for any two options A and B, either $U(A) > U(B)$ or $U(A) = U(B)$ or $U(B) > U(A)$. In other words, there must be a means for making the choice, and it is not possible for both $U(A) > U(B)$ and $U(B) > U(A)$, so the utility function must preserve the order of preference.

Later, in Chapter 9, when we discuss the application of game theory to cooperative decision-making among libraries, the specific mixes of quantitative and qualitative objectives appropriate to decisions concerning interlibrary cooperation will be discussed.

1.2.3 Representation of the Decision Problem

Given the existence of a utility function, it is then possible to represent the decision problem simply by the assessment of the value of the utility function for each of the alternatives available for solution of the problem. Expressed in that way, the decision problem appears to be almost trivial (even recognizing the possible difficulties in assessing the alternatives).

But, of course, real decision problems are not trivial for the very real reason that there are usually uncertainties that must be recognized. To represent those uncertainties, game-theoretic models place the decision problem in the framework of potential contexts over which the decision-maker has no direct control. Thus, while the decision-maker may face and be able to evaluate a set of alternative solutions to a problem, each solution must be assessed for its util-

---

[10] It is important to recognize that optimization of a cost/effectiveness measure usually is in the context of boundary conditions (such as "the cost must be less than some maximum" or "the effectiveness must be at least some minimum" or both).

ity in each context and, more to the point, the likelihood of each context must also be assessed.

Graphically, the game-theoretic model is simply a matrix the rows of which are the options for alternative solutions, the columns are the contexts, and the elements are the utility function assessments:

		Contexts	
Options	1	2	3
1	$U11$	$U12$	$U13$
2	$U21$	$U22$	$U23$
3	$U31$	$U32$	$U33$
4	$U41$	$U42$	$U43$

For example, the assessments of utility might be as follows:

		Contexts	
Options	1	2	3
1	−3	−4	5
2	−5	2	4
3	1	2	2
4	0	−2	3

The usual frame of reference for a game-theoretic model is a competitive game, in which the contexts represent the opponent's strategies for play and the utilities, if positive, are payments to the decision-maker from the opponent (or, if negative, from the decision-maker to the opponent). Note that the player and the opponent each have a utility and that they are negatives of each other: (U_{ij}, V_{ij}), with $V_{ij} = -U_{ij}$.

With utilities as shown above, the decision-maker might prefer option 1 because its utility is 5 in context 3, but there is the risk of a loss of −4 if the opponent plays context 2. How is the best choice to be made?

1.2.4 Max-Min Solution of the Decision Problem

The classical answer to the choice is "maximize the minimum utility"— the "max-min" solution. That is, for each option, across the set of contexts there is a least utility for the decision-maker and the choice should be that option for which the least utility is the largest. In the numerical example above, the answer is option 3, if the three contexts are equally likely. Note that the set of minimum utilities for the four options is (–4, –5, 1, –2) and the maximum of that set occurs at option 3 in context 1.

If the set of contexts are treated as the potential moves of a competitor, that person is similarly trying to maximize the minimum utility for him (which would be the negatives of the values shown), and the minimum utilities would be (–1, –2, –5), the maximum of which again occurs in context 1, option 3. In either case the result, G, from the game is payment of 1 from the competitor to the decision-maker.

In the example, as a game, the best strategies for the two competitors produce the same solution, option 3 and context 1. Such a game is one with a "saddle-point."

There are games without saddle-points and determining how best to decide for them requires introduction of what are called "mixed strategies," which entail basing the decisions on relative frequencies rather than fixed choices. For example, in the children's game "paper, scissors, rock," the best strategy is to make the choice among the three options as randomly as possible (unless the opponent reveals an evident bias). Using such mixed strategies, the decision process always will have a solution, in the form of relative frequencies for each option, that will produce at least the minimum expected return (as a counterpart of the max-min solution).

Determination of the best mixed strategy (i.e., best set of relative frequencies for selection of each option by the decision-maker and of the contexts by the opponent) entails solution of a set of linear equalities and inequalities. First, each set of relative frequencies must sum to 1:

$$A_1 + A_2 + \ldots + A_n = 1, \text{ and } B_1 + B_2 \ldots + B_m = 1$$

Second, each player wants the results, G, from the game to be the best possible for himself.

$$\Sigma A_i U_{ij} \geq G, j = 1, 2, \ldots, n \quad \text{and} \quad \Sigma B_i U_{ji} \leq G, j = 1, 2, \ldots, m$$

The need is to determine the values for the set of frequencies, A_i and B_i, and the value, G, of the game. In general, the solution of a set of linear inequalities (called "linear programming") is an iterative process of searching for values that are potential solutions and then finding the best among them. It is beyond the scope of this book to go into details about that process, and the reader will need to go to a standard text for operations research or linear programming to find them.[11] However, to illustrate the results, consider the following game,

[11] Churchman, C. W., Ackoff, R. L., and Arrow, F. L., *Introduction to Operations Research*. New York: Wiley, 1957. (The numerical examples presented in the text above are taken from this textbook.)

which does not have a saddle-point (i.e., max-min for the options is at option 1, context 2 but min-max for the contexts is at context 1, option 1):

	Contexts		
Options	1	2	3
1	2	−2	3
2	−3	5	−1

The inequalities for the decision-maker are $2A_1 - 3A_2 \geq G$, $-2A_1 + 5A_2 \geq G$, $3A_1 - A_2 \, A_2 \geq G$.

Those for the opponent are $2B_1 - 2B_2 + 3B_3 \leq G$, $-3B_1 + 5B_2 + B_3 \leq G$. $B_3 \leq G$.

The solution is $A_1 = 2/3$, $A_2 = 1/3$, $B_1 = 7/12$, $B_2 = 5/12$, $B_3 = 0$, and $G = 1/3$.

The result from each of the inequalities except the third one for the decision-maker is equal to G, but for that one it is greater than G. That means that the opponent does not want to select option 3 under any conditions, which is why B_3 should be zero.

1.2.5 Multiple Players

So far, the number of players has been just two—the decision-maker and the opponent. What happens if there are more than two players, say N of them? The crucial point in such games is that players may form coalitions with the objective of gaining advantages by doing so. Of course there is the implication that there will be mutual agreement among the players forming a coalition with respect to the division of utilities among them and that the utilities can be transferred among the participants in a coalition in accordance with that agreement (what are called "transferable utilities").

The representation of an N-player game is essentially parallel to that for the two-player game, except that there will be N components to the payoff vectors instead of two. That is, instead of simply (U_{ij}, V_{ij}) as a pair of utilities, there will be $(U^1{ij}, U^2{ij}, ..., U^N{ij})$ as an N-fold set of utilities with, for the moment, the sum of the utilities being equal to zero. Again, each player has a set of options among which to choose, with a coalition entailing agreed-upon choices among the options for the players forming that coalition.

The question at hand is then what the value of such a game is, as represented by the expected returns for each player, given the possibilities for forming the entire range of coalitions among the players. The answer is a beautiful formula, developed by Lloyd S. Shapley.[12] Consider S as one among the possible coalitions, with s players joining in it, and let $v(S)$ be the sum of the payoffs to the members of the coalition if they cooperate (and do not cooperate with any other player). Then, the payoff that each player can expect from the game is given by:

$$Ui = \Sigma[v(S)\star(s-1)!\star(N-s)!/N!] - \Sigma'[v(S)\star s!\star(N-s-1)!/N!]$$

where the first sum, Σ, is taken over all possible coalitions that include player i and the second sum, Σ', is taken over all coalitions that do not include player i. The sums together include all possible coalitions.

1.2.6 Non-Zero-Sum Games

Note that, in the matrix representation of the game-theoretic model for the N-person game, as shown above, the sum of the utilities equals zero. In particular, for the two-person game, only one utility function has been included and, in the numerical illustration, there are only single numbers in each element of the matrix. Further, in the discussion above, the utility function for the competitor was taken simply as the negative of that for the decision-maker, with the view that the results of the game were simply the transfer from one person to the other.

Clearly, it is possible, even likely, that competitors can have fundamentally different utility functions that cannot be expressed simply as the negatives of each other. If so, the matrix representation must consist of two values in each cell. To illustrate, with a two-person game, let U_{ij} be the utility function for the decision-maker and V_{ij} that for the competitor:

		Contexts	
Options	1	2	3
1	U11,V11	U12, V12	U13, V13
2	U21,V21	U22, V22	U23, V23
3	U31,V31	U32, V32	U33, V33
4	U41,V41	U42, V42	U43, V43

The sum of the two utility functions, $U_{ij} + V_{ij}$, would then represent the total value of that combination of options and contexts for both payers togeth-

[12] Shapley, Lloyd S., "A Value for N-Person Games," in Kuhn, H. W. and Tucker, A. W., *Contributions to the Theory of Games, II.* Annals of Mathematics Studies 28. Princeton: Princeton University Press, 1953, pp. 307–317.

er. If $V_{ij} = -U_{ij}$, as the illustration represented, the game is called a "zero-sum" game. If the two utility functions are not simply the negatives of each other, the determination of strategy by a given player would still be based on maximizing the minimum utility for that player.

As a principle, game theory assumes that the players in a game are "rational," in the sense that they will each make decisions that are best for their individual interests, as expressed by their respective utility functions. That implies, in particular, that the relative frequencies of the options and contexts (as defined above) will be determined by the optimal strategy of the player whose plays they represent. It is further assumed that both players have complete knowledge of the utility functions for each.

There are good reasons to question either of those assumptions in any context more complex than a game. Furthermore, the facts are that while the choice of a play in a game may well be made randomly, so that the opponent in making the opposing play is not sure of what it will be, the choice in virtually any real situation is likely not to be based on any element of randomness but instead will be made as directly as possible.

1.2.7 Cooperative Decision-Making

In particular, there are applications of game theory for which the assumption of maximizing individual interests, with max-min as the resulting criterion for choice and with the use of randomization as the means for creating mixed strategies, may be changed. The means for doing so is called "bargaining" and the resulting games are called "cooperative games."

Basically, bargaining is a process of making offers and demands with the objective of achieving total, joint results that are better than can be obtained from simply the competitive game. In such bargaining, of course, the competitive game sits in the background as the fallback position in the event that bargaining fails and that there is no cooperation in arriving at the solution.

Cooperative games are of special importance for libraries, for which cooperation in joint solution of operational problems is part of the underlying ethic as well as an economic and operational necessity. These kinds of applications therefore will be considered in Chapter 9 in the context of national information policy decisions and of library cooperation within them. As the background for that discussion, the following is a brief review of the theory underlying cooperative games.

The basis for the theory of cooperative games was developed by two quite remarkable individuals, each a combination of mathematician and economist—John F. Nash and John C. Harsanyl—who, together with Reinhard Selten, jointly received the Nobel Prize in Economics in 1994 for their work.

The seminal articles, though, were by Nash, and the following description draws primarily from them, supplemented by material from Harsanyi.[13]

Utility Functions in Cooperative Games

As was discussed above, to develop any game-theoretic model, one first needs a measure of utility, a means by which one can express the decision-maker's preferences. While such a utility function normally need only represent and preserve the order of preferences, there are two further requirements for application to cooperative games.

The first added requirement is "transitivity": If A is preferred to B and B is preferred to C, then A is preferred to C. Expressed in terms of the utility function, if $U(A) > U(B)$ and $U(B) > U(C)$, then $U(A) > U(C)$. The second added requirement is "linearity": Given a value p, $0 \leq p \leq 1$, with a possible option represented by $C = p \star A + (1 - p) \star B$, then the utility of C is the same linear combination of the respective utilities of A and B. Expressed in terms of the utility function, $U(C) = p \star U(A) + (1 - p) \star U(B)$. Note that the linearity requirement necessitates that the utility function be quantitative.

The Mechanism of a Cooperative Game

The theory developed by Nash treats situations involving individuals whose interests are neither completely opposed nor completely coincident. Decision-making in such situations is expected to require mutual discussion and agreement on a rational plan of joint action.

It is assumed that each participant has a set of possible mixed strategies (i.e., weighted combinations of simple strategies) that represent the actions that can be taken independent of the other participant. Typically the weights for the mixed strategies may be determined by a random process with specified averages.

For each combination of strategies, say (S_1, S_2), there will be resulting utilities $U(S_1, S_2)$ and $V(S_1, S_2)$ for the two players. Each utility is a linear function of S_1 and S_2 (because of the assumed property of linearity for the utility function).

Now, the issue in cooperation is to make a joint decision concerning the choice of S_1 and S_2 that would maximize the joint utility. Nash identifies a process of negotiation by which that joint decision is made and then identifies the properties that any "reasonable" solution must have.

Specifically, (1) there should be a unique solution, (2) any other potential solution cannot be better, (3) order-preserving transformations of the util-

---

[13] Nash, John, "The Bargaining Problem," *Econometrica* 18, 2, pp. 155–162.

Nash, John, "Two-Person Cooperative Games", *Econometrica* 21, 1 (Jan. 1953), pp. 128–140.

Harsanyi, John C., *Rational Behavior and Bargaining Equilibrium in Games and Social Situations.* New York: Cambridge University Press, 1977.

ity functions will not change the solution, (4) the solution is symmetrical with respect to the two players, (5) if, for some reason, the set of pairs of strategies should be reduced but still contain the solution, it will continue to be the solution, (6) restricting the strategies for one player cannot increase the value of the solution for that player, and (7) there is some way to restrict the strategies for both players without increasing the value of the solution for a given player.

Based on those axioms, Nash proves that there is a solution to the game that will maximize the total utility. The bottom line is that the solution to the game is that pair of strategies that maximizes the product of the possible gains over the fallback positions:

$$[U(S_1, S_2) - X_1] \star [V(S_1, S_2) - X_2]$$

where X_1 and X_2 are the expected payoffs for the respective fallback positions of the two players (i.e., the results from the strategies which would be used without cooperation). The following table (the example used by Nash in his article) illustrates a set of choices and the two utility values for each.

Choice	Cost to A	Value to B
1	−2	4
2	−2	2
3	−2	1
4	−2	2
5	−4	1

Choice	Value to A	Cost to B
6	10	−1
7	4	−1
8	6	−2
9	2	−2

Risk Factors

In the bargaining process, a crucial element is the relative degree of risk faced by each player at any given point. It is measured by the "risk factors" for each player:

$$R_1 = (U(S_1', S_2') - U(S_1, S_2))/(U(S_1', S_2') - X_1)$$
$$R_2 = (V(S_1', S_2') - V(S_1, S_2))/V(S_1', S_2') - X_2)$$

If $R_i > R_j$, then player i should prevail over player j in the choice between (S_1', S_2') and (S_1, S_2), since player i has relatively more to gain and player j has relatively more at risk.

Implementation in *LPM*

A process for solution of a cooperative game has been implemented in *LPM* for options (i.e., strategies) that are either independent or are based on combinations of possible choices, such as in the example given above. Note that in the example there are $2^9 = 512$ possible combinations. A given option then is one of those combinations of the nine possible choices. The value to each player of a particular combination is simply the sum of the costs and values associated for that player with the choices included in it. The case where there are no choices represents the noncooperative option in which the max-min solution, with a value of zero to both players, would arise if the players did not cooperate.

The crucial point is that by cooperation, the players can do much better, both individually and together. As Nash identifies, the optimum combination of choices is (1,2,3,4,6,7,8). For that combination, the payoffs are 12 for A and 5 for B, with the criterion product $(12 - 0)\star(5 - 0) = 60$. (The values of zero represent the fallback position of noncooperation.)

One might ask? Why not include all of the choices except number 5 (in which it is evident that there would be a net loss)? Well, note that the values of the combination (1,2,3,4,6,7,8,9) are 18 for A and 1 for B. Although the total, at 19, indeed is greater than the total, at 17, for the optimum choice, it is clear that B is subsidizing A and is not getting all that should come from the collaboration. The criterion product is $(18 - 0)\star(1 - 0) = 18$ and reveals the inequity by being much less than the 60 for the optimum answer.

1.2.8 Transferable Utilities

This does raise the possibility that one might do better. To illustrate the possibilities, in the example given above, let's change the values for choice 9 from (2,–2) to (3,–1). It turns out that there are then two combinations of options that have equal values for the Nash criterion: (1,2,3,4,6,7,8) and (1,2,3,4,6,7,8,9). The criterion product for the first is still $12\star5 = 60$, but that for the second is $15\star4 = 60$. In other words, the Nash criterion for each is 60, but the total utility of the second is 19 versus 17 for the first.

There are two reasons for looking at this new set of values. First, it serves to highlight one of the crucial features of the axioms that underlie the Nash solution. Specifically, the remarkable contribution that Nash made was not only to provide a simple criterion but to prove that it would provide the optimum answer and that it would be unique. How then can we have two options with the same Nash criterion value? The answer is that, given two values, there are linear combinations of them lying between them that are also potential answers.

Thus, let (X_1, Y_1) and (X_2, Y_2) be two options. Then $[a \star X_1 + (1 - a) \star X_2, a \star Y_1 + (1 - a) \star Y_2], a \leq 1$ is also an option. The linearity of the utility function then allows us to calculate the Nash criterion function:

$$N = [a \star U(X_1) + (1 - a) \star U(X_2) \star [a \star V(Y_1) + (1 - a) \star V(Y_2)]$$

To maximize N, set to zero the derivative of it with respect to a:

$$2 \star a[U(X_1) - U(X_2)] \star [V(Y_1) - V(Y_2)] + V(Y_2) \star [U(X_1) - U(X_2)] + U(X_2) \star [V(Y_1) - V(Y_2)] = 0$$

Then $a = (1/2) \star (V(Y_2)/[V(Y_1) - V(Y_2)] + U(X_2/[U(X_1 - U(X_2)])$.

In the example given above, $U(X_1) = 12$, $U(X_2) = 15$, $V(Y_1) = 5$, and $V(Y_2 = 4$. In that case,

$$A = (1/2) \star [4/(5 - 4) + 15/(15 - 12)] = 1/2$$

The Nash criterion value is then $F = (0.5 \star 12 + 0.5 \star 15) \star (0.5 \star 5 + 0.5 \star 4) = 13.5 \star 4.5 = 60.75$, and that is the unique maximum value.

The second reason for looking at this example, though, is that it highlights the potential for bargaining between the players with respect to the distribution of the total maximum utility. For them to bargain, the utilities must be *transferable*, so that player A would be able to give units of utility to player B as an incentive to cooperate in such a way as to increase the total utility.

In the example, player A might agree to give player B one and a half units if they can cooperate on the option that gives 15 units to A and 4 units to B. The result would be that A winds up with 13.5 units and B with 5.5 units. Each is ahead of the option that gave only 12 units to A and 5 units to B.

Later, in Chapter 9, we will use this example to illustrate the application of cooperative games in the context of decisions concerning library cooperation.

1.2.9 Optimization over Total Utility

So far, the optimization has focused totally on criteria that relate to the individuals separately. But as the discussion just above should demonstrate, there is great potential value if the optimization can consider the total utility, combining those for each of the two players.

Here is where Harsanyi provides another beautiful answer.[14] Without going into the details (as given in the reference), the bottom line is to maximize the Harsanyi criterion function:

[14] Harsanyi (op cit), p. 192.

$$H = [U(S_1,S_2) - X_1]^\star \, [V(S_1,S_2) - X_2]^\star \, [U(S_1 \, X_2) + V(S_1, S_2) - (X_1 + X_2)]$$

The Harsanyi criterion has been included in the implementation in *LPM*. But beyond the Harsanyi criterion is that of Shapley, which provides the basis for maximum collaboration among all of the participants. Again, the Shapley criterion has been included in the implementation in *LPM*.

1.2.10 Econometric Models

Econometric models draw upon a variety of mathematical methods, beyond those of game theory, to represent various aspects of economic decision-making.

A specific econometric model of significance to libraries is the Cobb-Douglas model, which measures the relative importance of capital investment and operating costs. It will be considered in Chapters 5 and 6, in which the collection of materials in a library, together with the costs in technical processing, will be considered as the capital investment of a library. In the same vein, it will be considered in Chapter 7, in which the library and other information resources (such as computing and telecommunication equipment) will be considered as part of the capital investment of the institution. Finally, it will be considered in Chapter 9, in which "information" and especially "published information" will be considered as part of the capital investment for industry in general.

A second econometric model of exceptional importance is the input-output matrix for use in large-scale macroeconomic decision-making. Developed by the Russian-born American economist and Nobel Prize winner for Economics in 1973, Wassily Leontief, it shows the expenditures by each industry for purchases from each industry within a national economy. This model will be of specific importance in Chapter 9 with respect to the role of "information industries" in national economies.

1.3
Models for Planning and Design

During the 1960s and 1970s, the use of the computer for both management and decision-making led to the introduction of a new approach to systems and procedures called *total management information systems*. Specifically, the combination of modern communications with the computer allowed the integration of administrative information to an extent previously impossible. As a result, data about an organization can easily be acquired, stored, processed, and used for management control. Even more important are the implications for scientific management. Whereas before it was at best difficult to acquire and process the data required for management decision-making, the availability of integrated files which can be easily processed makes it easy to do so. The most complete exposition of the role of a total management information system in industrial organizations was put forward by Jay W. Forrester.[15] He used the phrase "industrial dynamics" to describe the application of modern engineering control techniques to the management of a company.

When the management information system is a very large-scale one, the design and evaluation of alternatives for it requires a methodology, which started as a part of operations research but now generally is called systems analysis. It depends heavily upon the use of models but it is also concerned with issues which are not amenable to quantification. Therefore, other techniques have also been required. In particular, systems analysis must be especially concerned with the definition of objectives which the system is to meet. Although some objectives can be measured, others are essentially qualitative, relating to policy and politics or to social and ethical values. As a result, systems analysis has had to be concerned with the balance between costs (usually measurable) and benefits (frequently unmeasurable). The concepts of cost/effectiveness or cost/benefits evaluation have therefore been an integral part of systems analysis.

Of course, from the earliest days of scientific management, it was recognized that an adequate criterion for evaluation required some balance between cost and benefits derived. Harrington Emerson, around 1910, expounded the use of "cost/effectiveness," or efficiency, as the appropriate measure. Since then, it has become the characterizing feature of systems analysis, perhaps best represented by the work of Charles Hitch. In 1960, Hitch defined the concepts and problems in a cost/effectiveness criterion when applied to the policy issues in national defense.

1.3.1 Overview

There has been an image built around the concept of systems analysis which implies an unprecedented ability to resolve problems. The systems approach thus is invoked as the answer to any major issue. The facts are, of course, that systems analysis is simply an approach to problems and a body of techniques to aid in their solution. As an approach it follows the long history of scientific management theory; as a body of techniques it draws on mathematics, operations research, and the use of the computer. As the most recent mani-

[15] Forrester, Jay Wright, *Industrial Dynamics.* Cambridge, MA: Productivity Press, 1961.

festation of scientific management, systems analysis reveals one thing—each generation struggles with the task of discovering new principles which continually turn out to be the old ones.

But the problems change and become more complex, so even though the principles we rediscover may have been known, the difficulties in applying them require using even more powerful techniques. Systems analysis is merely the name we give at the moment to the most recent rediscovery of principles. Systems analysis is therefore neither new nor revolutionary nor a panacea. It is simply the latest version of the application of the scientific method to problems. However, there are some features of systems analysis which particularly characterize it—its use of cost/effectiveness as the ultimate criterion for evaluation of operation, its view of any problem in the context of the larger situation within which it occurs, and its attitude of question toward the very definition of the "problem."

1.3.2 Steps of Systems Analysis

The systems approach to problems can be summarized in a simple set of steps:

1. *Define* the problem, including its scope, the environment within which it occurs, and the constraints on solutions to it. It is here that the attitude of questioning arises, since the system analyst is continually asking whether the purposes as defined truly represent the requirements. Perhaps more than any other methodology of analysis, systems analysis adopts a teleological view. Even though the systems analyst may accept a definition of purpose as given, there is still an attitude of question. In part, this is a direct result of the recognition that any system exists as a component in a much larger system whose total purposes might be better met otherwise.

2. *Analyze* operations and, in doing so, describe them in detail, showing the relationships among the parts. It is here that the body of techniques is used. The systems study, the analysis of statistics and forms, the drawing of flowcharts, etc., provide the formalized tools to aid in this step.

3. *Synthesize* alternate solutions. This is the really creative part of "systems analysis" and perhaps the part around which the image has been built. Sometimes a solution is found by viewing the system as simply a part of a larger system, sometimes by a very simple change in the character of the operation. This is the creative side of the process, although we try to develop formalized tools to aid it.

4. *Evaluate* the alternatives according to defined criteria. It is here that the usage of cost/effectiveness has become characteristic of systems analy-

sis in general. Although implicit in all cost accounting systems, it has been made explicit only in the most recent applications of systems analysis. It is now the standard criterion in the Department of Defense, the Bureau of the Budget, and an increasing number of governmental agencies and industrial concerns. Even though issue may be taken with its applicability to essentially nonquantifiable issues, it is likely to be the criterion in library system analysis as well.

5. *Iterate* these steps to increase the detail and to modify the results if they do not adequately solve the problem.

1.3.3 Definition of a System

For answers to the basic question—"What is a system?"—there are well-established definitions of both a structural and a functional nature. Perhaps the most general picture is that provided by the following figure. As shown, systems

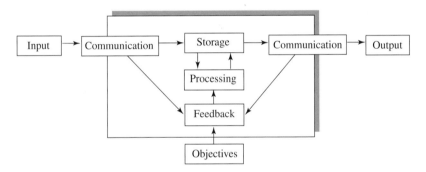

are configurations of components which are interrelated with each other in organized structures. The components in information systems include communication, storage, and processing, with the input and output of data representing the world external to the system. The "system" is contained within the boundaries, but with communication providing means for setting goals, for input of data, and for output of the results from system operation. Aside from input of data, though, there is another, even more important input from the external world—the objectives of the system. By comparing those objectives with the data coming into the system and the data going out, a process of feedback can determine the processing so as to bring the system into conformance with the identified objectives. If the objectives change, the process of feedback can then modify the processing in a dynamic fashion.

Within this general framework, several types of systems can be distinguished, primarily in terms of the particular components which represent the problem in a given situation. For example, a communication system is a specialized example of an information system in which the critical problems are involved with the communication components in the system—control of error in the presence of noise, and maximization of the amount of data transmitted. As another example, a storage and retrieval system might be considered as one in which the critical problems relate to the organization of a storage file for maximum effectiveness. A third special case is the servo-system—an information system whose problems arise from dynamic effects, particularly with respect to stability, which arise from the feedback time-cycle compared with response times in the remainder of the system. Finally, one could define a class of "processing systems" in which the problems of principal concern relate to the routine logical processes in operation of the system; presumably most systems for engineering computation and business data processing (such as inventory control, billing, accounting, etc.) fall in this class.

1.3.4 Defining the Scope of the System

The decomposition of a system into component parts (as exemplified in the figure above) is the result of an analytical process. Each component can now similarly be treated as a system, with its own input and output as determined by the other components. As such, it can be analyzed into exactly the same kinds of components as the original system—communication, storage, processing, and feedback. Reversing this view, it is evident that any system can itself be considered as a component in a larger system. One of the significant problems in system design, and one of the difficulties in defining the concept of an information system itself, is therefore the determination of its scope. In fact, the psychological bent of the system designer is to increase that scope continually, to consider larger and larger contexts, to reach for a "total system." It is also evident that valid system design requires a precise definition of the scope of the system and cannot tolerate grasping at ever-larger fields to conquer.

Therefore, before a system can be studied its scope must be defined. The way a person thinks of a system depends on the individual perspective from which the world is viewed. What one person defines to be a system may be a subsystem to another person. What this means for systems analysis is that all aspects of the operation must be considered, as well as some aspects of the operations of organizations outside that operation but which interface with it. The source of inputs and the destination of outputs for a system will need to be traced far enough to determine their actual impact on the operations.

1.3.5 Analyzing the Operations

A systems study then proceeds by assembling all available documentation covering the existing operations of the library. These include: samples of forms, reports, and publications; descriptions of files, equipment, physical plant; and copies of written procedures, policy statements, organization charts, position descriptions, externally imposed regulations, and existing system descriptions.

These materials are then organized and significant missing documentation is identified. It will almost always be necessary to bring much of the existing documentation up to date and will usually be desirable to prepare documentation covering those areas which previously have not been documented (for example, position descriptions prepared years ago may be out of date). As documentation is assembled and organized some omissions will become obvious. It is probable that a large number of undocumented policies will be in effect and it is likely that many policies thought to be generally understood will be differently interpreted by personnel. Getting the generally understood policies into a written form will in itself contribute to a more smoothly running and effective operation. Documenting the existing service policies will permit the need for the various service activities to be assessed. With this documentation assembled the detailed description of operations can be produced. The primary purpose of this phase of the systems analysis is the identification of inputs, constraints, and outputs for each component of the system, together with some measure of their actual importance. It therefore is clear that the analysis cannot be concerned exclusively with the existing systems operations. Forms and work flow are traced through the system as a means of determining the real requirements.

The Dimensions of an Information System

The process of systems analysis can well be pictured in terms of four dimensions: Data, Functions, Components, and Time. Each of these dimensions provides an essential point of view on a system, and the relationships among them serve as the means for description of the operation of the system.

The data involved in an "information" system are the foundation dimension, since they are the fundamental basis for operation of such a system. Those data must be identified; the structure of them must be described; the input sources of the data and the output destinations of the data must be identified; both input and output must be related to the objectives of the system.

The functions are the means by which "information" is derived from data (as will be discussed in detail in Chapter 8, with a definition of the term "information"). They are thus the characterizing dimension. They provide the means by which data are input, stored, retrieved, processed, and output. The technical analysis will deal with the means for identifying the essential operations, structuring and organizing them, and implementing them within a system.

The components are the means by which functions actually are carried out. They therefore constitute the structural substance of a system. Again, as with the first two dimensions, the components must be identified; their structural relationships with each other must be described.

The dimension of time serves as the means for describing the sequential flow of system operations. The primary issues arise in the interrelationships within the other dimensions, but some of them are fundamental to time itself, representing the relationship between a system of focus and the context within which it functions. The system will function within the time frame of external events and requirements; these must be identified and the sequence of them determined.

Interrelationships Among Dimensions

Much of the process of analysis is focused on describing the interrelationships among the four dimensions: the changes that occur in data as a result of the functions; the responsibility of components for specific data and specific functions; the time sequence of data flow, functional processes, and interactions among components. For each of these, there are well-established means for description and analysis of these interrelationships—the Gantt chart for showing time sequences, matrices for showing assignments of responsibility, tables for showing the structure of data as exemplified in relational databases.

1.3.6 Designing Alternate Solutions

The results will usually imply a need for a new design or for significant changes to the existing design. The justification for initiating such changes will involve improved effectiveness of the organization's performance and/or a reduction in costs, the primary objective of a systems program being the reduction of the cost/effectiveness ratio.

The means for systems design fall into two main categories: (1) change in the scope of the system of focus, and (2) modification of one or more of the fundamental dimensions of system description.

Change in Scope of System of Focus

Changing the scope of the system of focus is a standard method for system design. Usually it involves expanding the scope, though there may be times when the appropriate approach is to reduce the scope, an example of which would be making a subsystem independent of the original system of scope.

To illustrate, let's consider some examples that fit within this category of design approach: The system of focus might be a single library, but alternatives might be to expand the scope to include other facilities (such as computing), or to include a set of several libraries. The system of focus might be a single function within the library, but alternatives might be to expand to the full range of functions so as to achieve an integration of the system design, with sharing of data among functions and efficiency of total operation.

These examples illustrate expansion of scope, but sometimes a narrowing of scope is called for. The initial scope might be a group of branch libraries treated as an integrated whole, but an alternative might be to narrow the scope to just one of them if the services to that branch are not effectively being met by treatment of all libraries in a unified manner. This alternative is frequently exemplified by conversion from a function-oriented structure to a project-oriented one. It is likely that such a narrowing of scope will immediately be followed by expanding the scope but in a different context. Thus, focusing on a specific library might immediately be followed by expansion of scope to encompass the full range of information services all being considered together within the branch.

Changes in Dimensions of Description

In the methods presented for system analysis, four dimensions provide the structure both for description of specific aspects and for description of the relationships among them. Each of them provides a frame of reference for identifying alternatives. The dimension of function is the most frequent starting point for identifying alternatives. Probably this is a result of the fact that the effects of the actual operations carried out by an information system are the most evident aspects, the most likely to be the causes of problems and concern. One can consider adding new functions (either immediately or in a planned future); one can consider reorganizing functions, logically grouping them together in alternative arrangements; one can consider changing or even deleting existing functions.

One can consider changing workloads on functions, as a result of adding new demands or shifting demands from one function to another One can consider changing the structure of functions—the means by which they are logically implemented—resequencing the flow of routines, for example, performing some in parallel rather than in sequence.

Changes in the dimension of data may entail new data, new structures, new workloads.

The dimension of components frequently serves as the rationale for undertaking a systems analysis and design project: There is the lemming-like urge to rush into automation which has driven so many systems analysis efforts. Again, one can consider adding new components (a microcomputer or a CD-ROM unit, for example), reorganizing the structure of them (modifying the organization chart for the library, for example) or changing or deleting some of them (replacing professional staff by clerical staff or reducing the number of clerical staff, for example). And one can consider changing the workload handled by components—shifting the keyboarding workload from professional to clerical staff or reducing the keyboarding workload for all staff by use of OCR equipment and software.

Each of the other three dimensions involves that of time, so one can change the time sequence of operations, of data flows, of component operations. In that same vein, one can change relationships among the other three dimensions: assignment of data to different components, of function to different components, of functions to different categories of data.

1.3.7 Evaluation

Early in the formulation of system specifications a number of trade-off studies should be made. What are the advantages and disadvantages of on-line and batch mode processing of data at various points in the system? What equipment is available and what are the good and bad features of each? What are the different ways that data can be organized in machine files and what are the strengths and weaknesses of each file structure? Where do persons best fit into the system and where should machines be used? Equipment vendors are always anxious to propose alternatives using their equipment. Recognizing that a vendor has a solution for which he or she is seeking a problem instead of the converse, they can provide valuable assistance. Where the dollar volume warrants it, equipment manufacturers will prepare detailed proposals for the application of their equipment to solve a set of specified problems. However, their proposals should be treated with caution, preferably as input to the design work of the library's system staff.

Once the preliminary system specifications have been drafted it will be possible to prepare an estimate of implementation and operating costs for the new system for comparison with the cost of the present system, as estimated during the study of it. If the costs of the new system (including amortization of the one-time-only implementation costs) are estimated to be less than those of the old system, the decision to proceed with the development of a new system is easily justified. However, usually the cost of the new system exceeds that of the old system and its development must be justified on the basis of a more effective operation, including the provision of new services not previously provided. The information needs throughout the system and the required system outputs will have been determined during the systems analysis. Just how these needs are to be met will require a great deal of work. Certainly, it would be possible to design some portion of the system to meet a limited number of the needs and objectives, but the procedures developed likely would not be compatible with other procedures developed later on. Thus, it is really better to outline the entire system and to show in a preliminary fashion how the various parts of the system relate to one another (for example, converting a file to a machine-readable form could significantly alter the procedures of many secondary users of the file). In other words, the total system concept should be outlined before the detailed specification of a specific part of it is undertaken.

Bibliography

The following references provide a starting point for literature relevant to the background of operations research in general.

References of Historic Interest

Brandeis, Louis. "Economies through Scientific Management," in *Evidence taken by the Interstate Commerce Commission in the Matter of Proposed Advances in Freight Rates by Carriers* 8, pp. 4756–4803 (Aug.–Dec. 1910). This is a remarkable historical event. Brandeis brought together the persons who created scientific management during the decades around the beginning of the twentieth century.

Churchman, C.W., Ackoff, R.L., and Arrow, F.L. *Introduction to Operations Research.* New York: Wiley, 1957. This is the first textbook for operations research and still is probably the best.

Emerson, Harrington. *The Twelve Principles of Efficiency.* New York: Engineering Magazine Co., 1912. Emerson was one of the pioneers in scientific management, and this was his statement of principles.

Hayes, Robert M. *Handbook of Data Processing for Libraries,* 2nd ed. New York: Wiley, 1972. Chapter 3, Scientific Management of Libraries, Chapter 4, Cost Accounting in Libraries, pp. 74–121. This provides a review of history followed by a description of several of the models that will be discussed in this book. It concludes with an introduction to systems analysis.

Malthus, Thomas Robert. *An Essay on the Principle of Population, as it Affects the Future Improvement of Society with Remarks on the Speculations of Mr. Godwin, M. Condorcet and Other Writers.* London: Printed for J. Johnson, 1798. Although not strictly in the scope of scientific management, this is included as an excellent example of the use of quantitative models. More to the point of understanding operations research, though, it also serves as the basis for two other books that are listed below: *Limits of Growth* and *Models of Doom.*

Nash, John. "Two-Person Cooperative Games," *Econometrica* 21, 1 (Jan. 1953), pp. 128–140.

Nash, John. "The Bargaining Problem," *Econometrica* 18, 2 (Apr. 1950), pp. 155–162.

Pacioli, Luca. "Ancient Double Entry Bookkeeping," in Bursk, E. C., et al. (eds.), *The World of Business,* Vol. I. New York: Simon and Schuster, 1962, pp. 89–115. Pacioli was a mathematician and was responsible for the development of double entry bookkeeping, which is certainly part of the foundation for modern scientific management and, more specifically, managerial accounting.

Rathe, Alex (ed.). *Gantt on Management.* New York: American Management Association, 1961. Gantt was another of the founders of scientific management.

Taylor, Frederick W. *Principles and Methods of Scientific Management.* New York: Harper, 1911. Taylor was perhaps the founder of scientific management.

Von Neumann, John, and Morgenstern, Oscar. *Theory of Games and Economic Behavior.* Princeton, Princeton Univ. Press, 1944, 641 p. This remarkable work literally created operations research. Von Neumann was one of the world's great mathematicians and played a central role in the development of the computer. He wrote this book in collaboration with an economist, Oscar Morgenstern, as a formalization of decision-making in the context of uncertainty.

Zipf, G.K. *Human Behavior and the Principle of Least Effort.* Cambridge, MA: Addison-Wesley, 1949; (see also in Simon, H.A., *Models of Man.* New York: Wiley, 1957.) In this book, Zipf showed how many social phenomena are governed by J-shaped curves for the distribution of activity.

These three websites contain some interesting commentaries on the historical development of scientific management and operations research:

http://darkwing.uoregon.edu/~dapope/363taylor.htm
http://access.tucson.org/~michael/hm_2.html
http://www.shef.ac.uk/~psysc/staff/rmyoung/papers/shmt.html

References for General Scientific Management

Ackoff, R. Gupta, Shiv K., and Minas, J. Sayer. *Scientific Method: Optimizing Applied Research and Decisions.* New York: Wiley, 1962.

Archibald, Russell, and Villoria, R.L. *Network-Based Management Systems (PERT/CPM).* New York: Wiley, 1967. Project management, at least for major projects such as automation or building, requires sophisticated tools. Today, they are based on what Gantt did over 100 years ago, but go far beyond the simple Gantt chart of that time. This is an excellent text covering the range of such tools, but doubtless there are more recent ones.

Barnes, Ralph M. *Motion and Time Study: Design and Measurement of Work,* 5th ed. New York: Wiley, 1963. Time and motion study, first created by the Gilbreths, is one of the central tools of scientific management. This is a relatively modern textbook for it, but doubtless there are more recent ones.

Baumol, William J. *Economic Theory and Operations Analysis.* Englewood Cliffs, NJ: Prentice-Hall, 1961.

Bierman, Harold, Jr., et al., *Quantitative Analysis for Business Decisions.* Homewood, IL: Richard D. Irwin, 1961.

Bisio, Attilio. *Turning Research and Development into Profits: A Systematic Approach* New York: AMACOM, 1979.

Bursk, Edward C., and Chapman, John F. *New Decision-Making Tools for Managers.* Harvard, 1962.

Forester, Jay. *World Dynamics.* Cambridge, MA: Wright-Allen, 1971. This was the study that led to the *Limits of Growth* and *Models of Doom.*

Harsanyi, John C. *Rational Behavior and Bargaining Equilibrium in Games and Social Situations.* Cambridge: University Press, 1977.

Meadows, Donella H., et al. *The Limits of Growth.* New York: Universe Books, 1972. This book is based on Jay Forester's study, *World Dynamics,* building on the model of population growth first identified by Malthus.

Models of Doom: A Critique of the Limits of Growth, edited by H.S.D. Cole, et al. New York: Universe Books, 1973. This book attempts to counter the arguments of *The Limits of Growth.*

Novick, David (ed.). *U.S. Bureau of the Budget. Program Budgeting: Program Analysis and the Federal Budget,* Washington, D.C.: Superintendent of Documents, 1965.

Rigby, Paul H. *Conceptual Foundations of Business Research* New York, Wiley, 1965.

Rubinstein, Moshe F. *Concepts in Problem Solving.* Englewood Cliffs, NJ: Prentice-Hall, 1980; Rubinstein, Moshe F. *Patterns of Problem solving.* Los Angeles: Engineering Systems Department, School of Engineering and Applied Science, University of California, Los Angeles, 1973. These two books are consistent with the general approach represented by scientific management, but they broaden the range of methods to include more than just quantitative ones.

Stockfisch. J.A. *Planning and Forecasting in the Defense Industries.* Belmont, CA: Wadsworth, 1962. Though focused on planning in the defense industry, this book illustrates the role of quantitative models in making long-range management decisions.

White, D.J. *Decision Theory.* Chicago: Aldine, 1969.

"U.S. Agencies Get Order: Join McNamara's Band: Cost System Imposed by the Defense Secretary on the Pentagon Will Be the Model for All Federal Departments," *Business Week* 182 (Nov. 13, 1965).

References for Systems Analysis

Checkland, Peter. *Systems Thinking, Systems Practice.* New York: Wiley, 1981. Checkland is especially valuable in his recognition of the limitations of quantitative methods and the necessary use of qualitative methods in conjunction with them. He contrasts "hard" and "soft" methods and then brings them together in a integrated approach.

Hitch, Charles, and McKean, Roland. *Economics of Defense in a Nuclear Age.* Cambridge, MA: Harvard University Press, 1960. Charles Hitch brought scientific management and operations research into use by the U.S. military. He was the leader of what became known as "MacNamara's band." Later, he became President of the University of California.

Neuschel, Richard F. *Management by System,* 2nd ed. New York: McGraw-Hill, 1960.

References for Management Information Systems

Kelly, Joseph F. *Computerized Management Information Systems.* New York: Macmillan, 1970.

Laden, H.N., and Gildersleeve, T.R., *System Design for Computer Applications.* New York: Wiley, 1963.

Le Roux. H.S. *Top Management and Environmental Information.* Pretoria: University of South Africa, 1979.

Li, David H., *Design and Management of Information Systems.* Chicago: Science Research Associates, 1972.

Neuner, J.J.W. *Office Management: Principles and Practices.* Cincinnati: South-Western Publishing, 1959.

Optner, Stanford L. *Systems Analysis for Business Management.* Englewood Cliffs, NJ: Prentice-Hall, 1960.

Ross, H. John. *Techniques of Systems and Procedures.* Office Research Institute, 1949; *The Office: Magazine of Management, Equipment Methods.* New York: Office Publications Inc.

References for General Management

Argyris, Chris. *Integrating the Individual and the Organization.* New York: Wiley, 1964.

Bennet, Carrie Lynn. *Defining the Manager's Job: The AMA Manual of Position Descriptions.* New York: American Management Association, 1958. Research study (American Management Association) no. 33.

Bittel, Lester R. *Management by Exception: Systematizing and Simplifying the Managerial Job.* Bombay: New Delhi: Tata McGraw-Hill, 1964.

Blanchard, Kenneth H. *Leadership and the One-Minute Manager: Increasing Effectiveness Through Situational Leadership.* New York: Morrow, 1985.

Bursk, Edward Collins, et al. *The World of Business. A Selected Library of the Literature of Business from the Accounting Code of Hammurabi to the 20th-Century. "Administrator's prayer."* New York: Simon and Schuster, 1962.

Communication in Organizations. Compiled by James L. Owen, Paul A. Page, and Gordon I. Zimmerman. St. Paul: West, 1976.

Drucker, Peter Ferdinand. *An Introductory View of Management.* London: Pan Books, 1979.

Drucker, Peter Ferdinand. *The Concept of the Corporation.* New York: New American Library, 1964.

Haire, Mason (ed). *Modern Organization Theory: A Symposium of the Foundation for Research on Human Behavior.* New York, London: Garland, 1987.

Heyel, Carl. *The Encyclopedia of Management.* New York: Reinhold, 1963.

Lewis, Roy. *The Managers. A New Examination of the English, German and American Executive.* New York: New American Library, 1961.

Miller, Stanley S. *The Management Problems of Diversification. A Pilot Study of the Corporation Diversifying from an Established Base.* New York: Wiley, 1963.

Murphy, John D. *Secrets of Successful Selling.* New York: Dell, 1958.

Packard, Vance Oakley. *The Status Seekers.* New York: Pocket Books, 1961.
Randall, Clarence B. *The Folklore of Management.* New York: New American Library, 1962.
Strauss, George. *Personnel. The Human Problems of Management.* Englewood Cliffs, NJ: Prentice-Hall, 1965.
Whyte, William Hollingsworth. *The Organization Man.* Garden City, NY: Doubleday, 1956.

References Reflecting Perversions of Mathematical Modeling

Block, N.J., and Dworkin, Gerald. *The IQ Controversy.* New York: Random House, 1976. This is the first of six references relating to the application of mathematical models in this highly charged arena; it should be read together with a closely related commentary by Jerry Hirsch, "To 'Unfrock the Charlatans.'" The third, *The Legacy of Malthus,* builds upon the original article by Malthus (referenced earlier). The fourth is *The Bell Curve.* The final two relating to Cyril Burt (*Cyril Burt, Psychologist* and "The Real Error of Cyril Burt") are included because they exhibit some of the fundamental pitfalls in the use of such models, especially as they reflect the role of objectives.

Chase, Allan. *The Legacy of Malthus: The Social Costs of the New Scientific Racism.* New York: Knopf, 1977.

Gould, Stephen Jay. *The Mismeasure of Man.* New York: Norton, 1981. Especially Chapter 6, The Real Error of Cyril Burt, pp. 234–320.

Herrnstein, Richard J., and Murray, Charles. *The Bell Curve: Intelligence and Class Structure in American Life.* New York: Simon & Schuster, 1994.

Hirsch, Jerry. "To 'Unfrock the Charlatans,'" in *Sage Race Relations Abstracts* 6, 2 (May 1981), pp. 1–56.

Hearnshaw, L.S. *Cyril Burt, Psychologist.* New York: Vintage Books, 1979. This reference to the life of Cyril Burt and the commentary by Gould (see above) are included because they deal with one of the most excruciating examples of apparent fraud in the use of quantitative data.

2

Library Decision-Making Contexts

Introduction

Today, the magnitude of the management problems faced by libraries seems to be at a critical point. As libraries grow further in size and services, as they participate in national networks, as they introduce mechanization, as they consider the impact of new forms of publication, they must develop tools for scientific management appropriate to the tasks they face. In doing so, they can draw on those already found to be of value in other organizations—time and motion study, project management, cost accounting, systems and procedures, management decision-making, and systems analysis. But particularly in the last two areas, libraries will need to develop tools of their own, attuned to the particular characteristics of the library, its management problems, and its information system functions.

Library administrators are continually faced with situations in which they must make decisions and choose among alternatives. Some decisions relate to strategic planning of the long-range objectives of the library, whether and how they should be changed, what policies are required to achieve them, and what effects they will have. Others relate to operational planning, where administrative decisions must be made about allocations of resources. Some simply relate to the management of specific operational tasks.

To date, most of these decisions are made by the librarian on the basis of intuitive judgment. The general high quality of operations in the face of severe budgetary restraints is attributable to the librarian. But are there any quantitative methods which the librarian can use to aid in making these decisions? The models that will be presented in Parts 2 and 3 of this book provide some of the answers to that. In this chapter, though, the emphasis will be on the kinds of decision contexts for which those models and methods are intended.

2.1
Library Operational Management

2.1.1 Operational Issues

Probably the main burden of day-to-day library decision-making is represented by the management of the tasks in technical services and readers' services. The rules and priorities for selection of material and for scheduling of work loads in technical processing require the continued attention of library management. The library literature is showing an increasing level of attention to the development of quantitative models to aid the librarian in the choices to be made. Whereas at one time there were only a few time and motion studies, a few costing studies, and a few systems and procedures studies, now there is a wealth of models. These areas for scientific management in libraries, of course, represent the main focus of concern for this book.

2.1.2 Planning and Documenting Operating Budgets

An obvious value in modeling is to plan budgets and provide the support for budget submission. The models that will be presented in Part 2 (Chapters 4, 5 and 6) have special value in this respect, because they provide generic criteria for assessment of staffing requirements.

Sometimes budget planning can be quite easy, especially when the institutional approach is to assume that the budget is essentially continuing and that next year's budget will be the same as last year's (with at most minor changes, such as a factor to accommodate inflation). Ann Prentice refers to this as "the outdated incremental approach" and points out that, under those conditions, perhaps nothing more is needed.[1] But it can also be an exceptionally complicated process, so it is worth reviewing some of the potential complications.

First, the institutional policy concerning budgets may entail the concept of "zero-based budgeting." In such a context the assumption is that the budget for next year starts at zero and that any increase from there must be based on programmatic justification. Even when the institutional approach assumes a continuing budget, programmatic changes may require budgetary changes. It is these kinds of context for which the models of Part 2 are of special value, since they provide means for translating programmatic requirements into staffing and funding requirements.

Second, budgets usually reflect planned expenditures, not actual expenditures or even commitments. For libraries the complications are especially evi-

[1] Prentice, Ann E., *Financial Planning for Libraries,* 2nd ed. Lanham, MD: Scarecrow Press, 1996, p. 28.

dent in commitments for acquisition of materials. They may be made in one fiscal year, but the associated expenditures may be incurred in some other fiscal year or may even be canceled. In such cases, budgeted funds may not be expended when planned but must be carried forward or even backward in time. There is therefore the necessity of assuring that the budget is not unduly constrained in this respect and that there is sufficient flexibility in policy to accommodate the reality of timing of commitment and expenditure. A somewhat similar complication arises with respect to salaries of staff, since budgeted positions may be unfilled for some period of time during a fiscal year. The result is "salary savings," and there may be constraints on expenditure of those funds.

Unfortunately, none of the models to be presented will assist in the planning for these kinds of policy-related issues. They will need to be dealt with through appropriate accounting mechanisms and the negotiation of policies that will permit the library director to maintain proper, accountable control over operations.

2.1.3 Assessing "What-If" Alternatives

One of the great values of a model, well exemplified in spreadsheet realizations of it, is the ease of testing "what-if" situations. What if the workload in circulation of materials were to increase by 10%? What if the university institutes a new degree program? What if some publishers decide to stop printing their journals and to institute delivery through the Internet? What if two departmental libraries were to be merged into one? What if the budget for acquisition of journals is kept fixed at 60% of the total acquisitions budget?

If a model has been properly designed, with variables and parameters represented in it in forms that will permit them to be easily changed, it is then easy to test the effects of such "what-if" situations. The values are set to reflect the hypothetical situation and the model should then exhibit the effects directly. The models that have been incorporated in *LPM* have each been structured so as to permit easy changes in both variables and parameters, and the effects of alternatives can be directly compared.

2.1.4 Setting Fee Structures

For a variety of reasons, libraries are charging fees for services. While they can be set arbitrarily, there is value in basing them on concrete evidence of costs. In particular, it is important to establish a solid basis for accounting for all costs associated with a given service, including proper allocation of indirect costs.

That does not mean that fees are then, of necessity, set at the full cost. They may be less (thus being subsidized) or they may be greater (thus generating a profit). Those kinds of decisions are likely to be made on the basis of policy, not economics. But it does mean, whatever the rationale for setting the fees may be, that the library should be fully aware of the consequences of the decisions.

Historically, this issue was well exemplified by fees for interlibrary borrowing.[2]

2.1.5 Making Outsourcing Decisions

In much the same vein, the assessment of outsourcing decisions should be based on concrete evidence of costs. In particular, it is important to establish a solid basis for accounting for all costs associated with a given function, including proper allocation of indirect costs.

It is interesting to note that many if not most libraries outsource at least part of their process of selection of materials to be acquired. They do so through what are called "standing orders" or "approval plans," in which a significant part of the selection decision is made by vendors. While this may appear to be a "free service," there are hidden costs in internal operations if not real costs in vendor fees, and those costs need to be assessed. For example, the effective acceptance rate for an approval plan may be so low that the time required in internal review becomes excessive. To make that assessment requires an adequate model of the elements of cost in such a process.

Managing approval plan acquisitions is an operational issue. Two types of approval plan procedures are typically operative. One of them involves receiving books on approval; the other involves receiving order forms for books that might be ordered. A concern may be with the apparent inefficiency represented by a high percentage of books received on approval that turn out to be returned (many of them later to be acquired by direct order).

In both cases—books on approval and order forms—the decision to acquire is based on an identification, by faculty or by library staff, that the book should be acquired. Given that as the procedure, it is by no means surprising that a high percentage of books received on approval would not be identified and therefore not be acquired.

The prima facie assumption might be that books sent on approval match well to the profile of needs at a specific library. Based on that, books sent on approval should be acquired unless someone says otherwise. The result surely would be a dramatic increase in the percentage of books sent on approval that are acquired. Elimination of the double or triple handling would be a great gain in efficiency.

---

[2] Palmour, V.E., et al., *A Study of the Characteristics, Costs, and Magnitude of Interlibrary Loans in Academic Libraries.* Rockville, MD: Westat, 1971.

In sharp contrast, of course, are the titles that are represented by order forms. For them, the prima facie assumption would be that they at best marginally match the profile. Based on that, they should be acquired only if someone explicitly says so.

Some libraries, though, have gone further in outsourcing their selection decision, and have contracted with external vendors to do the entire job. The most evident and controversial example was the Hawaii Public Library System, in which the results were seen as near catastrophic. As this example illustrates, more than simple assessments of costs are necessary. They must be balanced with effectiveness.

In the area of cataloging, outsourcing of original cataloging is now the accepted practice in virtually every library—public, academic or special—for the great majority of its acquisitions, even to the level of 90%. Some libraries, though, have gone even further and have outsourced the entire workload in cataloging. The most evident case in point was the University of Ohio, which contracted with OCLC for such outsourcing of cataloging.

2.2
Library Tactical Management

2.2.1 Tactical Issues

Despite the evident importance of issues in operational management, as outlined above, those in tactical management are likely to have far greater long-term importance. They involve decisions about allocating resources—money, people, equipment, space, and facilities. They will directly determine what operational management must deal with, so they will entail political negotiations as well as technical evaluations.

2.2.2 Staff Assignment

During the past several decades, the need to plan for reassignment of staff has been a continuing issue for library management, for a variety of reasons. Two reasons, in particular, have been of special significance.

One has been the effect of automation on library technical and user services. In particular, there has been dramatically increased use of copy cataloging in the decades since implementation of the MARC format, the establishment of cooperative cataloging, and the creation of the international bibliographic utilities (e.g., OCLC and RLIN). Of course, even before those developments, libraries used the Card Production Service of the Library of Congress and parallel commercial services as sources for standard cataloging. But still, for major research libraries at least, there was a high level of original cataloging. That changed dramatically as libraries began to introduce automated systems and needed to convert catalog data to machine-readable forms, both for current acquisitions and for retrospective conversion of existing catalogs. Clearly the need was to deal with conversion of catalog data as a cooperative task, sharing the workload and the resulting data. Hence the development of MARC and the bibliographic utilities.

The effect on cataloging staff, though, while not immediate became increasingly evident during the 1970s. From a situation in which virtually all of the cataloging in a major research library was likely to be original, today it will be less than 25% and, for the typical ARL library, even less than 10%. This implies a dramatic reduction in the number of professional catalogers needed in those libraries and an increase in the number of clerical staff using the bibliographic utilities as sources for copy cataloging and making relatively simple changes to reflect local needs.

Fortunately, counterbalancing the reduction in need for professional catalogers have been increased needs for reader services staff. In large part, this too has reflected the impact of automation on library services and the need to assist patrons in the use of online public access catalogs and the Internet. But management of this rather massive shift of personnel has required delicacy and wisdom.

A second reason that reassignment of staff has been a management issue is the effect of economic conditions. During the decade from 1985 to 1995, the major universities of the United States experienced severe reductions in budgets, by as much as 25% in some years. And of course the libraries of those institutions were directly affected. In most cases every effort was made to protect the acquisitions budgets, so the reductions in staff were the only means for dealing with such massive cuts.

In many cases, staff reductions were accomplished by early retirements (which were typically used for reductions not only of library staff but of academic staff—faculty—as well), the positions then remaining unfilled. But however the reductions may have been made, they necessitated reassignments of staff. Some academic libraries consolidated branches, with the view that they would gain efficiency in operations.

The task in management, of course, is to accomplish these kinds of reassignment is ways that will maintain operating effectiveness, that will meet the workload demands in both technical and readers services, and that will conform to budgetary requirements. For these kinds of management tasks the *LPM* has specific value. It provides means by which the effects of shifting of workloads— from original cataloging to copy cataloging, from cataloging to reader services, from departmental services to central services—can be assessed. The models for these decsions will be discussed in Chapters 4 and 5.

2.2.3 Collection Growth Management

Perhaps the most fundamental issue faced by the librarian in tactical planning is that of projecting the rate of growth of the collection. Budgets for operating personnel, capital investment for buildings, levels and kinds of service to be provided for—all ultimately tie back to this primary issue. How should the librarian predict such growth over a period as long as 20 to 30 years or more? Does the librarian depend solely on personal experience or the experience of colleagues? Must the community served be asked to make predictions of what they will need? Or does it simply depend upon a year-to-year balancing of immediate needs with apparently available funds?

The picture of exponential growth as the pattern for research library collections was first identified by Fremont Rider in 1938, but in the decades since then the management issue has repeatedly been revisited. Such growth rates have been predicated on the underlying facts of the production of information, especially in the sciences and technology. The facts are that the number of scientists has grown and continues to grow exponentially, so it is not surprising that the publication of books and journals in fields of science and technology have similarly proliferated.

The management problem, of course, is that library acquisitions budgets do not grow exponentially. In fact they tend not to grow at all, except as may be necessary to reflect inflation and even there they tend to grow more slowly. So faced with a steady-state budget and exponentially increasing information materials, what is the library manager to do? We will consider models for this decision in Chapter 6.

2.2.4 Collection Storage Decisions

In applying his exponential growth model to library growth, Rider was concerned with an operational planning problem: How were the resulting storage needs to be solved? The particular approach he was interested in exploiting was microimage storage (in the form of "Microcards"). Other approaches which have been suggested since then have included depository libraries, retirement policies, compact storage, sharing of resources through some form of network, and other forms of storage (such as digital).

The Center for Research Libraries, as a shared depository facility, was among the first and in many respects the most extensive attempts to deal with the collection storage problem. The State of California adopted a similar approach for its academic libraries of the University of California and State University and College System. It set up two regional depository facilities, one in the north and one in the south.

The management decision in this operational planning situation can be easily stated: How to choose among the alternative methods of storage, and how to decide what material to allocate to each alternative? A number of models have been proposed as possible answers, and they are discussed in Chapter 6.

2.2.5 Space and Facility Planning

Without question, the all-encompassing tactical issue is the planning for new space and facilities. It requires estimation of requirements over a long time into the future, as much as twenty to thirty years. It involves every aspect of operations—collections and their expected growth and requirements for storage, users and their requirements for services and facilities, and staffing to provide both technical and user services and their requirements for operations. Each of those is affected by policies of the institution, by operational realities, and by technological developments. Each not only must be projected over an uncertain future, but must be translated into specifications for space that will provide an adequate basis for an architect to design a new building, to modify an existing one, or in general to create the space required to serve the library over the identified planning horizon.

A separate issue in space and facility planning, aside from the amount of space that will be required, is the configuration of that space to meet the operational and service needs. Units of the library must be collocated so as to assure that the flow of persons and materials is efficient. One model for representing the needs in this respect is a matrix showing the frequency of traffic flow from one unit to and from another. That matrix can then be analyzed to identify groupings of units that have high degrees of interaction and which therefore should be collocated.

The models presented throughout this book have direct utility in making these kinds of assessments.

2.2.6 Information Acquisition Decisions

The past several decades have seen exponential increases in the prices of scientific and technical journals, of the magnitude of 15% to 20% per annum. The result has been a heart-wrenching erosion of the budget for acquisitions and a steady, almost catastrophic shift of that budget from monographs to journals. Some libraries have established a policy of maintaining the commitment to monographs by limiting expenditures for serials to something on the order of 60% of the budget.

Complicating this decision problem has been the uncertainties about the pace at which publishers will move to electronic distribution. Furthermore, it is not at all clear whether they will maintain the print formats, replace them by electronic formats, or provide a combination of both. Even for electronic distribution, the choices are not clear, since the potential is that there can be a mix of CD-ROM (or DVD) and online, through the Internet.

The models for dealing with this set of issues are discussed in Chapter 8.

2.2.7 Balancing Capital Investment and Operating Expenses

Given the pressure from these inflationary increases in costs of journals, one of the most challenging management issues has been the choice between collection development and information access, between investment in the future and meeting needs of the present, between "just in case" and "just in time."

Virtually every academic administrator has, at one time or another, seen the library as a fiscal black hole—growing exponentially, needing more and more resources, needing new, ever-larger buildings. In some states, construction of new library buildings has been absolutely stopped during the past twenty to thirty years, yet university library collections have continued to grow. What is to be done?

And now appears the answer to every academic administrator's dream— the promise of electronic distribution of information! Instead of acquiring more and more books and journals—so many of which appear never to be used—we can get them when we need them, by electronic access. No more acquisitions budgets; no more unused dusty old volumes taking up valuable space; no more library buildings which are so expensive to build.

But there are many institutions that can provide "access"; only the library is committed to assuring preservation of the published records of the past. If the library loses that and becomes merely another among the many agencies that provide access, where then will the library be? Like Esau, it will have sold its birthright, but this time for a "pot of messages" that, as they are used, will filter through fingers like sand and then disappear, with nothing left. The library will have lost its value, lost its role in society, lost its soul and birthright.

Clearly, access is important. Indeed, historically it meant "access to one's own collection"; it was that meaning that made it possible for the library to embrace the principle of "free access," since once it had made the capital investment in its collection there were minimal added costs in the use of it by any and all. In that historical context, ILL was not regarded as "access," but simply as the means by which materials could be shared.

But within the past decades, "access" has become something quite different; it now means not access to one's own collection but access to the entire world of materials. With such a meaning, in the future world of electronic information it increasingly will be tempting to shift the resources of the individual library from acquisitions to access; indeed in many contexts administrative pressures may well force such decisions. How else will we pay for steadily increasing costs in access?

And there are costs in access and resources must be committed to them. Access is not free nor will electronic publication and distribution be so simple and cheap as the enthusiasts appear to think. There are real costs in communication, even though the Internet may seem, for the moment maybe or for the near future perhaps, to eliminate them for the users; there are even greater costs incurred by the library or the individual in identifying materials and getting to the point of access; there will be increasing costs imposed from the sources as they achieve positions of virtual monopoly; and most importantly the basic cost of the information itself will not be reduced, whatever the means for distribution, whether electronic or print. Already we see charges for "document delivery" that are comparable to the costs incurred by lending libraries in interlibrary loan, and if there are truly significant shifts from "acquisition" to "access," those charges are bound to increase dramatically. Libraries and the users they serve will find that they have become captive markets, dependent on electronic access and with no other means for meeting information needs.

The crucial point is that by transferring resources from acquisitions to what are purely operating expenses in access, the library's investment in its collection will be diminished, perhaps eventually even reduced to nothing. Where, then, is the library?

It is this dilemma that underlies much of the modeling in Chapter 6 and in Part 3; Chapters 7 through 9.

2.2.8 ILL Operations

With respect to ILL operations, there are two issues of tactical importance. One relates directly to acquisition decisions and results from an exceptionally valuable policy now operational at some libraries. That policy directly uses the fact of an ILL borrowing request to assess whether the requested item should be purchased instead of being borrowed. If the item is in print and, indeed, has been published within the past five years, it is a prime candidate for being acquired, since experience clearly confirms that materials once needed are very likely to be needed again—and the request is clear evidence of a need.

This is very valuable as a means for strategic management of the acquisition process. It should apply not only to ILL borrowing but to document delivery requests as well, and it should enter into decisions concerning journal acquisition and deacquisition as well as to monograph acquisition.

The second tactical issue related to ILL operation concerns the cost for borrowing and lending. In fact, the costs in borrowing—primarily for staff time—have been estimated at twice the costs of lending, with a total for both on the order of $30 to $40 depending upon how indirect costs are handled. Given the real magnitude of costs for ILL, two developments are now underway.

First, there is an increasing move on the part of libraries that are "net lenders" to impose fees for borrowing from them; that has been facilitated by the implementation by OCLC of a "clearinghouse" service that makes it feasible to manage the accounting and billing without incurring uneconomic costs for doing so. While reciprocal agreements may still obviate such charging for a large percentage of borrowing, the likelihood is great that an increasing percentage of requests will require payment. And the level of fees being charged are virtually equivalent to those charged by commercial document delivery services. As a result, there may be a steady shift from ILL to document delivery as the means for serving needs.

Second, it is becoming increasingly feasible for the patrons to initiate requests themselves for both ILL and document delivery. The effect is greatly to reduce the costs incurred by the library, since staff time is significantly reduced. The operational question is whether such patron-initiated requests should be monitored by library staff both to assure that uses are economical and to provide the data for strategic decisions concerning acquisitions.

2.2.9 Location Decisions

It is well known that the use of a library or other information resource is inversely related to the distance that the user must travel in order to get to it. In their study of branch library system planning, Coughlin and his associates approach this issue as a marketing problem, and identify the serving area around a branch library by the geographic radius encompassing, as a representative value, 80 percent of its users.[3] With the ready availability of data from the U.S. census, it is possible to determine the socioeconomic characteristics of the population within that serving area and then compare it with the characteristics of the population in other areas. Although typically, as in the Coughlin study, this shows a clear correlation between socioeconomic level and degree of library usage, it can also be used to identify different patterns of library service needed to meet the needs of those population differences.

The various models available to support decision-making about library location are thoroughly and well covered by Christine Koontz.[4]

[3] Coughlin, Robert E, et al., *Urban Analysis for Branch Library System Planning.* Westport, CT: Greenwood Press, 1972

[4] Koontz, Christine M., *Library Facility Siting and Location Handbook* Westport, CT: Greenwood Press, 1997.

2.2.10 Automated Library Systems Development

Development of automated library systems for both services and internal data processing in libraries has been a tactical issue of continuing importance in libraries for the past three decades at least. In making such decisions, the application of systems analysis to the library is the crucial technical methodology in aid of management. Who is the library systems analyst? What is his or her role in data processing development and implementation? What is his or her relationship to the library? What are the tools and techniques which he or she uses?

Chapter 1 provided a brief general overview of the steps and methodologies involved in systems analysis. They are fully applicable in considering automated library systems. Of special importance among those steps is determining the proper scope of the automated library system. Today, unless there are reasons of overwhelming significance to do otherwise, the scope should be the total integrated system since the technology for that scope is now so well developed. Beyond that, though, the impact of the Internet is now so pervasive that there is good reason to expand the scope to include the wider, Internet-oriented issues, including access to reference resources, databases, and digital libraries as part of the system design requirements. In particular, in the design of an automated system today for a given library, significant external factors should be taken into consideration—the strategic effects of decisions by book publishers, by national cooperative library systems, by library funding agencies, and so on. The library systems planner must take them into account to insure compatibility of any new library systems with those of such external agencies.

2.2.11 Capital Equipment Expenditures

Academic libraries in general appear to deal with capital equipment funding on an ad hoc basis. Major items, such as equipment and software for an integrated library system will be acquired as a capital purchase, but little attention will be paid to the need to plan for additions, upgrades, modifications, and/or replacements. Furniture may be acquired as part of the construction of the library building, but little attention will be paid to the effects of wear and tear. Equipment may be installed as part of the working structure of a building, but little attention will be paid to the need to upgrade and repair. Audio-visual and microform equipment may be acquired in implementation of a program, but little attention will be paid to the need for newer equipment.

The result is that capital equipment needs will come as budgetary surprises, not as a planned progression of commitments.

2.3
Library Strategic Management

2.3.1 Strategic Issues

As the term "strategic" is used here, it is concerned with issues over which the library manager has little if any control and yet which have direct effect upon the internal decisions at the operational and tactical levels.

2.3.2 Institutional Policy Effects

Institutional policies that will be examined include those for governance of libraries, telecommunications, computers, media centers, and similar information resources. Various models for such governance will be discussed. While the models are all essentially nonquantitative, there may be elements that can be quantified, and that will be the focus of discussion. Others policies will include those related to staffing, to space allocation, and to budget determination. Again, the focus of discussion will be on the extent to which they can be quantified.

2.3.3 Interlibrary Cooperation Effects

The role of library networks will be examined again with respect to policies for governance, operations, and charging. Again, while these are largely nonquantitative, the focus of discussion will be on the extent to which they can be quantified. The most far-reaching solution to the problems posed by library growth is the creation of cooperative library networks. By depending upon the availability of material from other libraries and depository centers, the individual library can limit the size of its own growth and specialize in those materials it regards as of particular importance or high frequency of use. The design and evaluation of library networks is therefore a task of real strategic importance to individual of libraries as a whole. It is in part a function of cost; in part a function of the volume of traffic among libraries; and in part a function of the response time both to be expected and to be actually achieved, Models have been developed which represent one or more of these considerations.

2.3.4 National Information Policy Effects

A range of national information policies will be discussed. Some of them will relate to the models discussed in Chapter 9, with special focus on the implications in development of information economies—issues such as taxation, intellectual property rights and fair use, and information security. Again, while these are largely nonquantitative, the focus of discussion will be on the extent to which they can be quantified.

2.4
Data Acquisition for Use in Models

In the following chapters, as each kind of model is considered, the nature and sources for data appropriate to it will be specifically discussed, but it is important to identify from the outset the kinds of sources that can be considered, the problems that arise from them, and the means for solving those problems.

2.4.1 Sources of Data

Potential sources of data include (1) published literature, (2) published statistics, (3) documents specific to individual institutions, and (4) observation and experiment. Each of these sources, especially the published sources, exhibits various kinds of problems that must be recognized—in definition of data elements, in consistency in reporting, in reliability of data acquisition, and in interpretation and use. Methods for dealing with those problems will be discussed. Among them is the use of the *LPM* as a means for calibrating and assessing the reliability of data, since it provides a standard or benchmark against which to compare specific data.

Published Literature
There are many articles that report data that may be usable in models. Some research articles provide details of the data used in the reported studies. The published reports of some libraries contain data about their operations.

Published Statistics
Throughout the book there are some sources for published statistics that will be of specific value. The bibliography for this chapter includes a listing of them. Among them, for the academic library field, the two primary sources of published statistics are the Association of Research Libraries (ARL) and the Association of College and Research Libraries (ACRL). Each publishes yearly statistics for its members and has done so for many years (ARL, since 1964–65, although some data are available going back to 1907–08; and ACRL, since 1978–79). Together they provide data of inestimable value. The definitions of

the statistical categories were specified to be those given in *Library Statistics* (ALA, 1966). This specification has not changed over the years.

More broadly, for academic libraries the Department of Education publishes yearly statistics derived from the Higher Education General Information Survey (HEGIS). The HEGIS database is accumulated from a questionnaire sent to 3200 institutions.

Documents for Specific Institutions

One would think that at least documents that are specific to an institution would be reliable, consistent, and accurate sources of data. Such documents might include annual reports, internal operating reports, and accumulated statistics. Unfortunately, though, these are as unreliable, inconsistent, and inaccurate as any of the other sources. There are literally no guarantees and sometimes no means for assessment. Sometimes, even the internal documents that, in principle, will represent the sources for submission to HEGIS, IPEDS, ARL, or ACRL will be inconsistent with the published data. Annual reports will differ from year to year in their coverage of data and even in the definition of data elements.

Personal Observation and Experiment

This data source may turn out to be necessary as means not only for obtaining data but for calibrating data obtained from other sources.

2.4.2   Generic Problems with Data

Unfortunately, the data from almost any sources suffer from a variety of problems. The published literature is a notoriously unreliable source of data.[5] Leaving aside the question of whether the data as reported are reliable, the most common problem is the fact that two articles will typically use very different frames of reference for the data they present. Just to illustrate, one article may be reporting "time and motion" data and another reporting total costs. To use such data, at least in combination with each other, it is crucial that they be carefully analyzed to reduce them to a common frame of reference. One means to do so is to convert one to the other by using estimates of the ratio of the two kinds of costs, based on prior experience or by analysis of the reported data. Later, as part of the discussion of means for determining workload factors, some

---

[5] Bourne, Charles P., *Summary Cost Data from 300 Reports of Library Technical Processing Activities.* Berkeley: University of California, June 1977.

Bourne, Charles P., and Kasson, Madeleine S., *Preliminary Report of the Review and Development of Standard Cost Data for Selected Library Technical Processing Functions.* Prepared for the Council on Library Resources. Palo Alto, CA: Information General Corporation, Nov. 4, 1969.

typical rules of thumb will be presented for such ratios among various means for reporting data.

In the case of published statistics such as ARL and ACRL, just to illustrate, studies have repeatedly identified a wide range of inconsistencies in definition and in reporting by the participating libraries.[6] While the HEGIS survey in principal should be accurate, again there are many inconsistencies and some values must be imputed (i.e., calculated or estimated on the basis of historical data or implied relationships among fields of data). Fortunately, the Department of Education is careful to report such calculations, so the user will be aware of them, but still they create real problems. The types of inconsistencies for any of these sources are really generic:

1. The context for the data (e.g., the set of libraries or institutions covered) can change from year to year, both in number and in qualitative character. Even the definitions of what institutions are covered may be unreliable.
2. The definitions of categories of data may change over time and may vary among reporting institutions.
3. The values reported for a given category may be unreliable for a variety of reasons.

The problems are further complicated by the fact that in some cases a library simply may not adhere to the definition; in other cases, while the library may follow the definition, it does so with significant differences in interpretation. Just to illustrate, the most amazing changes in definitions in ARL statistics have occurred over the years in such categories of data as "Total Staff" and "Expenditures—Current Periodicals." A number of other categories have had significant changes in name but without discerniable changes in content (the changes being identified by the footnotes in the table).

Even documents for specific institutions will present problems. For example, data reported from one year to the next frequently will not be comparable because the respective documents have different purposes or different definitions for the data.

2.4.3 Specific Problems with Data

These kinds of generic problems are exhibited for each category of data.

---

[6] Hayes, Robert M. with Pollock, Ann M., and Nordhaus, Shirley, "An Application of the Cobb-Douglas Model to the Association of Research Libraries, *Library and Information Science Research* 5, 3 (Fall 1983), pp. 291–325 (see especially about ARL inconsistencies).

Problems with Data About Staffing

The problems with the reporting of staff can perhaps best be illustrated by simply quoting from the ARL Instructions for Completion of the Questionnaire (1978–79, p. 3): "Since the criteria for determining professional status vary among libraries, there is no attempt to define the term 'professional.' Each library should report those staff members it considers professional, including when appropriate, staff who are not librarians in the strict sense of the term, such as computer experts, systems analysts, budget officers, etc."

The category of "Nonprofessional FTE" obviously depends upon the definition used for professional, which as noted above can vary widely. Beyond that, some instances can be found in which student assistants were included in this category (despite the fact that there is a separate category for those data). Two other kinds of problems arise with respect to data about student staff. First, there are differing practices with respect to counting federally funded work-study student employees. Second, the estimates for FTE for student workers, because of the variability in work schedule, seem to vary widely.

Another category of staff is "Volunteers." In many public libraries and even some academic ones, they play a crucial role. Yet, libraries will vary greatly in whether they will report them and in what way. In a similar vein, some staff may be funded outside the library's own budget.

Since total staff is the sum of some or all of the three categories we've already discussed, it is subject to the variability resulting from them. Unfortunately, while some variability may balance (e.g., the assignment of a person to one subcategory or another), some will not.

Another problem arises in the difference between "budgeted position" and "filled positions." On the surface of it, this would seem to be easy to resolve, but doing so is complicated by the use of "volunteers" and by midyear changes in positions. Definitions for a given library in these respects may well change from year to year.

Beyond the inconsistencies due to variations in the definitions, there are also inconsistencies due to time lags in implementing changes in definition. Frequently, libraries will retain the prior reporting practice for varying numbers of years after a change has presumably been effected. In addition to the fact that libraries will vary in the time during which they retain prior reporting practice despite official changes in defintion, they will also vary in their interpretation of those definitions. And that vagueness or drift in definition will itself be inconsistent for a given library over time. All categories of data seem to suffer from this type of inconsistency to some degree. Items of data reported in one year will frequently be corrected or revised in subsequent years.

Problems with Data About Collections

The data for collections similarly differ in both definition and interpretation. Do the reported holdings include materials being processed, materials still uncataloged, and materials awaiting processing? How are nonbook materials (e.g., manuscripts, scores, calendars, A-V materials) counted? How are government documents reported and do they include both bound and unbound, cataloged and uncataloged? How are specialized materials (such as standards, pamphlets, reprints, theses, technical reports, analyzed series) treated?

Taking microforms as a specific example, reconciling the data from one institution with those from other institutions may be impossible for any of the following reasons: (1) The number of microforms may not be reported. (2) Only some cataloged microforms may be included, but there is no estimate of the number. (3) The volume count may be physical, but the microform count is bibliographical. (4) The volume count may be bibliographical, but the microform count is physical.

Libraries will determine the data for their holdings using a variety of methods: a bibliographical count (the unit presumably being the "title"), a physical count, combinations of those two (e.g., "physical count for monographs but bibliographic count for serials," "initial count bibliographical and later years count physical," "varies with the several units reporting"), and other methods (e.g., "linear foot estimation," "figure based on recent estimates," etc.).

Problems with Data About Budgets and Expenditures

Each of these categories is subject to wide variation with respect to whether they include expenses paid from grants, from special allocations (such as for computerization and file conversion projects), federally funded work-study student assistants, and other sources of noncontinuing funding. Costs for computer use may or may not be included (since in some cases they are not charged against the library's budget). Beyond these general sources of variability, there are the following more specific sources of variation in some of the subcategories.

Libraries differ in whether they report only binding expenses incurred out-of-house or include those incurred in-house, and usually the practice followed is not specified.

Salary expenses may or may not include fringe benefits. Sometimes fringe benefits will be included in other operating expenses; sometimes they won't be included anywhere at all and presumably are covered in the institutional budget for benefits.

Problems with Data About Workloads

Interlibrary lending was first reported in 1973–74. In some cases the reported data may include data for medical libraries, in some cases not, but there is rarely any note identifying what the practice has been. Lending data may or may not include loans provided through networks or consortia; similarly for photocopies in lieu of loans. Furthermore, the data for photocopies are reported sometimes as number of requests, sometimes as number of prints made. It is likely that the parallel category, PHOTOCOPIES BORROWED, suffers from the same inconsistency. If so, both the TOTAL LOANED and the TOTAL BORROWED categories will be similarly inconsistent.

Problems with Data About Universities

Data related to each library's institution are also subject to widely varying practice. For example, the categories PH.D.'S AWARDED and PH.D. FIELDS were first reported in 1971–72. Although from the beginning the "Instructions…" state that statistics for all other advanced degrees were to be excluded, even the 1980 volume contains a footnote from one member which reads "Ph.D.s awarded 12 degrees that could be Ed.D." The several libraries adopt varying definitions for "fields," and the very definition of the category is explicitly different from that of the HEGIS form: Although HEGIS form requests figures for all doctoral degrees, only fields in which Ph.D.s are awarded should be reported (1979–80, p 44).

In general, the caution that the data are "unverified" is applicable to all of these categories. The HEGIS data for enrollment statistics, in particular, are all unverified.

2.4.4 Means for Solving Problems with Data

Given the array of problems, both generic and specific, the task of using data for management purposes is at best difficult. Indeed, among the most critical needs is to identify that there are problems with the data. Are there means for identifying that there are problems and for solving them?

Use of *LPM*

In fact, one of the primary purposes in creating the *LPM* is to provide a tool for exactly this purpose. For this purpose, data derived from whatever may be the source are entered into *LPM* and the results from *LPM* are compared with other data. For example, workload data reported for the library will be used and then the staffing estimates from *LPM* can be compared with reported data for actual staffing; estimates from *LPM* for the level of use of specific services can be compared with reported data for actual levels of use; estimates from *LPM* of expenditures can be compared with reported data for actual expenditures.

If *LPM* estimates agree with the reported actuals, one can proceed with the operating assumption that the data are reasonably accurate. But if *LPM* estimates differ substantially from the reported actuals, one is faced with a red flag. Either *LPM* is not appropriately representing things or something is wrong with the data. In either case, the existence of a potential problem has been identified.

Now, the potential that *LPM* is not appropriately representing things is very real and indeed likely, not necessarily because of inadequacies in it (though that is possible) but because of a lack of understanding of the nature of the specific library, the workloads, the staffing, or the budget. Just to illustrate with a real example: In one library the estimates for staffing provided by *LPM* were 25% less than the actual staffing. That is a huge difference, and the immediate question was, "What is wrong?" Are there problems with the data? Is *LPM* in error? Or is there something that was missed?

The answer turned out to be simple. The library was responsible for the publication functions for a large number of scholarly journals, and that fact had not been included in the initial application of *LPM*. Once that function was recognized, the estimates matched the reality exactly.

The potential that there are problems with the data, though, is even more likely. The variables for which discrepancies occur between *LPM* estimates and reported data allow one easily to determine where there may be erroneous data. As a result, one can examine those data, test them for reliability, determine whether the errors are a result of definition or measurement, and know what needs to be done to correct them.

Use of Standard Conversion Factors

Perhaps the simplest problems to resolve are those that reflect different units for physical measurement. For example, collections of materials may be reported in terms of number of items, number of linear feet, amount of square feet, and numbers of cabinets or drawers. The following table lists some conversion factors with representative values for them:

Representative Space Conversion Parameters	
Microform drawers per cabinet	17
Square feet per microfilm cabinet	11
16mm reels per drawer	135
16mm reels per square foot	209
16mm reels per linear foot	20
35mm reels per drawer	80
35mm reels per square foot	124
35mm per linear foot	10
Microfiche, items/drawer	2,500
Microfiche, square feet/drawer	1
Archives, linear feet/square foot	3
AV & electronic, items per linear foot	15
AV & electronic, items per square foot	30
Bound materials per linear foot	10
Bound materials per square foot	15

Use of Imputed Values

The HEGIS data exemplifys the use of imputed values as means for solving some problems with data, such as missing values or variant definitions. The imputed values are determined by calculating values from historic data and trends, by comparison with averages across comparable institutions, and by deriving them from combinations of other variables (for example, by subtracting "graduate students" from "total students" to determine "undergraduate students"). Any such imputations are potentially in error, but they do permit the analyst to proceed even if some data are missing or appear to be so in error that they must be replaced.

Calibration of Data

A powerful tool for identifying potential errors in data and even for correcting those errors is to calibrate them with other sources of data. Is the calculation from reported data for "average number of volumes per square foot" consistent with generally expected values? Is the calculated "ratio of students to faculty" consistent with generally observed ratios for similar institutions? Is the "price per journal" consistent with general experience?

In each case, the calibration is valuable primarily in identifying a potential problem. After examination of the data, it may well turn out to be correct, of course, but if not the means for calibration may well be used to determine what is erroneous in the data and what is needed to correct them.

2.4.5 Summary

As this recounting of problems with data should demonstrate, every source of data is very slippery. It is possible, of course, to make fairly reliable corrections for explicit changes in definition, either in the overall or as interpreted by individual libraries in specific years. In some cases, data can be flagged for inclusion or exclusion to allow for valid comparisons among data for various years or institutions. But there are so many cases in which these kinds of corrections are impossible that one must examine data very carefully, both individually and as a whole.

Bibliography

References for Library Location Analysis

Coughlin, Robert E., and others. *Urban Analysis for Branch Library System Planning.* Westport, CT: Greenwood Press, 1972.

Hayes, Robert M., and Palmer, E. Susan. "The Effects of Distance upon Use of Libraries: Case Studies Based on a Survey of Users of the Los Angeles Public Central Library and Branches," *Library Research* 5, pp. 67–100.

Koontz, Christine M. *Library Facility Siting and Location Handbook.* Westport, CT: Greenwood Press, 1997. This is an excellent example of modeling. It provides both descriptive and quantitative material and covers the crucial models for library facility siting and location.

Morrill, Richard L. *The Spatial Organization of Society.* Belmont, CA: Duxbury Press, 1970.

Shishko, Robert. *Centralization versus Decentralization. A Location Analysis Approach for Librarians.* Santa Monica, CA, Rand Corp. 1971. Rand Corporation, Paper P-4687.

Thompson, James Howard. *Methods of Plant Site Selection Available to Small Manufacturing Firms.* Morgantown. West Virginia University, 1961.

References for Outsourcing

Woodsworth, Anne, and Williams, James F. *Managing the Economics of Owning, Leasing, and Contracting Out Information Services.* Aldershot, England: Gower; Brookfield, VT: Ashgate, 1994. An excellent coverage of the issues involved in using external contractors.

References for Data Sources

A Classification of Institutions of Higher Education; with a foreword by Ernest L. Boyer, 1987 ed. Princeton, NJ: Carnegie Foundation for the Advancement of Teaching, 1987. Series title: Original edition: A Carnegie Foundation technical report, Carnegie Foundation technical report. (This is background for the Carnegie Classification of institutions of higher education as used in IPEDS, q.v.)

Annual Statistics of Medical School Libraries in the United States and Canada, compiled by Houston Academy of Medicine, Texas Medical Center Library. Houston, TX: Houston Academy of Medicine, Texas Medical Center Library, 1978. Annual 1977/1978. Related titles: Medical library statistics.

ARL Academic Law and Medical Library Statistics, Association of Research Libraries. Washington, DC: The Association. Annual began with: 1977–78 to 1991–92. (Print and Diskette).

Association of Research Libraries. *ARL Academic Law and Medical Library Statistics, 1992–93 to 1994–95,* compiled and edited by Martha Kyrillidou, Kimberly A. Maxwell. Washington, DC: Association of Research Libraries, 1996. Related titles: Academic law and medical library statistics.

Higher Education Revenues and Expenditures, 1987–88. Washington, DC: Research Associates of Washington, 1990.

Integrated Postsecondary Education Data System: Higher Education Finance Data, IPEDS. From ICPSR (Interuniversity Consortium for Political and Social Research).

Keynote/Boardwatch: Index of Backbone Providers. Downloaded on Aug. 20, 1998 from http://www.keynote.com/measures/backbones/backbones.html.

Medical Library Statistics, 1974–75. Dallas: Library, University of Texas Health Science Center, Dallas, 1976.

Medical Library Statistics, 1975–76 compiled by Donald D. Hendricks. Dallas: Library, University of Texas Health Science Center at Dallas, 1977.

Molyneux, Robert E. *ACRL Academic Library Statistics: 1978/79–1987/88.* Chicago: Association of College and Research Libraries, 1989.

National Center for Educational Statistics: *Academic Library Survey.* Available online at http://nces.ed.gov/surveys/academic data. U.S. Department of Education, National Center for Education Statistics, ICPSR 2738A-8, yearly.

National Center for Educational Statistics: *Public Library Survey.* Available online at http://nces.ed.gov/surveys/librarydata. U.S. Department of Education, National Center for Education Statistics, ICPSR 2738A-8, yearly.

Network Wizards, *Internet Domain Survey* (as of July 1998). Downloaded on Aug. 20, 1998 from http://www.nw.com/zone/www/top.htlm.

Research Library Statistics. Washington, DC: Association of Research Libraries (published yearly). Available online at http://www.arl.org/stats/arlstats.

Statistical Abstract of the United States (current year). (available at website www.census.gov/statab or on CD-ROM).

Statistics for Academic Business Libraries: http://cubl.johnson.cornell.edu/.

Statistics on Worldwide Publishing: http://ironwood.lib.utexas.edu/cird/publishing.html.

The first site listed here is the home page for the National Center for Educational Statistics. It leads directly to the pages for public and academic libraries and to the related data files, as shown in the other websites listed.

> *http://nces.ed.gov/, http://nces.ed.gov/surveys/libraries/public.html,*
> *http://nces.ed.gov/surveys/libraries/academic.html,*
> *http://nces.ed.gov/surveys/libraries/data.html#public*

United States Department of Commerce, Bureau of the Census. http://www.census.gov/. This site will lead directly into the array of reports and databases available online from the Bureau of the Census. Among them are "mrts" data for current retail sales, for example.

References for Library Applications of Scientific Management

Baker, Norman R., and Nance, Richard E. *The Use of Simulation in Studying Information Storage and Retrieval Systems.* Lafayette, IN: Purdue University, Nov. 22, 1967.

Bergman, Jed I. *Managing Change in the Nonprofit Sector: Lessons from the Evolution of Five Independent Research Libraries.* San Francisco: Jossey-Bass, 1996.

Bohem, Hilda. *Disaster Prevention and Disaster Preparedness.* Berkeley: Office of the Assistant Vice President—Library Plans and Policies, Systemwide Administration, University of California. This book is probably irrelevant to the book, but is included because it reflects such a well done, reasoned, even scientific approach to dealing with an important library management problem.

Chapman, Edward A., et al. *Library Systems Analysis Guidelines* New York: Wiley-Interscience, 1970. This book provides a classical review of methods and tools for systems analysis, applying them specifically to library automation.

Coney, Donald. "Management in College and Research Libraries," *Library Trends* 1, 91 (July 1, 1952).

De Gennaro, Richard. *Libraries, Technology, and the Information Marketplace: Selected Papers.* Boston: G.K. Hall, 1987. This compilation of papers written by De Gennaro covers a wide range of topics, from early stages in library automation to the most current issues related to the impact of digital libraries.

Dougherty, Richard M., and Fred J. Heinritz. *Scientific Management of Library Operations,* 2nd ed. New York: Scarecrow Press, 1966. This is an excellent expository introduction to the application of scientific management to libraries. It focuses on tools and techniques for data gathering, data analysis, project planning. Among the techniques included are flowcharting, time and motion study, forms management.

Erickson, E. Walfred. *College and University Library Surveys, 1938–1952.* Chicago: American Library Association, 1961. The surveys presented really relate to issues in library management, serving "as means of measuring the effectiveness." The kinds of management issues discussed include governance, organization, administration; technical services; readers' services; cooperation; library buildings; personnel; collections; financial administrion. All of them are critical and important to this book.

Fingerman, Joel. *Applied Statistics for Libraries: A Primer in Statistical Techniques and Library Applications.* Houston: Association of Academic Health Sciences Library Directors, c1986. (Book and related Computer File).

Goldhor, Herbert. *An Introduction to Scientific Research in Librarianship.* Urbana, IN: University of Illinois, Graduate School of Library Science, 1972. Goldhor covers both qualitative methods (e.g., historical research) and quantitative methods (statistical tools, in particular).

Goldhor, Herbert. *Research Methods in Librarianship: Measurement and Evaluation;* papers presented at a conference conducted by the University of Illinois Graduate School of Library Science, September 10–13, 1967. Urbana: University of Illinois Graduate School of Library Science, 1968. It must be said that the papers presented here are almost universally descriptive, but they do provide an introduction to some issues in scientific management of libraries.

Hamburg, Morris, and others. "Library Objectives and Performance Measures and Their Use in Decision Making," *Library Quarterly* 42, 1 (Jan. 1972), pp. 107–128.

Kent, Allen. *Library Planning for Automation.* Washingtons DC: Spartan Books, 1965.

Lancaster, F. Wilfrid. *The Measurement and Evaluation of Library Services.* Washington, DC: Information Resources Press, 1977.

Leimkuhler, Ferdinand F. "Mathematical Models for Library Systems Analysis," *Drexel Library Quarterly* 4 (July 1968), pp. 18–196.

Morelock, M., and Leimkuhler, F. F. "Library Operations Research and Systems Engineering Studies," *College and Research Libraries* 25 (Nov. 1964), pp. 501–503.

Morse, Philip M. "Measures of Library Effectiveness," *Library Quarterly* 42, 1 (Jan. 1972), pp. 15–30.

Morse, Philip M. *Library Effectiveness: A Systems Approach.* Cambridge, MA: MIT Press, 1968.

Operations Research: Implications for Planning. Proceedings of the 35th Annual Conference of the Graduate Library School, University of Chicago. *Library Quarterly* 42, 1 (Jan. 1972).

Osborne, Larry N. *Systems Analysis for Librarians and Information Professionals.* Englewood, CO: Libraries Unlimited, 1994. A standard coverage of the methods and tools of systems analysis with focus on library automation.

Research in Librarianship, Mary Jo Lynch, issue editor. Champaign, IL: University of Illinois Graduate School of Library and Information Science, 1984. *Library Trends* 32, 4.

Research in Librarianship, Library Trends 6, 2 (Oct. 1957). Champaign, IL: University of Illinois Graduate School of Library and Information Science, 1957). Though completely qualitative in the methods, this is an important historical reference.

Research Methods in Librarianship, Library Trends 13, 1 (July 1964). Champaign, IL: University of Illinois Graduate School of Library and Information Science, 1964. The focus is still almost totally on qualitative, descriptive methods.

Shaw, Ralph R. *Scientific Management in Libraries.* An issue of *Library Trends* 2, 3 (Jan. 1954). Urbana, IL: University of Illinois Library School, 1954. Ralph Shaw was one of the great figures of modern librarianship. He was Director of the Library of the Department of Agriculture, the librarian who experimented with the Rapid Selector (a microfilm-based retrieval system), and Dean of the School of Librarianship at Rutgers University. This issue of *Library Trends* contains articles that are essentially descriptive but still useful in identifying issues and means.

Srikantaiah, Taverekere. *An Introduction to Auantitative Research Methods for Librarians,* 2nd ed. rev. Santa Ana, CA: Headway Publications, 1978, 1977.

References for General Library Management

Advances in Library Administration and Organization: A Research Annual, Vol. 10 (1992), editors, Gerard B. McCabe, Bernard Kreissman. Greenwich, CT: JAI Press, 1991.

Biehi, W. J. "Libraries Need Good Management," *Library Quarterly* (December 20, 1962), pp. 317–319.

Hayes, Robert M. *Strategic Management for Academic Libraries.* Westport, CT: Greenwood, 1993; Hayes, Robert M. *Strategic Management for Public Libraries.* Westport, CT: Greenwood, 1996. These two books, as well as providing a pair of commentaries on library management, contain chapters that have specific relevance to this book.

Influencing Change in Research Librarianship: A Festschrift for Warren J. Haas, edited by Martin M. Cummings with the assistance of Ellen B. Timmer. Washington, DC: Council on Library Resources, 1988. Jim Haas was among the most important modern librarians. He was Director of Libraries at Columbia University and then became the third President of the Council on Library Resources (after Verner Clapp and Fred C. Cole). He played crucial roles in funding of automation developments in academic libraries.

Planning in OCLC Member Libraries, edited by M.E.L. Jacob; Sondra Albanese, editorial assistant. Dublin, OH: OCLC Online Computer Library Center, 1988.

Shera, Jesse Hauk. *The Foundations of Education for Librarianship.* New York: Becker and Hayes. 1972

Taylor, Robert S. *The Making of a Library: The Academic Library in Transition.* U.S. Dept. of Health, Education and Welfare, Office of Education, Bureau of Research, 1970.

Wheeler, Joseph Lewis. *Practical Administration of Public Libraries,* rev. ed. Completely revised by Carlton Rochell. New York: Harper & Row, 1981.

Wilson, Louis Round. *The University Library: The Organization, Administration, and Functions of Academic Libraries,* 2nd ed. New York: Columbia Univ. Press, 1956. These two books are the classic texts for management of their respective types of libraries. Unfortunately, they each pay at best limited attention to such technical areas as accounting or tools of scientific management.

Appendix

The CD-ROM associated with this book includes, in addition to the operating copy of LPM—The Library Planning Model, four files of academic library data. Permission has been received from the ARL (Association of Research Libraries) to include years 1997/1998 and 1998/1999) of their data and from the ACRL (Association of College and Research Libraries) to include years 1994/1995 and 1996/1997) of their data.

The following description of their program of academic library statistics was provided by the ARL.

ARL Statistics and Performance Measures

One of the longest-running and most recognizable activities of ARL is the statistics program. Quantitative and descriptive statistics have been collected and published annually by ARL since 1961-62. The publication ARL Statistics describes the collections, expenditures, staffing, and service activities of the member libraries of ARL. Before 1962, annual statistics for university libraries were collected by James Gerould, first at Minnesota and later at Princeton. These data cover the years 1907-08 through 1961-62 and are now called the Gerould Statistics. The whole data series from 1908 to the present represents the oldest and most comprehensive continuing library statistical series in North America.

The ARL Annual Salary Survey, first published for 1972-73, currently compiles data for over 12,000 professional positions concerning average, median, and beginning salaries; salaries by position and experience, sex, and race/ethnic background; and salaries in different geographic regions and sizes of libraries. Published annually since 1992-93, ARL Academic Law and Medical Library Statistics reports data on collections, expenditures, staffing, and user services in the law and medical libraries of ARL university members. Preservation Statistics, published annually since 1988-89, includes data tables on personnel, expenditures, conservation treatment, preservation treatment, and preservation microfilming, as well as an in-depth analysis of data by size of library. In 2000, ARL Supplementary Statistics, with data on the size and kind of member's electronic resources, was first made available to the public, after being used since 1983 as a test for collecting information on new measures in libraries. Developing Indicators for Academic Library Performance: Ratios from the ARL Statistics, which presented 30 selected ratios that describe changes in internal library operations, as well as resources per facility and per student, for the ARL university libraries over a two-year period, was published for the years 1992 through 1999. Those ratios can now be generated from the interactive website<http://www.arl.org/stats>.

For many years the traditional statistics projects, ARL Statistics and the Salary Survey, were supported through volunteer efforts from member institutions. Kendon Stubbs, of the University of Virginia, served as the consultant for the main statistics and Gordon Fretwell, University of Massachusetts at Amherst, was the salary survey consultant. They were instrumental in establishing the data collection activities and ensuring the consistent high quality of the data. In 1994, the program was expanded to include a full-time program officer and the data gathering activities were made available over the web; more extensive custom reports were made available to members; and the Association became ever more active in other national library and higher education data gathering efforts.

A timeline of program activities <http://www.arl.org/stats/program/timeline.html> highlights the Association's interest in statistics and descriptive data about research libraries. These data have been used both for comparative purposes and also to track the trends of investment in research libraries for the better part of the twentieth century. The timeline also demonstrates the attempt by ARL over the years to respond to the need to look at more than descriptive data. In the early 1980s, the Statistics Committee began to look for ways to objectively measure organizational performance and began to collect supplementary statistical data that provided information on a variety of measures including those that address access to information resources.

In 1999, the ARL Statistics and Leadership Committees, and other interested member leaders, began what has become the ARL New Measures Initiative. The initiative is an effort to address the need to develop methods to measure how well libraries meet institutional and user needs and how well libraries use their resources and services. One area of interest is how to measure user expectations and perceptions of library services. The 1999-2000 LibQAL + pilot project tackled these questions. In 2000, ARL was awarded a grant by the U.S. Department of Education Fund for the Improvement of Postsecondary Education (FIPSE) to continue development work on the LibQUAL + protocol for three years. The goals of the project include the establishment of a library service quality assessment program at ARL; development of web-based tools for assessing library service quality; development of mechanisms and protocols for evaluating libraries; and identification of best practices in providing library service.

Another area of interest is how to measure the collection and use of electronic resources. The goals of the ARL E-Metrics project are to develop, test, and refine selected statistics and performance measures to describe electronic services and resources in ARL libraries; engage in a collaborative effort with selected database vendors to establish an ongoing means to produce selected descriptive statistics on database use, users, and services; and develop a proposal for external funding to maintain the development and refinement of networked statistics and performance measures.

These and other new projects that focus on higher education outcomes assessment, including the role that the library plays in support of learning, teaching, and research; identification of cost drivers; and applying the results of the ILL/DD Performance Measures cost study, can be followed at <http://www.arl.org/stats/newmeas/newmeas.html>.

3

The Library Planning Model

Introduction

This chapter provides an overview of the Library Planning Model *(LPM)*, a computer spreadsheet that provides a structure within which the several models presented in the following chapters of this book can be interrelated and easily brought together for application to operations in specific libraries and to the several policy contexts.

3.1

Menu Structure

LPM is "menu-driven," which means that all of its operations are initiated by the use of menus rather than commands. The *LPM* menu structure consists of nine main menu options: **File, Edit, View, Data Entry, Results, Modify, Strategic, Batch, Help.** The following sections will discuss the set of these as a whole and then discuss each of them in turn.

Fortunately, if you are among those who prefer to control things more directly, the series of menus you must move through to get to desired functions is quite shallow—just two or three levels deep.

Thus, in addition to the opening message, you will be presented with the main menu at the top of the screen, the entries being the main menu entries or top level of the menu structure shown below. If you use the cursor keys, each of the choices in the menu will be highlighted in turn. Alternatively, you can use the [ALT] key together with the underlined character in the name of the desired menu. To select the highlighted choice, press the [ENTER] key or click on the menu choice.

The result, after a series of selections, will be the initiation of an *LPM* function and the display of an *LPM* screen. Some functions call for you to perform an action (such as entry of data, in the Data Entry Menu or the Modify Menu), others, for *LPM* to display something (in the other menus). You specify the initiation of the action by choosing the [ENTER] key or clicking on the menu entry.

The menu structure to two levels is as follows (the ">" at the end of several submenus indicates that there is a third level for them):

Main Menu Entry	Sub-Menu Entry	Main Menu Entry	Sub-Menu Entry
FILE	Context	RESULTS	Show Results >
	Save		Allocation Options >
	Save As		Compare with Actuals >
	Page Setup		
	Print Area	MODIFY	Definitions >
	Print Preview		Workload Factors >
	Print		Facilities Factors >
			Cost Factors >
EDIT	Un-Do		Parameters
	Repeat		
	Cut	STRATEGIC	University
	Copy		Cooperation >
	Paste		
VIEW	Normal		National Policies
	Full Screen		
	Zoom	BATCH	Load Batch
DATA ENTRY	User Data >		Select from Batch
	Materials Data >		Process Batch
	Library Publishing >		Results from Batch
	Library Structure >		Append to Batch
			Save Batch File
		HELP	Return to Initial Screen
			Access to Help

The following description will lead you through the successive menu levels.

3.1.1 Main Menu

The main menu provides nine options: File, Edit, View, Data Entry Menu, Results Menu, Modify Menu, Strategic Menu, Batch Menu, and Help Menu. The first provides means for managing the current *LPM* file, including identifying the context for analysis, printing displayed screens, and saving the current file. The second provides the standard means for editing data (copying, deleting, and pasting highlighted data, using the clipboard, as well as undoing the results of immediately prior data entry). The third provides means for changing the display. The fourth provides means for entry of data into *LPM*, including defining the workload for services and materials. The fifth shows results of application of the model to those data, including comparing the results with data for actual operations. The sixth provides means for changing the default values in the model, of special importance to workload factors. The seventh provides means for dealing with a range of external, strategic contexts. The eighth provides means for processing a file of data for entry into *LPM* in a batch. The ninth and final one provides means for access to context-specific help.

3.1.2 File Menu

This menu provides means for saving the current *LPM* file with all changes made to that point in time. It also provides means for printing out the currently displayed screen. The value of each of these is that they allow you to include the results from a given use of *LPM* in other contexts.

The File Menu also provides means for entry of data describing the context for a given use of *LPM*. Possible contexts might include documentation in support of budget submissions, assessments of alternative "what if" conditions, evaluation of change for a given library over time, and differences among constituencies.

Other data input from the Context screen include identification of the analyst or person entering data, the date of entry (with the current date as the default), the purpose for the analysis, and the time period represented by the data. They are stored in files to provide means for auditing and control of data entry.

3.1.3 Edit Menu

The Edit Menu provides means to perform simple data editing by use of menu operations, though each of them can also be done by CTR-key operations. They include undoing the results of the most recent keying (CTR-Z), copying highlighted text (CTR-C), deleting text (CTR-X), and pasting text from it (CTR-V); each of those operations use the clipboard as the means of storing or retrieving data.

3.1.4 View Menu

The View Menu provides means for changing the appearance of the screen by, for example, zooming out so as to see more data or zooming in so as to see fewer data but larger characters.

3.1.5 Data Entry Menu

There are screens for entry of data about the populations served, materials acquired, services provided to the populations served, processes involved in acquiring, cataloging, and preserving materials, and facilities related to both users and materials. For definition of any term used in data entry see the definitions section of the *LPM User's Guide and Reference Manual* accessible through the Help Menu of *LPM*.

Populations Served

These data provide the basis for measuring the workload generated by the set of populations served by the library. They are therefore fundamental input to the model, serving as the basis for estimating FTE (i.e., "Full-Time Equivalent") staff required to handle those workloads.

There is a row for each type of population and columns for data that are used to characterize the workload, ultimately measured by "Total Uses," generated by each.

Materials

These data provide the basis for measuring the workload generated by the set of materials acquired by the library. They are therefore fundamental input to the model, serving as means for estimating FTE (i.e., "Full-Time Equivalent") staff required to handle those workloads.

There are two entry screens needed to provide data about the workload. The first is concerned with the current holdings and the status of processing of them. In this screen, there is a row for each type of material and columns for data that are used to characterize the holdings and the status of processing of them, measured by numbers of volumes or linear feet to be processed for each.

The second screen provides data on the planned additions to the holdings and planned workload for the various levels of processing. In this screen also, there is a row for each type of material. The columns are for data that are used to characterize the workload, measured by numbers of volumes or linear feet to be processed at various levels for each type of material.

Services

The extent to which the uses by each of the populations served requires one or another of the services provided is represented by two screens, one for the use of materials and the other for the use of reference services.

In each screen there is a row for each type of population and columns for data that are used to characterize the relative frequency with which uses involve the various kinds of services, measured by percentages.

Processes

The extent to which each of the several kinds of materials acquired uses one or another process is represented by three screens: the first for acquisition processes, the second for cataloging and related processes, the third for preservation and conservation processes.

In each screen there is a row for each type of material and columns for data that are used to characterize the relative frequency with which each type of material involves the various kinds of processes, measured by percentages.

It should be noted that the handling processes are related to each other in the respect that various kinds of activity may be shifted easily from one context to another and may even be handled differently for each type of material. It would enormously complicate the model to try to represent the full diversity of such assignments, so the user will need to make appropriate judgments about how best to represent the reality of work assignments.

It should also be noted that each of the handling processes is really part of a more substantive set of processes (acquisition, cataloging, or conservation). Therefore, in calculating results, the related staff and costs are assigned to those substantive processes.

Library Publishing

Publishing already is a significant activity in many academic libraries and the potential is that there will be increasing interest in it in others. Therefore *LPM* includes provision for input of data about the magnitude of publishing activities and the distribution of them over various processes involved in publishing. To do so, there are two screens within the Library Publishing menu.

Publishing Workload.   This screen provides for entry of data measuring the magnitude of workload for various kinds of library-based publications.

Distribution Over Processes.   This screen provides for entry of data showing the extent to which functions involved in publishing (authorship, editorial, production, marketing, distribution, fulfillment, etc.) are entailed for each type of publication.

Library Structure

First, *LPM* provides a set of matrices by which you can provide data about the large-scale structure of libraries within an institution, including those related to branch libraries and independent libraries.

Second, *LPM* includes means for you to create organization charts for the library using the "Structural Elements" matrix, which lists the units of the library in the sequence of the chain of authority.

Specifically, the organizational matrix has the following format:

Row	Level	Name of Unit	Responsible Person	Other Data
1	0	Library Organization Chart		
2	1	Central Operations	James Jones, Director	Staff, budget
3	2	General Administration	Flo Williams	etc.
4	3	Budget & Accounting	Jane Smith	
5	1	Readers Services	etc.	
6	2	Reference Services		
7	2	Circulation Services		
8	3	Chargeout		
9	3	Reserves		
10	3	Reshelving		
11	0	SubUnit to Be Detailed		
12	3	Top Level of Subunit		
13	4	Next Level of Subunit		
14	0	Another Chart		
15	2	Top Level		
16	3	Next Level		
17	End			

In this matrix, the second column contains the level of the unit (which is to be represented by the row) in the chain of command or hierarchy of administrative responsibility in the library. Thus, units at level 2 report to the head of the preceding unit at level 1 and similarly those at level 3 report to the head of the preceding unit at level 2, and so on. There is no limit to the number of levels, but even 10 would be far beyond any reasonable library administrative structure. The third and fourth columns respectively contain the names of the unit and of the person responsible for it; those names will appear in the box for the unit in the organization chart. Other columns, to the right, can be used to contain data that are relevant to the unit. (Eventually, those data will serve as input to *LPM,* but for the moment they are simply there for you to have a place to put data of potential interest to you.)

LPM will permit you to define any number of separate organization charts in a single matrix. This is primarily of use to provide greater levels of detail than a single chart can effectively show. Thus, the first chart might be an overview of the library as a whole, then successive ones might provide details about the subunits shown in that overview. The row for the title of each of the charts to be included is identified by the value 0 (zero) in the column for level, as illustrated above by the titles "Library Organization Chart," "Subunit to Be Detailed," and "Another Chart."

Following the row containing the title for an organization chart are rows identifying the successive units to be included in that chart. It is important to note that that there cannot be any gaps in the hierarchy entered into a chart. That is, the level for each unit must not be more than one greater than that for the just-prior unit. It can be one more than or less than or equal to that for the prior unit. Thus, the sequence of levels 1,2,3,1 shown in the example above would be acceptable, but a sequence like 1,3,1 would not be, since the level 3 would not have a level immediately superior to it (level 2 is missing). If the sequence of levels does not conform to that requirement, the chart in which that happens and all subsequent ones will not be produced. You will be alerted to the row of the matrix in which such an error occurs, so you will know what to correct. Note that each chart can start at any level (as illustrated above in the entries for "Subunit to Be Detailed," which start with level 3, and for "Another Chart," which start with level 2).

Note that the matrix ends with a row in which the word "End" appears in the column for level. This is a signal to *LPM* that there are no more organization charts to be produced. A similar signal would be given by a blank or a space in that cell of the matrix, but it is recommended that you put the word "End" at the end of the entries to be considered simply to alert yourself to the fact. Parenthetically, it would be possible to have entries following that row, but they will not be included in the resulting output of organization charts.

LPM will give you means for choosing whether the final level included in each chart will be presented as a list or as a set of boxes (with a list being the default choice). Use of the list option will reduce the width of the chart and thus allow the font used to be larger.

3.1.6 Results Menu

Results are presented in two ways: first, simply as they are derived by *LPM* and second, as they compare with data input to reflect the actual situation. The latter provide ready means for comparison of estimates with reality and thus serve as means for determining what changes in data or *LPM* workload factors may be required to have estimates conform with the real situation.

Staffing
The first and perhaps most important result from the model is the estimation of the staff required, both for each category of service or process and in total. Staff estimates are in two categories, Direct FTE and Indirect FTE, and for three levels of personnel (professional, nonprofessional, and hourly).

Comparison with Actual Staff Distributions
To calibrate the staffing estimates from the model, it is useful to compare them with actual staffing, distributed both by administrative units and functional areas (using the categories of the model). The screen for this menu function

provides the means to do so. Data should be entered into the body of the matrix showing the number of FTE in each category of staff (the rows) that are assigned to each functional area (the columns). The column totals can then be compared with the estimates from the model. The calculation of the model's estimate requires separating out of the indirect FTE of those items, such as training and unallocated, adding them to the direct FTE time.

If there is a publishing workload, the display will include a row for the staff required to process that workload.

Staffing for Publishing

A similar table is provided for the staff that *LPM* estimates are needed to support the identified workloads in publishing.

Budget

Another result from the model is the estimation of budget, both for salaries and for various kinds of expenses. These budget estimates are derived by combining the staff estimates with data for the average salaries in each category and for various kinds of direct and indirect expenses. Among the indirect expenses are such things as salary-related benefits and overhead costs (such as supplies, space, and utilities).

Workload Estimates

There are screens that present the estimates from the model of the workload involved for each service or process. They are especially valuable as means to calibrate the estimates from *LPM* and to provide the basis for changes in entry data or workload factors.

Facilities

These identify the requirements for facilities—for services to users, for storage of materials, and for accommodations for staff—as estimated by *LPM* and for comparison with facilities as may actually be provided. Among the estimates made by *LPM* are those for queuing (i.e., lengths of lines for persons waiting to use facilities) as implied by the estimated numbers in comparison with the specified traffic loads.

Allocation Results

A separate set of results relate to the allocation model. First, they provide a basis for balancing between acquisition of materials and access to them from elsewhere; those results can be used as input to the Acquisitions Matrix. Second, they provide a basis for decisions about alternative means or locations for storage of acquired materials; those results can be used as input to the assessments of facilities for storage.

3.1.7 Modify Menu

The primary purpose of *LPM* is to provide a structure for incorporating data for an analysis into a common frame of reference. Default values are provided for all essential variables (such as workload factors, overhead factors, salaries, acquisition costs, direct costs, and parameters) so that the model is complete. However, the default values may not adequately represent reality for a specific analysis. *LPM* therefore provides means to modify all variables. The Modify Menu identifies those elements that can be so modified.

Modify Definitions

First, it is possible to modify the definitions of any of the populations, types of materials, services, library processes, facilities, types of publication, or processes for publication. It is also possible to modify the description of the various categories of indirect staff FTE and indirect expenses. It is possible to add new types of populations, materials, or publications with the definitions associated with them, and the additions will appear in all related matrices, thus allowing the user to enter data about them that will be included in *LPM* estimates.

Adding or Changing Populations.   Please note that if you add new types of population served you will need to add data in the client workload matrix and the two distribution matrices (for use of services and for use of materials) to represent patterns of use for the new population. In the same vein, if you change the definition and nature of an existing population, you will need to review the data in those three matrices to make sure they properly represent those for the new definition.

Adding or Changing Type of Materials.   Please note that if you add new types of material you will need to add data in two matrices for collections (one for holdings and the other for additions) and five distribution matrices (for acquisitions processes and means, for cataloging, and for conservation of holdings and additions) to represent patterns for the new type of material. In the same vein, if you change the definition and nature of an existing type of material, you will need to review the data in those seven matrices to make sure they properly represent those for the new definition.

Adding or Changing Type of Publications.   Please note that if you add new types of publications you will need to add data in the matrix for numbers of each type and that for distribution for publishing processes to represent patterns for the new type of publication. In the same vein, if you change the definition and nature of an existing type of publication, you will need to review the data in those two matrices to make sure they properly represent those for the new definition.

While in principle additions could be made for services to users or processes for materials, doing so would require major changes in the structure of *LPM,* so no provision has been made to accept additions. Instead. you should change existing ones to represent whatever you may want to do.

Adding or Changing Types of Facilities.   The definitions for all three types of facilities—user, storage, and staff—can each be modified.

Adding or Changing Cooperation Contexts.   Finally, additions and changes can be made to the array of cooperation contexts.

Modify Workload Factors

As discussed in detail in Chapter 4 on the conceptual structure of the model, workload factors play a crucial role in relating FTE staff requirements to the workloads in services and processes. Each of the several categories of services and processes is represented by a screen in which those workload values related to it can be changed. There are also workload factors related to the indirect staffing and expenses.

From the *Modify Workload Factors* submenu you may select any of these screens. You will then see a screen showing the array of associated functions and processes. For each, the current value of the workload factor will be displayed, though if that value is zero it may show as a blank. Using the cursor keys, you can move the cursor to any workload factor and then enter a replacement value. Press the [ENTER] key and it will become the new value. Continue this process for all values you wish to modify.

Caution about Changing Workload Factors.   Please note that the default values for workload factors reflect experience in assessing them at literally hundreds of institutions. They truly represent generic values that have proven to be widely applicable. They are, admittedly, at low precision but that actually is valuable as a recognition that these kinds of data inherently are of low precision and even questionable accuracy. In any event, you should very carefully assess whether change in the workload factors is necessary or appropriate. If you do make changes, limit them to one at a time.

Modify Costs

The estimation of budgets is based on sets of costs—for salaries, materials, and direct expenses associated with each service or process. Built into *LPM* are current default values for these costs, but a set of screens permits you to replace those defaults with values that are more accurate for the given context for analysis.

Modify Parameters

There is a set of parameters that affect various operations. *LPM* has default values for each of them, but the screen associated with this menu selection permits you to change any of them.

3.1.8 Strategic Menu

Library planning is affected by and, in many cases, largely determined by events that are outside of the library itself. They include things related to the institution served by the library. They include the sources of information acquired or accessed by the library and the information technologies used by the library. They include the mechanisms for cooperation with other libraries and the bibliographic utilities which play an especially important role in library operations. They include national policies which determine the economic, political, and legal framework within which libraries operate.

In *LPM,* these are called "strategic contexts," and the Strategic Menu provides means for relevant data to be derived from each of them. The conceptual structures underlying the Strategic Menu are discussed in Section 3 of this chapter.

Institutional

The first submenu provides means for assessing the effect of institutional objectives, especially with respect to needs for acquisitions and distribution of budgets.

Information Publishing and Distribution

The second submenu provides means for assessing the effect of means for publication and distribution, especially as reflected in decisions by the publishers. Of special importance is the increasing role of electronic media and of the Internet.

Information Technology

The third submenu provides means for assessing the effect of developments with respect to the information technologies (computers, telecommunications, and multimedia).

National Information Economy

The fourth and final submenu provides means for assessing the effects of national information economies, with special emphasis on the role of libraries in serving the needs in operation and development.

3.1.9 Batch Menu

It is sometimes valuable to apply *LPM* to data concerning a number of libraries. For example, the Association of Research Libraries (ARL) and the Association of College and Research Libraries (ACRL) each annually publish data concerning their member institutions. In much the same way, data are available for medical school libraries and business school libraries. Such data can serve as means for calibrating values used in *LPM* or as the basis for comparing your own library with similar libraries. Obviously, you could do so by entering such data into *LPM* for each library in turn, but that would be tedious and error prone. Therefore, *LPM* provides means for dealing with such data in a batch, directly using what is called a "source file."

Source File

The "Batch Menu" is the means in *LPM* for you to input data from an Excel formatted source file. To be used by *LPM,* the file *must* be an Excel file (with extension ".xls"), and the first row of a source file must contain headers identifying the fields represented by each column of data. In the case of ARL or ACRL files, there are well-established fields of data, although they sometimes change from year to year. These files usually are in Lotus 123 format (i.e., files with extension ".wkl"). They must be converted to Excel files to be input to *LPM,* but that is easy to do. Simply input the Lotus 123 file into Excel and then save it as an Excel Workbook.

A subsidiary use of the Batch Menu is to input data for a single institution into *LPM*. To so do, simply create a file with headers that are *LPM* variables and then enter just a single row of data representing the values for the given single institution. With that as the source file, the Load Batch submenu will insert those values into *LPM* just as though you had entered them directly through the Data Entry Menu.

Load Batch

Given such an Excel source file, the "Load Batch" submenu allows *LPM* to access it. You will be presented with a form that provides means for you to identify the name of the file. The name of the file *must* include the path and the Excel extension ".xls" so that *LPM* can know exactly where to find the file. The form also provides means for you to specify the number of entries (rows) to be input from the source file. Normally, that will be the total number of entries in the source file, but it could be fewer if the source file contains many rows of which only the first few are of interest to you. However, there is no way to be selective beyond specifying the number of rows to be input starting at the beginning of the source file.

Once you have entered the source file name and number of rows, you then click on the button labeled "Click here when finished" and *LPM* will access the source file. If you entered a file name that does not lead *LPM* to an acceptable file, you will be told so, and you will then need to launch the "Load Batch" submenu again.

Assign *LPM* Variables to Source Variables

When *LPM* is able to find the file you specify, it will present you with a form that permits you to assign fields (variables or columns) from the source file to *LPM* variables. The form will present you with two lists, the one to the left showing *LPM* variables and the one to the right showing source file variables. You assign a source variable to an *LPM* variable by clicking on each of them in the respective lists and then clicking on the button labeled "Click Here to Assign." You continue doing that for each *LPM* variable to which you want to assign a source variable.

If you make a mistake or forget to click on the button, there is no problem. Just repeat the assignments as you want them to be. The list of the *LPM* variables will always show the assignments that have been made to each *LPM* variable, including both the name of the source variable and the column for it in the source file. That means that you can easily review the assignments you have made and, if necessary, correct any that you want to change. Indeed, it is strongly recommended that you always make such a review before proceeding to the next steps.

Once you have made all of the appropriate assignments, click on the button labeled "Click Here When Finished with All Assignments." The "Load Batch" submenu will then read the data from the source file, placing them into a file within *LPM* itself, with values from the source file inserted in the columns for the *LPM* variables to which they are assigned.

Opportunity to Make Changes

You will then have the opportunity to make changes in the data as derived from the source file. For example, in some cases data that are missing in the source file may be specially coded in it (such as by a value of "−1" or an alphabetic code), and you may want to change such codes. In other cases, you may want to calculate some *LPM* variables from the source data because of differences in definitions between the source file and *LPM*. To illustrate, the source file for ARL libraries contains data for "Graduate Students" and for "Total Students" but not for "Undergraduate Students." You would need to calculate values for "Undergraduate Students" as the difference between "Total Students" and "Graduate Students." Do so by entering the difference into the first row of the column for "Undergraduate Students," and then copy that calculation into the remainder of that row. In still other cases, some data may not be available from the source file at all, and you may want to calculate values using the data that are available. To illustrate, the ARL file does not contain data for number of staff in the institution; if you want such data to be considered by *LPM,* you might want to calculate "Number of Staff" by multiplying "Faculty" by some parameter.

The important point is that you have the opportunity to make whatever changes you may think will best represent your objectives in subsequent processing of this file. It is strongly recommended that you carefully review the display to be sure that changes in the data are not needed before proceeding to the next steps.

Select from Batch

Once a file has been loaded you can select an individual row from it to serve as direct input into *LPM.* In this way, you can select an entry from an external file for entry into *LPM* and process the data for it as though you had entered it directly into *LPM.* This is especially valuable if your library is one among those included in a file (such as an ARL or ACRL database), since you can simply use the source file to provide the data needed. Of course, you can use Batch menu operations as means to use a file that you have created externally to *LPM* as means for entering it into *LPM* as a totality.

The selected item from the source file will be stored into *LPM* and can then be processed just as though it had been directly entered. The data that had originally been in *LPM* will be stored at the end of the source file so that it can be restored into *LPM* if you wish. To do so, you need merely select the row identified as "Current Data Values."

Process Batch

You can at any time call on the "Process Batch" submenu. It will present you with a message that will review the status to that point and permit you either to continue with processing or to cancel it. If you decide to continue, the process first will save the current values so they can be reentered into *LPM* at the conclusion of the processing. Then, it will apply *LPM* to each of the rows in the file derived from the source data. It does so by entering data for populations served and materials acquired into the matrices in *LPM* to which they related. Then, it stores the results from *LPM* calculations into the relevant variables in the derived file.

Results from Batch

You can then see the results from *LPM* operation for all of the cases and, in particular, can compare values for variables from the source file with those for related *LPM* variables. The "Results from Batch" submenu is the means to do so. It allows you to identify each of the variables to be displayed at a given time. By repeatedly using Results from Batch, you can examine many different aspects of the comparisons among the libraries from the source file.

Of special value are comparisons on source data such as "circulation" or "reference use" with the estimates derived by *LPM*. That will reveal changes that might be needed in underlying *LPM* values, such as those for distributions of use of the library or of services or of materials, in order to represent the workload experience in the source file libraries. You can then make changes in those values and repeat the "Process Batch" submenu to see the effect of those changes on the entire set of institutions. In this way, you can explore the implications of changes in *LPM* variables for their effect on many different libraries.

Append to Batch

The current data for workloads in *LPM* can be appended to the loaded file. In this way, data that have been entered into *LPM* can be stored as part of a standard file for easy retrieval and automatic reentry into *LPM*.

Save Batch File

For that purpose, this submenu provides means for saving the batch file, including any appended entries. The saved file can be given any appropriate name and can then be processed separately as an Excel file. In this way you not only can save data entered into *LPM* but you can modify it to change or update data.

3.1.10 Help Menu

First, the Help Menu provides means for Return to the Initial Screen, in which some of the aspects of use of *LPM* are described. Second, the Help Menu provides Access to Help in use of *LPM* and, perhaps even more important, information about the theoretical concepts that underline it. It is called the *LPM User's Guide and Reference Manual*.

The help screens include tabs for Contents, Index, Find, and browsing (i.e., "<<", ">>"). The Contents tabs will bring up a display of the complete contents of the *LPM User's Guide and Reference Manual:* by double-clicking on any entry in it you will immediately be presented with a display of that section of the manual. The Index tab is a listing of the sections of *LPM User's Guide and Reference Manual* in alphabetical order, again, double-clicking on any entry will lead to display of that section of the manual. The two browse tabs permit you to move forward and backward in the sequence of sections (in the order of the listing in the Contents tab).

On some screens, there will be words that are highlighted in dark green. Such words provide hypertext jumps to sections of the manual that are related to them or to pop-up displays of comments that are specific to them.

At the very top of each help screen is a menu of options available to you. They include means for printing the displayed section of the manual, returning to prior displays, looking at a history of the sequence of displayed screens, and a variety of other things you can do. Given the ability to print displayed sections, you can obtain a printout of the full *LPM User's Guide and Reference Manual* simply by starting at *"LPM,"* the title page, and then browsing section by section through the manual, printing each as you proceed.

3.2
Conceptual Structure for Operational Contexts

The most central elements of the *LPM* relate to operational contexts in services to staff and in processing of materials. Most of the menu structure involves the entry of data relevant to these applications and to the presentation of the results. The theory underlying these elements is presented in Part 2 of this book, in Chapters 4 through 6. Within *LPM,* that theory is represented by a set of matrices.

3.2.1 Matrices for Clients and Materials

LPM models for operational applications are based on eight matrices, four of clients and services for them and four of materials and technical processes for them. In each case, the first matrix contains data for determining workloads involved; the second contains data for the extent to which workloads use specific services or processes; the third contains workload factors as means for estimating required staff and costs; the fourth contains factors for estimating the need for facilities.

3.2.2 Matrices for Workloads in Library Publishing

Publishing already is a significant activity in many academic libraries. Most libraries provide relatively brief newsletters, for example. Beyond that, though, some universities (the University of Sao Paulo, in Brazil, being an example) produce scholarly journals, and frequently their libraries serve as the publisher. The potential is that there will be increasing interest in such scholarly publishing in other universities. In particular, many universities in the United States, faced with what they regard as unconscionable increases in prices of commercial journals in technical and scientific fields, have responded by saying, "Why must we pay such prices for access to the research that we produce?" And they have considered asking their university presses and their libraries to become publishers of their scholarly product.

Perhaps even more important is the effect of the Internet. First, it may be feasible for the universities to use it as the vehicle for distribution of scholarly product, and the university libraries might well serve as the editorial managers; second, the move is well underway to create online digital libraries based on the resources available from the collections of major academic libraries, so they are already potentially in the position of publishers of that material. In recognition of these possibilities—indeed, with respect to the online digital libraries, the reality—*LPM* includes means for estimating the effects of publishing activities upon library planning.

Three matrices in *LPM* relate to publishing. The first provides data about the workload involved in the publishing activity, measured by number of pages (or equivalent) for each type of publication. The second shows the distribution of workload over publishing functions. The third provides workload factors for each publishing function.

Types of Publications

Several types of publications are identified in the first two matrices. They include:

Types of Publication	Units	Description
Monographs	Title	Regular books
Scholarly Journals	Article	Refereed journals in specialized academic fields
Popular Journals	Issue	Journals for general reading
Digital Libraries	Megabytes	A variety of publications for digital distribution
Special Collections	Items	Materials such as maps, photographs, etc.

Most of the types of publication are self-evident, but it is worth commenting on the role each of them might play in academic libraries. The first, regular books, is unlikely to be significant and is included only to be comprehensive. The second, scholarly journals, is important in some libraries and may well become very important if universities attempt to take greater responsibility for scholarly publishing; while the responsibility may well be delegated to university presses, there are good reasons for it to go to the library. Most academic libraries publish counterparts of popular journals—newsletters and similar means for informing patrons and supporters of the library.

The type of publication with the greatest future potential is digital libraries. Academic libraries are a primary source for materials, and most large academic libraries are now participating in experiments to establish state and regional digital library networks. Special collections have particular importance.

In the description above of the types of publication, units for measurement have been identified for each. In *LPM* those units are all converted into "number of pages" as the means for combining them into a single calculation, illustrated as follows:

Publication Workloads	Units of Measure	Units per Year	Pages per Unit	Pages per Year
Monographs	Titles	1	300	300
Scholarly Journals	Articles	100	10	1,000
Popular Journals	Issues	12	25	300
Digital Libraries	Megabytes	3	500	1,500
Special Collections	Items	10	100	1,000

Distribution of the Use of Publishing Processes

The second matrix has the same rows as the first, but the columns now relate to the set of functions involved in publishing. As with other distribution matrices, the values in this matrix identify the percentages of units (measured by pages) for each type of publication that will involve the process.

Chapter 9 brings together a variety of data related to functions in publishing to provide a first step in developing workload factors for them for inclusion in *LPM*. The functions and related default values for their workload factors in *LPM* are as follows:

Publication Processes	Workload Factors		
	Intellectual	Procedural	Physical
Editorial	20		
Copy Edit	10	20	
Data Enter		20	
Compose	10	20	
Distribute		5	10
Fulfillment		5	

Editorial functions are essentially intellectual and substantive, involving decisions about content, its quality and organization, about market and publishability, and about format and means for publication and distribution.

Typically, the editor will work closely with the author or creator of a publication to assure that all of those issues have been properly dealt with.

Copy editing is the process of assuring that the source material conforms to accepted standards. It entails intellectual issues, especially in review of text to assure that it communicates what is intended and to assure that it is accurate and consistent. But it also involves essentially procedural issues, especially with respect to format.

Data entry and composition are the essentially mechanical processes involved in translating the source into a master from which copies can then be made for distribution.

Distribution and fulfillment are the means by which the publication is made available and, if it is a journal, fulfillment of contractual obligations is assured.

The workload factors associated with publishing processes are preliminary and much more uncertain than those for traditional library services and processes. They are based in part on experience in management of a publishing activity, in part on examination of a few academic libraries at which publishing is a major activity, in part on examination of data reported about publishing in a variety of sources, and in part on discussion with those responsible for operations in a variety of commercial, scholarly, and university presses.

Note that the publishing processes list above does not include those in authorship (i.e., creation of materials to be published). This is important because the academic library may well find itself in a dual role, as author or creator and as publisher, and it will be necessary carefully to distinguish what is involved in each.

In particular, the collection of an academic library is likely to be a source from which digital library products may be produced. The assemblage of those materials and preparation of them in a form to be considered for publication are essentially counterparts of authorship, not of publishing. The processes in publishing then follow those of creation. Therefore, the part of *LPM* that deals with publishing does not include the costs in assembling and converting the source materials. For the library producing a digital library, those costs will be substantial, and they will need to be assessed separately. One means for doing so might be to treat them in the context of Conservation, using the function of preservation of content in digital form, which represents precisely the process involved.

In general, the costs incurred in authorship appear to be substantially greater than the typical return to the author, as represented by royalties on sales. For example, a professor on the average might have two articles a year accepted for publication, each of about ten pages in length. The cost of authorship is likely to reflect 25% of the yearly salary (taking that as the commitment of time in research), amounting to say $20K (including benefits). For those articles, the professor usually receives no royalties and in some cases may need to pay page charges to cover some of the costs of publication.

In the same vein, the costs to the library in creating a digital library package will almost certainly not be recovered from income, but the costs in publishing that package probably can be and perhaps should be.

3.2.3 Roles of Parameters

There are several parameters that enter into calculations in *LPM* so as to serve as means for accommodating differences among libraries. Those related to operational applications of *LPM* fall into four major groups: (1) materials, (2) time, (3) user interactions, and (4) cataloging. The following table shows the set of these parameters, together with the default values for each.

Parameters	Group	Value	Purpose
Finding-Aids/Linear Foot	Cataloging	5	To determine cataloging workload for materials measured in linear feet
Volumes/Monograph Title	Materials	1.50	To measure space required for additions
Volumes/Serial Title	Materials	1.50	To measure space required for additions
Pages/Photocopy Request	Interaction	10	To translate pages into request workloads
(Peak Load)/(Average Load)	Interaction	5	To determine queuing requirements
Hours/Year at Reference Node	Time	2,000	To determine number of reference workstations
Days in Working Year	Time	210	To shift from working year to full year
Hours in Working Day	Time	8	
Minutes/Working Year	Time	100,800	Calculated from the above two
Days in Service Year	Time	350	
Hours in Service Day	Time	12	
Minutes/Service Year	Time	252,000	Calculated from the above two
Direct Time/Service Time	Time	1.5	To relate WLF to service times

Parameters Related to Materials

To deal with differences between measure of materials by titles and measure by volumes, there are two parameters: "Volumes/Monograph Title" and "Volumes/Serial Title." Each is intended to represent the average for the given library for its holdings and/or current acquisitions.

Parameter Related to Cataloging

"Finding Aids/Linear Foot" is a parameter used to represent the workload involved in cataloging of materials such as archives, manuscripts, photographs, and so forth. Usually, the nature of such materials is that there will not be catalog entries for each individual item but, instead, there will be catalog entries for identified collections of them. However, in addition to the major catalog entries there are likely to be what are called "finding aids," which identify subgroups of items within collections. Each finding aid really represents a separate cataloging task, so this parameter provides means for measuring that workload.

Parameters Related to User Interaction

Two parameters relate to interaction with users. The first, "Pages/ Photocopy Request," is a means to make the workload in staff-operated photocopying service more nearly commensurate with that for other kinds of tasks. The default value of 10 represents a typical journal article, for example. Of course, the value of this parameter could be taken as 1 (i.e., "one"), but if so the related workload factors will need to be divided by 10 (i.e., "ten").

The second parameter "(Peak Load)/(Average Load)" is conceptually quite interesting. It is discussed in more detail in Chapter 5, as part of the coverage of queuing, but briefly it reflects the need to recognize that the number of facilities provided must accommodate not simply the average traffic load but, to some extent at least, the possible peak traffic loads.

Parameters Related to Time

Finally, eight parameters relate to time. The first, "Hours/Year at Reference Node," provides the basis for translating the hourly traffic load on reference services into the number of reference stations required to serve it. The second, "Direct Time/Service Time," provides the means for reflecting the fact that the time in direct performance of work does not represent the total time of service for a staff member.

The next six parameters relating to time provide the means for dealing with alternative policies concerning the working year, the working day, and the service day. The final parameter provides the basis for relating workload factors (which are based on the working day) into the context of the service day.

3.3

Conceptual Structure for Tactical Contexts

The term "tactical" is interpreted as relating to the allocation of resources. *LPM* includes means for dealing with two tactical contexts: (1) the allocation of materials to alternative means for storage and access and (2) the allocation of budgets between acquisition of materials and the provision of services. The theory underlying these applications of *LPM* is included in Chapter 6. Again, that theory is represented in *LPM* by a set of matrices.

3.3.1 Matrices for Allocation of Materials

The theory underlying the allocation of materials is presented in Chapter 6. That theory is represented in *LPM* by equations that determine the point of optimum allocation (i.e., that which minimizes the total costs). To implement the theory and equations, there are two matrices in *LPM*. One provides means for entry of data for determining whether to acquire materials or to depend upon access elsewhere (through interlibrary borrowing or document delivery).

The second matrix provides means for entry of data for determining where to store materials, given an array of alternative means and locations. The specific options included in the default matrix are (1) open stack shelving in a central library, (2) open stack shelving in a branch library, (3) closed stack shelving, (4) compact shelving, and (5) automated storage (using industrial methods for storage and access, for example).

Parameters Related to Acquisition vs. Access Elsewhere

A number of parameters relate to the application of the Allocation Model to the decision concerning "acquisition or access." They are listed in the following table, along with the default values for them:

Normalizing Parameter	10000000
Proportion of Uses in Serials	0.4
Ratio of Year-to-Year Change in Use	0.8
Years to Reach Steady-State of Use	7
Planning Horizon	20
Ratio of Cumulative Uses to First Year Uses	6.68
Interest Rate (for current value calculations)	0.05
Present Value for Access Cost	5.03
ILL/(Unmet Uses)	0.2
Distribution Factor	8

The first, the Normalizing Parameter, serves as a means for normalizing holdings data in the calculation of the scope of the collection in the Allocation Model equations. The second, Proportion of Uses in Serials, provides means for allocating total numbers of uses of the collection between serials and monographs, so that acquisition vs. access decisions can be made independently for each.

The next two, Ratio of Year-to-Year Change in Use and Years to Reach Steady-State of Use, are intended to represent the distribution over time in the use of a collection. The first reflects the fact that, for most materials, use decays over time. The second reflects the likelihood that after some time, there will not be further decay but instead a steady, though low, amount of use. Together, these enter into a calculation of the ratio of Cumulative Uses to first-year use which, though not strictly a parameter, is included in this list to highlight the role of the underlying parameters. Cost for access in future years needs to be translated into "current value" in order to enter into the calculation of optimum and so there is a parameter for the interest rate to be used; that enters into a calculation which, again though not strictly a parameter, is included here to highlight the role of the underlying parameters.

Beyond the parameters listed above, there are parameters that relate to other aspects of *LPM* as well as to the Allocation Model: Volumes per Serial Title, Volumes per Monograph title, and Planning Horizon. There also are several elements of cost that enter into the Allocation Model and are derived from other *LPM* operations: Monograph Purchase (per title), Serial Purchase (per title), Acquisition Staff Costs (per title), Acquisition Direct Costs (per title), Cataloging Staff Costs (per title), Cataloging Direct Costs (per title), Processing. Direct Costs (per volume), Costs for Processing of Serials, Binding Costs (per volume bound). Storage Costs (per volume per year), ILL Staff Costs (per ILL Borrow), and ILL Direct Costs (per ILL Borrow). Finally, there are statistics for number of publications of various types (i.e., Population of Current Serial Titles. Population of Monograph Titles, Population of Electronic Serial Titles, Population of Multi-Media Titles. etc.) that are derived from the Information Sources data.

Parameters Related to Decisions Concerning Allocation to Alternative Means of Storage

The other application of the Allocation Model is to decisions concerning allocation of materials to various locations and/or means for storage. The relevant parameters are listed in the following table, along with the default values for them:

Storage Choices	Yearly Storage Cost	Access Cost	Access Time (minutes)
Branch Open Stack	$2.00	$0.00	5
Central Open Stack	$1.00	$0.00	10
Closed Stact	$0.75	$3.00	20
Compact Shelving	$0.50	$7.50	25
Automated Storage	$0.20	$10.00	30

The first three of the storage options are self-explanatory. Compact shelving can take a variety of forms, but is perhaps best represented by some form of movable shelves; the result is an effective doubling of the capacity of a given space because the interstack access space is shared among the stacks.

The final option, automated storage, also can take a variety of forms. At the extreme might be the kind of facility used at Cal State Northridge (until it was destroyed by the 1994 earthquake), in which the materials were managed by a computer-controlled system. The computer controls the means for access, storage, and retrieval by identifying where a given item is to be stored or has been stored and then directing a mechanical access unit to retrieve the bin in which the action of storage or retrieval is to occur. The item is manually (i.e., by a person) stored in the selected bin or retrieved from it.

For each storage option, the matrix as shown above identifies the yearly cost for storage, including the cost of space, or the means for storage (e.g., shelving), and of equipment used for Control of storage and retrieval (in the case of some level of automated operation). The cost of open-stack shelving for a branch is taken at twice that for a central library on the assumption that the branch is likely to occupy space that was not designed for library use.

The matrix also identifies the access cost, as it might represent the time of staff in paging materials. Finally, the matrix identifies the average time that access is expected to take; this represents both the cost to the user and something that might affect the likelihood of use.

3.3.2 Allocation of Budgets

LPM includes means for representing the Cobb-Douglas econometric model as the basis for assessing the allocation of budgets between acquisition of materials and provision of information services.

3.4
Conceptual Structure for Strategic Contexts

As has been previously described, the term "strategic" is used to refer to those contexts which affect library management but over which the individual library manager has little, if any, control. The theory underlying the application of *LPM* to these contexts is presented in Part 3, Chapters 7 through 9. Again, as with other parts of *LPM,* the theory is represented by a set of matrices.

3.4.1 Matrices for Institutional Context

The institution within which the library falls has programmatic objectives that affect the library's decisions concerning acquisitions, staffing, administrative and operational structure, and budgets.

Acquisitions Decisions

LPM represents the effect of institutional objectives on acquisitions decision by two matrices. The first describes the institutional program. In the case of an academic library, the relevant programmatic elements are shown in the following matrix:

Academic Structure	Programs	Staff	Faculty	Graduate Students	Undergrad Students	Researcher
Administration	1	550	24			
Humanities	4	10	190	500	4,500	2
Soc Science	4	10	190	500	4,500	2
Biol Science	4	10	190	500	4,500	2
Phys Science	4	10	190	500	4,500	2
Professions	2	5	95	250		1
Total	25	595	879	2,250	18,000	9

The second matrix presents the weightings given to each programmatic element in making acquisition decisions. It is based on the Voigt-Susskind formula but with modifications. The product of the weightings by the program elements from the first matrix then provides both a total target for acquisitions and a distribution of that total among types of program:

Programmatic Element	Number of Programs		Acquisitions per Program		Product of Columns 2 and 3	
			Books	Journals	Books	Journals
Basic Acquisitions	Campuses	1	35,000	5,000	35,000	5,000
Humanities	Grad Fields	4	1,500	500	6,000	2,000
Social Sciences	Grad Fields	4	1,000	1,000	4,000	4,000
Biological Sciences	Grad Fields	4	500	1,500	2,000	6,000
Physical Sciences	Grad Fields	4	500	1,500	2,000	6,000
Professions	Grad Fields	2	3,000	6,000	6,000	6,000
Undergrad Students	Per 2,000	9	1,000		7,000	
Sponsored Research	Per $15M	5	200	800	1,000	4,000
Total					65,000	33,000

3.4.2 Matrices for Interlibrary Cooperation

There is a tentative set of matrices related to interlibrary cooperation. The rows of these matrices identify specific cooperative contexts, including Multiversity Systems, Statewide Systems. National Systems, Contractual Arrangements, and International Agreements. The tentative matrices are focused on specific reasons for cooperation, such as Resources, Acquisition, Digital Libraries, Reference Services, Automation, and Storage Facilities. These contexts and reasons are discussed in Chapter 9.

The application of cooperative game theory is represented by a program within *LPM* that provides means for assessment of joint strategies for two participants in a bargaining process. It assumes that strategies to be considered are expressible as combinations of choices, and it applies the Nash criterion for evaluation. The Nash criterion maximizes the product of the gains for each participant to be derived from cooperation.

3.4.3 Matrices for Information Production and Distribution

There is a matrix of data for current patterns of publication.

3.4.4 Matrices for National Policy

The theory underlying models for national information economies in *LPM* is discussed in Chapter 9. That theory is represented in *LPM* by four matrices. The first matrix is derived from national economic statistics for distribution of the workforce by industry and by function. The second matrix describes the intensity of information use by various types of industry and functions. The third matrix identifies the level of development of the information economy in a given country.

4

Library Operational Requirements

Introduction

This chapter discusses models for assessing the requirements for library staff. In principle, they should reflect the workload to be handled.

4.1
Approaches to Staff Estimation

This section discusses the roles and relationships between various means for estimating staff requirements: (1) time and motion studies and (2) *ex post facto* accounting of data concerning direct staffing and related workloads. It then provides specific data for workload factors that reflect the results from the use of these methods. It discusses the use of those workload factors based on identified workloads (with reference to the succeeding two chapters in which the means for determining those workloads will be discussed).

The following schematic summarizes various approaches to staff estimation and costing together with some rules of thumb for the ratios among them.

Level	Means for Evaluation	Rule of Thumb Ratios
Minimum	Time & Motion Study	
		(Basic)/(Minimum) = 1.50
Basic	Direct Labor	
		(Full Salary)/(Basic) = 1.50
Full Salary	Salary & Benefits	
		(Burdened)/(Full Salary) = 1.50
Burdened	All Costs	

It is important to recognize the differences among these approaches, since they result in dramatically different estimates of cost that are difficult to reconcile. Various mixes of means for evaluation can produces ratios anywhere from 1.5 to 3.375, and ratios of that magnitude and more are well exhibited in the data reported by Bourne.[1]

The most accurate and complete is a true cost accounting based on records at the time costs are incurred and properly allocated. The most detailed will be the time and motion study, but it will usually account for only the most specific costs, not dealing with benefits or with allocable costs since it measures only the actual time in performance of a defined set of tasks. At the other extreme, the total cost approach provides no detail and no means for analysis of functions; it is the least accurate of the methods and may grossly misestimate the costs, both under and over, in ways that make it impossible to calibrate. The ad hoc accounting approach used in *LPM* is an effort to establish a standard means for dealing with quoted costs that will include all components in a framework that permits analysis.

4.1.1 Time and Motion Studies

There are several purposes for time and motion studies. First, they provide the basis for assessing the effect of changes in patterns of work on the productivity or efficiency of workers. Sometimes simply changing the sequence of component motions or the locations of materials to be processed will have a dramatic effect on productivity, and a time and motion study can be used to test the effect of such changes. Second, they can provide the data, in the form of "workload factors," on which to assess the staffing required to handle a given workload. A workload factor identifies the staff time per unit of work required to perform a given task so, when multiplied by the workload to be handled, it serves as the basis for calculating the required total staff time (and therefore number of staff). Many of the workload factors that will be presented in this chapter were derived, in part, by carrying out time and motion studies for typical generic tasks (such as keyboarding, sorting, and filing).

4.1.2 Direct FTE Staff Accounting

A second approach to staff estimation is an "*ex post facto* accounting" for direct staff FTE (i.e., "full-time equivalent"). That is, data reported in a wide variety of ways are reduced to a common accounting structure, from which is then calculated the implied associated staffing. This approach is in contrast to the typ-

---

[1] Bourne, Charles P., and Kasson, Madeleine S., *Preliminary Report of the Review and Development of Standard Cost Data for Selected Library Technical Processing Functions.* Prepared for the Council on Library Resources. Palo Alto, CA: Information General Corporation, Nov. 4, 1969.

ical time and motion study, in which careful measurements are made of the time actually taken for each of a sequence of operations, and to a "total cost" approach, in which reported costs for an operation are taken as a whole and simply divided by the total workload. Finally, it is in contrast to a true cost accounting, in which data are recorded and analyzed in standard categories when incurred.

In this approach, data are acquired for numbers of staff and for workloads for each of the internal, technical services functions and reader service functions of a library. The data for numbers of staff are assigned to appropriate categories based on the nature of the tasks assigned to persons (for example, managerial tasks, intellectual tasks, procedural tasks, and physical tasks). The data for workloads are similarly assigned to the same kinds of categories so that the ratios of workload divided by staff can then be used as workload factors, in much the same way as would have been obtained from a time and motion study. The difference, though, is that the workload factors from an *ex post facto* accounting reflect data reported from actual operations rather than from scientific study and experiment. (It would be much better if the data were based on a solid cost accounting system which accumulated the relevant staff time as assigned to identified tasks, services, or product. Few if any libraries have instituted such a cost accounting practice, though.)

All of the workload factors presented in this chapter were, in part, derived from and were tested by *ex post facto* accounting of data from literally hundreds of libraries, of all types and sizes, as visited during studies conducted over several decades or as derived from sources of reported data. Of course, the time of staff in direct labor is only part of the story. Provision must be made to represent salary-related benefits, including benefit time (holiday, vacation, sick leave, sabbatical, etc.) as well as such costs as medical insurance, retirement, and so on. These will be discussed as "indirect" costs.

4.1.3 Total Staff Budget

The third approach, as implied in the table above, is to estimate staffing requirements on the basis of total staff budgets. The problem, of course, is that this provides absolutely no basis for allocating the staff among functions or workloads. It provides no basis for management, for decision-making, or for planning.

4.2
Direct Labor and Costs

4.2.1 Workload Factors

LPM uses a matrix of "workload factors" as the means for estimation of the staff required to handle a defined workload, measured in appropriate "units of work." For each of the set of library services and processes, such units of work have been defined. The workload factors then are expressed in terms of "minutes per transaction." They are translated by *LPM* into percentages of FTE (yearly full-time equivalent) staff for the performance of 1000 (i.e., 1K) units of work for each library function and subsidiary process. (The translation from one to the other is based on the fact that a working year is almost exactly 100,000 minutes—that is, 40 hours per week for 42 working weeks is 100,800 minutes—so 1 minute per transaction would be 1 FTE per 1,000 transactions. However, *LPM* provides means for you to change the number of minutes in a working year and then adjusts the conversion appropriately.)

  LPM incorporates default values for the workload factors, as has been illustrated in the displays of workload factor matrices in Chapter 3, but you can modify them to reflect your own library experience. The default values currently used in *LPM* are, with very few exceptions, identical with those first published in 1974.[2]

  The default workload factors in *LPM* are consciously and deliberately used with minimal precision—typically on the order of 10%. This reflects the fact that there is great variability among institutions and, even within a single one, differences in the qualitative character of the workload. It would be spurious to imply high levels of precision simply not warranted. As a result, there is no reason to anticipate that use of these default values in a given library will match actual data any closer than the precision implies—within say 10%. It is for that reason that *LPM* provides means for you to change the defaults to your own estimates. You may have sufficient confidence in your data to warrant use of workload factors of higher precision than is represented in these default values.

4.2.2 Determining Values for Workload Factors

  As indicated above, the default values for the workload factors were developed by an iterative process that involved hundreds of libraries, of all kinds and sizes, over a period of decades. The uniform base of the process was the fundamental cost accounting structure into which the observed data were fit. Estimates at a given point in time were matched with actual and/or reported costs for a visited library and operations within it as of that time. If estimates matched library data to within about 10%, they were regarded as further confirmed.

  But if the estimated costs differed by substantially more than 10% from the reported ones, they were carefully examined for possible reasons for the differences. Were they caused by flaws in the workload factors; if so, should there be changes in them? Did they reflect differences in functions and processes; if

[2] Hayes, Robert M, and Becker, Joseph, *Handbook of Data Processing for Libraries,* 2nd ed. New York: Wiley, 1974, Chapter 4, Cost Accounting in Libraries, p. 118.

so, should there be additions to them? Were there differences in efficiencies; if so, how should the efficiencies be treated?

Beyond the use of actual data from visited libraries, other means were used to determine default values. A number of time and motion studies were conducted to determine production rates on typical generic library activities. The rich array of published data were reviewed and reduced to a consistent accounting structure. Analogies were drawn among various kinds of operations, both within libraries and between them and industrial and commercial counterparts. To put these various sources of data into a common framework, the rule-of-thumb ratios (shown above in the discussion of levels of costing) were consistently used for conversion to fully burdened estimates.

4.2.3 Direct Costs

Associated with each library service or technical process there are likely to be direct costs, beyond the staff time involved. For example, the use of OCLC for copy cataloging will involve fees for those services; the processing of books will involve costs for labels, covers, and security tabs. *LPM* includes default values for these kinds of direct costs, but they are simply to provide tentative values. They should be replaced by accurate data for the costs as currently incurred by the library.

4.3
Indirect Labor and Costs

The next major component of the *LPM* cost-accounting model is "indirect." In general, indirect or, as it is frequently called, "overhead" or "burden," includes those costs that cannot be directly attributed to "productive work." That in no way means that such costs are not necessary or significant. It simply means that it would be difficult or irrational to attempt to associate them directly with productive work. Supervision, for example, is clearly necessary, but it in no way in itself produces catalog entries, binds volumes, films pages, or does the actual work, whatever it may be. Holidays, vacation, and sick leave are necessary components of a compensation package, but usually no productive work is accomplished during such time.

4.3.1 Alternative Bases for Allocation of Indirect Costs

The purpose of "overhead" or "indirect costs" is to account for these kinds of costs. There are several potential means for allocating indirect costs. One is "proportional to direct labor costs," and that is the rule used in *LPM*. A second is "proportional to total labor costs." A third is "proportional to total costs (labor plus expenses)." Some illustrative values for overhead are presented in the following table, in order to show the differences between the first two alternative means for presentation of the overhead accounts. (The percentages shown are merely for the purposes of illustration, to show how each enters into the calculation.)

Category	Percentage of Total Salaries	Nonprofit Allocation	Commercial Allocation
Total Salaries	1.00T		
Direct Salaries	0.67T		0.67T = 1.00D
		1.00T	
Indirect Salaries	0.33T		
			0.67T = 1.00D
Salary Benefits	0.14T	0.14T	
Overhead Expenses	0.20T	0.20T	
Subtotal		1.34T = 1.00S	1.34T = 2.00D
General & Administrative		0.13T = 0.10S	0.13T = 0.20D
Total		1.47T	1.47T = 2.20D

It is important to recognize both the differences between these two and the essential equivalence of them. The one which treats "direct salary" as the foundation is typically used in commercial contexts; the other, which treats "total salary" as the foundation, is typically used in "not-for-profit" institutions. Whichever may be used, the total costs (leaving aside allocation of profit or amortization of capital costs, neither of which is included here) must be the same, if efficiencies are the same. And, with all due respect to the much vaunted efficiency of private enterprise, there is nothing inherent in the tasks here that implies greater efficiency as a result of different means in accounting for costs. For a variety of reasons, though, the commercial accounting model is the one used in *LPM*.

Specifically, as this illustrates, nonprofit organizations typically will use total staff salaries as the basis for overhead calculation. As a result, the overhead rate will be approximately 34%. In contrast, commercial and industrial organizations will use direct labor salaries as the basis for overhead calculation, with indirect labor costs treated as part of overhead. The resulting overhead rate typically will be 100%. In either case, as illustrated above, to the total must be added the costs for what are called "general and administrative expenses," to which we turn in the next section.

4.3.2 Workload Factors for Indirect Staff

Within *LPM,* there are two tables of indirect (i.e., overhead) workload factors, expressed as percentages of direct labor, one for Indirect Expenses and the other for Indirect Staff, with default values as follows:

Indirect Expenses	Intellectual	Procedural	Physical
Benefits	25.00%	20.00%	10.00%
Indirect Expenses	10.00%	10.00%	10.00%
Total	35.00%	30.00%	20.00%

	Workload Factors		
Indirect Staff	Intellectual	Procedural	Physical
General & Administrative	10.00%	5.00%	
Supervision by Professional	10.00%	5.00%	
Supervision by Nonprofessional		5.00%	10.00%
Supervision Clerical Support	5.00%	5.00%	5.00%
Training	2.00%	2.00%	2.00%
Unallocated	2.00%	2.00%	2.00%
Benefit Time	25.00%	15.00%	10.00%

Supervision and Clerical Support to Supervision

Note that supervision of the three levels of tasks (intellectual tasks, usually done by professional staff, procedural tasks, usually done by clerical staff, and physical tasks, usually done by hourly or casual staff such as students) is allocated among the three levels of staff. The default values assume that supervision is generally at 10% of the staff being supervised. They also assume that professional staff would normally be supervised by professional, clerical staff by a 50/50 mix of professional and clerical, and hourly staff by clerical. Obviously, though, the actual distribution in any given library would be determined by policies and by the realities of qualifications of individuals.

Clerical support for supervision includes such activities as typing, filing, scheduling, and similar kinds of tasks required in supervision. Note, though, that clerical work that is directly productive (such as online search of national bibliographic databases in copy cataloging) is *not* included here but is instead part of direct labor for the productive activities.

Training

Training is a critical activity at every level of operation in a library. It is required to assure that hourly staff and clerical staff have the skills necessary to carry out their assigned tasks, that they know what is expected of them in doing so, that they understand how they will be evaluated in performance, and that they have a basis for advancement in responsibilities. It is required even for professional staff so that they can maintain their skills, and so they can be aware of changes in policies both of the library and of the institution.

It is required for supervisory staff, especially when they move into their positions of responsibility but even later in order that they will maintain their awareness of personnel policies and procedures. It is of special importance for management staff so that they can maintain their skills in dealing with their strategic and tactical responsibilities.

The default values for training are 2% of direct labor. They reflect what appears to be reality in actual library operations, not what the level of commitment perhaps ought to be. The need for training is probably closer to 3% of direct labor.

Note that the value of 2% does *not* include the staffing required for the conduct of training programs but is limited solely to the time of direct labor staff that is spent in training programs. The conduct of training programs is part of the responsibility of supervision and, more formally, of central library administration.

Unallocated Time

The indirect time for "unallocated" is intended as a catch-all for such things as attending staff meetings or other such activities. It is called "unallocated" because, as a catch-all, it represents activities that in a real sense are unplanned or even unexplainable.

Benefit Time

Benefit time of course, is holidays, vacations, sick leave, and similar commitments that are part of a compensation package. There are two possible alternatives for measuring the working year. One excludes benefit days and the other includes them. A typical value for the former is 210 days (i.e., 42*5). That would then mean that the remaining 10 weeks of the calendar year would be benefit time. If benefit time is included in the working year, it is not assigned to indirect FTE. If not, it is necessary to include it in indirect FTE. To provide for a range of days in each alternative, *LPM* includes the number of days in the working year as a parameter, if the working year is more than 250 days LSM assumes it includes benefit time; otherwise, not.

4.3.3 Indirect Expenses

There are two categories of indirect expenses.

Benefit Expenses

Benefit expenses include the employer's payments for Social Security, medical insurance, retirement, and similar salary-related benefits. (Note that the employee's contributions to each of those are *not* included here, since they are part of the salary.) They also include pro-rated costs for sabbatical leave and sim-

ilar contractual commitments for future time off with pay. The default value in
LPM for benefit expenses is there simply to provide a value; it should be
replaced by the value that represents actual experience in a given library.

Indirect Operating Expenses

Indirect operating expenses include such things as office supplies, telephone, utilities, rental for space, and so on. (They do not include expenses that
are directly related to productive activity, however. Those are separately accounted for as "direct expenses.") The default value in *LPM* for indirect expenses is
there simply to provide a value; it should be replaced by the value that represents actual experience in a given library.

4.4
General Management and Central Administration

An academic library is a complex mix of services to users and internal
operations to provide the bases for those services. It requires not only supervisory management of the operational units that provide those services and operations but general strategic management of a high order and central administration that will assure effective operations.

As a result, general management and central administration are vital functions and must be recognized as such. In *LPM,* this is represented by an item
for G&A added in much the same way as "Indirect FTE," with default values of
10% for professional staff and 5% for clerical support staff. Functional responsibilities in G&A typically include the following:

The Library Director and directly related staff
Budget & Accounting Officer and staff
Personnel Office
Facilities Management
Formal Training Programs
Development Office and staff (concerned with funding development)
Systems Officer and staff (concerned with automated systems and
    equipment)
Other functions (such as publications, public relations, etc.)

4.4.1 Central Library Management

The strategic issues with which library general management must be concerned relate primarily to the needs of the institution being served and the pri-

mary constituencies it represents. The library manager must be in constant touch with those needs in order to ensure that the library continually meets them, within the constraints of available resources. The library manager must also, though, present the case for additional resources as may be needed to assure that the legitimate needs indeed are met.

Beyond those primary strategic issues, the library manager must also deal with a range of other strategic contexts: changes in patterns of publication, changes in information technologies, changes in laws and governmental policies, and changes in cooperative relationships with other libraries. Each of those requires that the library manager continuously be aware of what is happening in those contexts and of the effects they will have on library operations, services, and budgets.

4.4.2 Administrative Functions

Functions such as accounting, personnel, and facilities management deal with the resources needed to operate the library—money, people, and space. There are procedures needed to assure accountability for each of those administrative functions.

4.4.3 Training

Training is essential for staff at every level of operation. As new staff are hired, they must learn the specifics of their operational responsibilities as they fit within the structure of the specific library. As staff move into positions of supervisory responsibility, they must learn the policies and procedures to be followed in the library with respect to assignment of staff, supervision of them, and evaluation of their performance. As staff move into positions of central management responsibility, they need to deal with the requirements and expectations of the institution and clientele to be served.

Each of these implies the need for a formal training program, centrally managed but with the active participation of persons at each level of responsibility.

4.4.4 Development

The need to develop additional means of support, beyond that explicit in the institutional budget for support of the library, has become a necessary part of the funding strategy for libraries of every kind. Even the most heavily endowed private libraries (such as the Huntington, Morgan, Newberry, Folger, and American Historical Society libraries) have, during the past three decades, needed to turn to sources beyond the endowment income to support their operations.[3] Every major academic library has an active program to develop donations from wealthy alumni, corporations, foundations, and other sources. The federal government, through grants and, in some cases, contracts, has been a major source of funding for libraries of every kind, especially under the auspices of the Library Services and Construction Act (for public libraries and state library systems), the Higher Education Act (for academic libraries), and the National Endowment for the Humanities (for the endowed libraries).

Sometimes, these development programs have been needed to get support for specific activities. During the past three decades, a common example has been the development of automated systems. Another example has been conservation and preservation, with the objective of assuring that the world of culture does not disintegrate with the paper on which it is printed. In both of those examples, the Council on Library Resources has been a major source of funding, not so much for individual libraries as for the fundamental infrastructure.

In some cases, the funding of a major building for an academic library has been a very typical objective for a development program. In other cases, the support may be needed for augmentation to acquisitions, for support of new services, or for the addition of new clientele to be served. For the large endowed libraries, it has been needed simply to deal with the growth in programs.

In each case, the "development office," whether in the library or in the institution, serves as the focal point for management of the process of soliciting gifts, grants, and in some cases contracts as the means for funding operations.

4.4.5 Systems Management

The addition of a systems office to G&A staffing and costs in libraries is relatively recent and reflects the increasing role of computer-based systems in libraries. The likelihood is that it will increase in magnitude and importance in the future, especially for those libraries that actively participate as sources for electronic publication. The responsibility includes development and implementation of automated systems. It may well include management of the contract with the supplier of hardware and software. In most cases it includes coordination with institutional data processing systems. On a continuing basis, it involves management and maintenance of the central integrated library systems, the array of microcomputers and terminals, the local area network, and servers required to tie all of that equipment together.

---

[3] Bergman, Jed I., *Managing Change in the Non-Profit Sector.* San Francisco: Josey-Bass, 1996.

4.5
Library Administrative and Operational Structure

4.5.1 Administrative Structure: Organization Charts

The simplest model for representing the structure of the library is an *organization chart*. Primarily, it serves as a means for showing the chain of authority or administrative hierarchy of the library and the assignments of responsibility within it.

Aside from producing administrative organization charts, this capability in *LPM* can be used for other purposes. In particular, the list option makes it easy to use *LPM* to produce staffing lists for each of the units in the library. To do so, simply put the staff names into a structural element matrix with the units listed at level 1 (one) and the names of persons in each unit as subunit names at level 2 (two) following the unit to which they are assigned.

Organization charts can be used to show the structure of the library's automated system and the assignments of operations to specific pieces of equipment. A building can be described by organization charts which show the hierarchical arrangements of spaces and assignments to them of functional roles in operations of the library.

4.5.2 Operational Structure: The Matrix of Interunit Relationships

An organization chart shows the chain of authority and assignments of administrative responsibility. While that is important and serves as a useful starting point for picturing the structure of the library, it by no means represents the operational structure of the library.

Aside from providing means to produce organization charts, therefore, there currently are two matrices in *LPM* that represent elements of the operational structure of the library, one to provide data about branches and the other about independent libraries. These are still tentative elements in the conceptual structure of *LPM,* subject to change both in structure and content, since as yet there is no theoretical basis for assessing the effects of the operational structure on library operations and services. Indeed, that is far more complicated and difficult to represent, since it involves both the assignment of operational responsibilities (in contrast to administrative ones) and the flow of work among units.

The operational relationships between branch libraries and even independent libraries and central operations are of special importance. It is almost certain that responsibility for maintenance of the institution's automated library system will be centralized in the general and administrative systems staff, including system acquisition, installation, maintenance, and training. This is especially important if the OPAC (online public access catalog) is to reflect the holdings of the entire institution.

It is likely that responsibilities for all library personnel actions are focused in Central Operations, even for independent libraries, so as to ensure equity throughout the institution. Possibly, acquisition budgets may be coordinated through a central budget and accounting office.

Frequently, though, some independent libraries and even some branches may do their own technical processing—acquisitions and cataloging—while others may depend upon central technical processing. Branch libraries and independent libraries will probably each have their own reference staff, but the assignments, at least to branch libraries, may well be coordinated by central reference staff management.

4.5.3   Centralization and Decentralization

There are several aspects of the administrative and operational structure that are worthy of discussion. Some relate to historic and current rationales for one or another structure; some, to the effects on users; some, to the effects on staffing and on operational effectiveness and efficiency.

In the United States, because universities generally developed as integrated institutions, their libraries were created with structures that were largely centralized. Branch libraries have been established within them to meet specific needs of users, as will be discussed, but in general they have been tightly controlled by the central library administration, with their collections treated as part of the total institutional library.

Even within that framework, though, there have been specialized academic libraries that, to varying degrees, have operated independently. Two are especially evident—law libraries and medical libraries—but there are some institutions with independent libraries for other academic fields (music, art, or architecture, for example). The extent to which such libraries are operationally independent varies from institution to institution. At one extreme, in some cases they are totally independent, with policies, budgets, staffing, and services determined by the academic program they serve. At the other extreme, they are treated simply as branches of the central library of the institution, like any other branch. In between the two extremes, some aspects may be determined by the central library and others by the independent library. For example, technical processing (acquisition processing and cataloging) may be centralized, but all other aspects (selection and acquisition policy, budget, staffing, and services) may be determined by the independent library.

Beyond these formal independent libraries, there frequently are departmental libraries that operate more or less outside the control of the central library. Usually, they are staffed by students or clerical staff of the academic department; they are small collections of materials, acquired and paid for out of departmental budgets; the processing and cataloging will be of varying quality.

In most countries of Europe and Latin America, the administrative pattern for libraries is substantially different from that in the United States, primarily because universities there were created not as integrated institutions but as amalgams of what had previously been independent faculties. Each of those faculties came to the merger with its own library already in existence, and the independence of those faculty libraries usually continued after the amalgamation into a university. The "university library" is thus a combination of a central library, its collections serving the university at large and its staff and policies centrally determined, with a large number of independent faculty libraries whose staff and policies are separately determined by each faculty.

Effects on Users

There is little doubt that there is real value to users in bringing the materials they need close to them, both physically and administratively. Doing so increases their accessibility and the extent to which users can determine policies, especially with respect to collection development and services provided. This argues for branch libraries, if not for independent ones. The problem, though, is that where collections have value in a number of disciplines, they may be widely scattered and the policies may not adequately serve the needs of each discipline. And that argues for a centralized library, even with respect to the effects on users.

Effectiveness and Efficiency in Operations

If independent libraries have complete control over their staffing policies, there are likely to be substantial inequities across the institution. Beyond that, though, there are also likely to be losses in effectiveness and efficiency.

In particular, decentralized technical processing is likely to be inefficient because the staffing will be duplicative and at uneconomic levels. Even worse, though, is that the institutional catalog will become a mishmash of independent cataloging decisions. This is especially critical in the context of automated systems, in which the effectiveness of the institution's catalog depends upon conformance to standards of practice. Beyond that, decentralized user services are likely to be even more inefficient because they again will be duplicative and at uneconomic levels. Reference desks and circulation chargeout points must be staffed in the branches or independent libraries, even when the level of use may not justify doing so.

This can be characterized aa "structural inefficiency," and it has significant impact that needs to be recognized in *LPM*. The problem at the moment is how best to do so and that is the primary reason that this part of *LPM* is still under development.

Bibliography

The following references provide a starting point for literature relevant to costing and managerial accounting:

References Providing Introduction to General Accounting

Anthony, Robert N. *Accounting: Text and Cases*. London: McGraw-Hill, 1999.

Buckley, John W. *The Accounting Profession*. Los Angeles: Melville, 1974.

McCullers, Levis D. *Introduction to Financial Accounting*. Los Angeles: Melville, 1975.

Midgett, Elwin W. *An Accounting Primer*. New York: Mentor, 1992.

Myer, John Nicolas. *Accounting for Non-accountants; Key to an Understanding of Accounting*. New York: New York University Press, 1963.

Nickerson, Clarence B. *Accounting Handbook for Nonaccountants*. New York: Van Nostrand Reinhold, 1984.

Pyle, William W. *Fundamental Accounting Principles: Workbook of Study Guides*, 10th ed. Homewood, IL: Irwin, 1984.

References for Managerial Accounting

Bierman, Harold. *The Capital Budgeting Decision: Economic Analysis and Financing of Investment Projects*, 2nd ed. New York: Collier-Macmillan, 1967.

Buckley, John W., and Lightner, Kevin M. *Accounting: An Information Systems Approach*. Encino, CA: Dickenson, 1973.

DeCoster, Don T. *Accounting for Managerial Decision Making*, 2nd ed. Santa Barbara: Wiley, 1978.

Horngren, Charles T. *Introduction to Management Accounting*, 11th ed. Upper Saddle River, NJ: Prentice Hall, 1999.

Hyatt, James A., et al. *A cost Accounting Handbook for Single-Purpose Colleges and Universities*. Washington, DC: NACUBO, 1983.

Lazzaro, Victor (ed.), *Systems and Procedures: A Handbook for Business and Industry*. Englewood Cliffs, NJ: Prentice-Hall, 1959.

McCullers, Levis D., et al. *Contemporary Business Environment: Readings in Financial Accounting*. Los Angeles: Melville, 1975.

References Specific to Library Cost Accounting

Hayes, Robert M. "Managerial Accounting in Library and Information Science Education," *Library Quarterly* 53, 3 (July 1983), pp. 340–358.

Hayes, Robert M. *Handbook of Data Processing for Libraries*, 2nd ed. New York: Wiley, 1972. Chapter 4, Cost Accounting in Libraries, pp. 102–121.

Palmour, V.E., and Bryant, E. *A Study of the Characteristics, Costs, and Magnitude of Interlibrary Loans in Academic Libraries*. Rockville, MD: Westat, 1971. ILL has been the means by which libraries have dealt with the need to provide access to "all the world's information" without incurring the cost for each library to acquire it. But it is expensive. This study is one of the very few that directly applies methods of cost accounting. While it has some flaws, even they have value.

5

Services to Library Users

Introduction

This chapter presents models for representing data about users and their uses of libraries in a form that permits generation of estimates for workloads on user services based on readily available data about the population of users and library-derived data about historical patterns of use.

5.1
Populations of Users

This section discusses various different kinds of populations of users (e.g., in an academic library: faculty, graduate students, undergraduate students, researchers, general public, institutional staff, other libraries borrowing materials, etc.; in a public library: the general public, children, youth, elderly, business and professional, local government, etc.; in a special library: management, engineers, production, sales, etc.). It discusses the means for measuring their characteristics. It discusses relevant data on numbers of persons in each relevant type of population. It then discusses the nature of "J-shaped" curves representing the relative frequency of use. It concludes with a discussion of the absolute frequency of use by each type of population.

The Populations Served are used to represent contexts for providing services. Most of them relate to persons and, for those, the population is measured by number of persons. The populations of users currently included in *LPM* are shown in the following table. Most of them should be self-evident, but it is worthwhile being specific about each of them, so following the table is a brief discussion of each.

Population Types	Descriptions
Staff	Staff of representative institution
Faculty	Members of the teaching and research faculty
Graduate Students	Students pursuing studies beyond 4-year level
Undergraduate Students	Students studying up to the 4-year level
Institution	ILL-lending, document delivery
Informed Public	Frequent users
General Public	All other persons

Staff refers to staff of the institution, other than the members of the teaching and instructional faculty; although one can interpret that either broadly or narrowly, it is recommended that it be taken as inclusive of everyone, with the parameter for "Percent Users" providing the means for narrowing it to those who actually are users.

Institutions refers to those agencies that are served by the library through ILL (Inter-Library Loan) lending and/or document delivery (the latter referring to the delivery of a photocopy, fax copy, or electronic copy of the material). It is important at this point to reemphasize the fact that *LPM* derives workloads from the behavior of using populations. Workload for use of ILL in Borrowing (or for obtaining document delivery instead) is therefore derived directly from the behavior of the staff, faculty, and students as individuals; it is *not* separately entered into the model. However, the workload in use of ILL for Lending or for responding to requests for document delivery must be derived from the behavior of the population that uses it—the institutions that request those services from the library. Of course, ILL borrowing and lending are usually combined in operations, but conceptually they are really two quite different things.

Informed Public refers to those researchers that use the library in much the same way that staff, faculty, or students do but that do not have a formal affiliation. General Public refers to all other persons who come to the library for possibly casual reasons but who still represent a workload on reference or on use of materials and facilities.

The first matrix for the populations of users consists of rows, one for each type of population served, and four columns. The first column contains a measure of the overall size of the type of population; the second column, the percentage of that population that are regarded as users; the third, the average yearly frequency with which users actually use the library; and the fourth, the resulting total number of uses (calculated as the product of the first three). This matrix in *LPM* looks as follows:

Usage by Population Types	Total Population	User Percent	Uses/User	Total Uses
Staff	600	25%	50	7,500
Faculty	974	100%	90	87,660
Graduate Students	2,586	100%	60	155,160
Undergraduate Students	19,289	100%	45	868,005
Institutions (ILL Lending)	5,920	100%	1	5,920
Researchers	100	100%	25	2,500
Informed Public	100	100%	25	2,500
General Public	100,000	1%	9	9,000
Total Uses				1,138,245

For example, consider a single row from the illustrative matrix:

| Staff | 600 | 25% | 50 | 7,500 |

The type of population served is "STAFF" (currently defined to include all staff of institution-related activities, other than academic staff). The total size of that population (i.e., the number of persons in it) is 600. Of those 25% are regarded as real users (the remainder being, for example, security and mainte-nance staff, administrative support staff, etc.). Those users average 50 uses a year (on the average, about once a week). Total use for this population type is there-fore 600*.25*50 = 7500, shown in the fourth column.

Obtaining and verifying data for this matrix should be relatively simple. Of course, it requires that the set of populations be identified, but that surely derives directly from the identified mission of the library. The first three columns of data should be readily derivable from reports and internal records of operations in either the institution or the library itself.

5.1.1 Total Usage

Please note, though, that it is not necessary that data in the three columns each be accurate. They are intended only to assist in getting to the final column, the total use for each type of population, which is calculated as the product of the first three columns of data. The data in that final column can be compared with data on actual use, either directly from surveys of users or indirectly from actual workloads on various types of services or uses of materials.

5.1.2 Distribution of Frequency of Use

It is of interest to note that the two values, percentage and frequency of use, are two of the underlying parameters necessary for representing the typical highly skewed distributions of use of information resources—called "J-shaped" curves. The nature of J-shaped curves will be discussed in Chapter 6, when they will be applied to collection allocation decisions, but they are equally applicable to the behavior of users.

Distribution of Use Within Types of User

First, within a type of user there will be differences among individuals in the extent to which they will use libraries or other information resources. Such individual differences may reflect demographics, skills, priorities, the effects of distance, subject interests, or any of a wide range of other characteristics.

Intensity of Need and Amounts of Use

Second, there will be differences among groups or types of users in the intensity of their need for information and, as a consequence, of their frequency of use. The illustrative values presented in the matrix for "Usage by Population Types" show numbers of uses by faculty substantially greater than those for graduate students and even more so for undergraduate students. Actual data for the use of the UCLA library system show exactly that kind of difference, with values per user essentially as shown in the illustration.[1]

The underlying model is that the amount of use made by a type of user reflects the relative intensity of need for information or, at least, for access to library materials. Later, in Chapter 9, this assumption will be used to represent differential demands for services from various kinds of information industry. Here, though, the focus is more specific and deals with the individual library and, especially, the academic library.

Presumably, in universities the intensity of need for information increases with research demands. In research-oriented institutions, it is typical to expect that faculty members will devote between one-third and one-half their time to research, with the remainder devoted to teaching, departmental administration, and public service. That implies a continuing high level of need for information to support that level of research. In contrast, in institutions that are more oriented to instruction, faculty members will spend from 75% to 100% of their time in teaching. Their need for information to support research will be substantially less.

In either context, an undergraduate student is largely focused upon classroom instruction, with the assigned textbooks as the primary source of sup-

---

[1] The data were generously provided by the management of the UCLA Library System. The data were for the years 1997, 1998, and 1999 (the general picture for all analyses being essentially identical for each of the years). These data provided the basis for testing and confirming several of the default values included in *LPM,* including in particular those for relative intensity of use as shown here.

porting information. The use of the library typically is for assigned readings, especially through use of materials on "reserve." The intensity of need is therefore likely to be much less than for the faculty member.

The graduate student is somewhere between the two, with relatively intense research needs but leavened by commitment of time to classroom instruction as well.

5.1.3 Growth in Populations of Users

A crucial need in planning for the future is to recognize the potential, even the likelihood that there will be growth is the size of populations served. Underlying such growth is the fact that the overall number of persons in the world at large, and in communities within each country, are all growing exponentially. Indeed, the number of students enrolled in academic institutions is also growing exponentially, as is the number of faculty needed to teach them.

It is therefore necessary to establish a basis for estimating the expected future growth in populations served by the library. One easy means for doing so is to examine historic data to determine whether there has been a pattern of growth that can then serve as the basis for projecting continuation into the future. Another is to obtain external data, such as census of population, from which more fundamental factors determining future growth can be determined.

5.2
Distributions of Uses Over Materials and Services

This section discusses the various kinds of uses of materials (e.g., circulation use, in-house use, reference use, photocopy use, etc.). It then discusses the differences in the relative distribution of such uses by various populations of users.

The second matrix has the same rows as the first, but the columns now relate to the set of services provided by the library. In *LPM,* those services are:

Services	Description
Circulation	Page, circulate, deliver, reshelve, keep records
In-house	At shelf, at table, for browsing, reference, data
Reserve Use	Class-assigned readings
Photocopying	Copying done by library staff
A–V, Multimedia, Computer	Audio-visual and computer-based multimedia
Regular Reference	Staff reference desk, assist with equipment
Extended Reference	More than 15-minute reference work
Database Access	Access to databases, beyond OPAC
Access Elsewhere	Obtain materials (by ILL or document delivery)
Instruction/Analysis	Instruct users, consult, analyze

The distribution matrix itself is in two parts and looks as follows:

Materials Use by Population Types	Circulate Use	In-House Use	Reserve Use	Photocopy Use	AV, Multimedia
Staff	33.00%	67.00%		0.10%	0.10%
Faculty	33.00%	67.00%		0.10%	0.10%
Graduate Students	33.00%	67.00%			0.50%
Undergraduate Students	16.00%	33.00%	7.00%		1.50%
Institutions (ILL Lending)	50.00%			50.00%	
Researchers		100.00%			
Informed Public		100.00%			
General Public		100.00%			

Reference Use by Population Types	Reference		Database Access	ILL Borrow	Consult/ Instruct
	Regular	Extended			
Staff	5.00%	1.00%	0.20%	5.00%	0.20%
Faculty	5.00%	1.00%	0.20%	5.00%	0.20%
Graduate Students	5.00%	1.00%	0.10%	2.50%	0.20%
Undergraduate Students	5.00%	1.00%	0.10%		0.20%
Institutions (ILL Lending)	100.00%				
Researchers	2.00%				
Informed Public	2.00%				
General Public	2.00%				

The value in each column, for a given population, measures the percentage of uses of the library that will entail the service related to that column. It is these values that provide the means for *LPM* to derive the workloads on each of these services. In particular, the workload on in-person Reference is derived from Reference, Extended (Reference), Database Access, and Analysis; the workload on ILL-Borrowing (and document delivery), from Access Elsewhere. Any request for services not in person but by communication would be included in the values for it for each of the services.

Getting the values for this second matrix is clearly more difficult than for the first, but it is still quite feasible to do so. Values can be estimated from knowledge of the patterns of use of a given population and then be tested by observation. Other values can be estimated from statistics on services which may identify the category of each user. Some values may be obtained by sampling of users during a period of time, by interviews, or by questionnaires.

5.2.1 Relationship Between Use of Materials and Use of Services

Note that, in characterizing and measuring services to users, a distinction has been made between the use of materials and the use of services. A fundamental question is what the relative importance of the two may be, both in general and for a given library. The answer to that question affects the allocation of resources between the two kinds of service. Put in operational terms, "What should be the distribution of resources between collections and reader services?"

A partial answer to the question may be found in the Cobb-Douglas model, which is intended to reflect the effect on production of the allocation of resources between capital investment and labor. In application of the Cobb-Douglas to the library, the capital investment is taken as the collection of materials (including both the cost of acquisition and the cost of technical processing in selection, acquisition, processing, and cataloging). The labor is taken as the reader services staff.

Such application of the Cobb-Douglas model was considered in a paper in 1979 by Hayes.[2] The results in that paper showed that circulation of materials in public libraries, per library staff member, increases as the size of the collection increases, all else being constant. In a separate study, the same kind of behavior was exhibited for academic libraries.[3]

The implication of these results is that the use of materials and the use of services are interconnected, but the results from application of the Cobb-Douglas model are more specific. They imply what the appropriate division in expenditure between the two should be. Those results for academic libraries show that about two-thirds of the library budget should go toward capital investment (including both purchase costs and technical services costs) and one-third toward costs for services.

5.3
Workload Factors for User Services

The workload factors relevant to use of materials and to uses of services are illustrated by the following matrix, with the default values as shown:

| | Workload Factors | | |
Services	Intellectual	Procedural	Physical
Circulation Use		3	2
In-House Use			2
Reserve Use			5
Photocopy Use			1
Multimedia Use			5
Reference, General	10	10	
Reference Extended	50		
Database Access	50		
Access Elsewhere (ILB)	20	20	10
Analyze, Consult, Instruct	250		

[2] Hayes, Robert M., "The Management of Library Resources: The Balance Between Capital and Staff in Providing Services," *Library Research* 1, 2 (Summer 1979), pp. 119–142.

[3] Hayes, Robert M., with Pollock, Ann M., and Nordhaus, Shirley, "An Application of the Cobb-Douglas Model to the Association of Research Libraries," *Library and Information Science Research* 5, 3 (Fall 1983), pp. 291–325.

Recall that the values shown are intended to represent "minutes per transaction," a transaction being a request for service and/or the delivery of that service. The time per circulation transaction includes not only the procedural work in chargeout, renewal, billing for overdues, and so forth, but the physical work in reshelving. It is of more than passing interest to note that for closed-stack libraries, the physical work is likely to be at least double that shown for the default value because of the necessity for "paging."

The time shown for photocopy use is for staff-operated services, not for user-operated copying. The latter are separately accounted for in the assessment of needs for photocopy facilities. Furthermore, the default value is for copying a 10-page unit of work.

5.4
Needs for Facilities

This section discusses the various kinds of facilities needed to meet the needs of users (e.g., various kinds of terminals, seating, circulation chargeout stations, reference service points, photocopying, computers, etc.). It discusses the means for estimating the levels or amount of use required for each kind of facility. It discusses the role of queuing and the means for dealing with its effects.

5.4.1 User Facilities Models

Among all of the contexts for estimation, user facilities are the most subject to variability, the most dependent on policy decision, and as a result the most complex to represent. The variability arises from the fact that, while we can estimate and even measure the total number of uses, they are distributed over time—seasonally, monthly, weekly, hourly—and that distribution needs to be recognized. The policy decisions relate to whether the amount to be provided of a given facility will be chosen to meet peak load requirements or average requirements and to what is an allowable amount of queuing or delays in service.

To illustrate, let's consider terminals for access to the OPAC. Let's suppose that there are 1 million uses per year of the library. Accepting, for the moment, that virtually every one of those uses will require access to an OPAC terminal, how many terminals does that imply? Assume that there are 250 days in a service year, that there are ten hours in a service day, and that an average use will require a tenth of an hour (i.e., 6 minutes). If we were to calculate based solely on averages, terminal time would total 100,000 hours spread over 2500 service hours, which implies the need for 40 terminals. The point, though, is that use is not evenly distributed over the 2500 service hours. Use during some hours may be ten times the average and during other hours may be close to zero, but it makes little economic sense to provide a number of terminals that would meet a peak load of ten times the average, since for much of the year they would be unused.

This is well illustrated by data for uses of the UCLA Library System during the calendar year 1999.[4] The hours can be divided into two major categories. First are the hours during which the number of transactions per hour is substantially greater (i.e., more than 500 greater than the average over the surrounding week) than the surrounding hours. The following chart shows the distribution of them over the year, the anomalous hours being those that rise above the base rate at about 1000 per day.

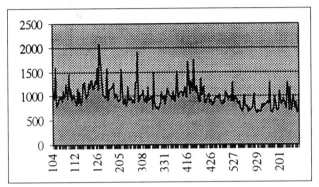

Such hours can be reasonably regarded as anomalous. These are hours that probably should not be the basis for queuing decisions. There were a total of 229 such hours of peak traffic load. The average traffic during these peak load hours was 992.29; the median was 946; the maximum was 2081 (on 26 January 1999, at noon). Of the total of 7270 hours, these represent 2% of the hours and 15% of the transactions.

The second is all other hours during opening. The following chart shows the distribution during the year: The total number of hours involved is 5699.

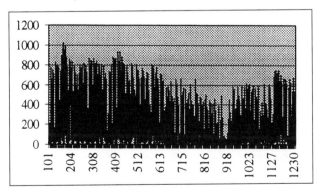

[4] This graph and the following one are based on the data provided by the management of the UCLA Library System. The use here was to test the default value of 5 for the ratio of maximum to average in nonanomalous hours.

The average traffic during these "normal hours" is 220.47; the median, 150; the maximum, 1022. (Note that the maximum occurs within a week during which the average workload is nearly 400 per hour). The ratio of maximum to average is 4.6. Of the total of 7270 hours, these represent 83% of the hours and 79% of the transactions.

The rationale for treating the normal hours separately from the anomalous ones is that it would be irrational to base queuing decisions on the anomalous hours. The queuing decision, instead, should be based on relatively normal, consistent behavior. Of course, one must still deal with handling maximum traffic loads within the normal, consistent patterns, but that is what the ratio of maximum to average is intended to recognize.

This is a classical "queuing theory" problem. Solution of it requires a policy decision about what length of queue and what time delays for patron waiting in a queue are acceptable. It is this combination of variability and policy decision that needs to be recognized in estimating each of the user facilities.

There are two separable parts in representing this problem in *LPM*. The first is represented by the number of uses of the library, the percentage of uses that require access to a user facility, and the parameters for days and hours in a service year. Those are all counterparts of elements in the matrices for users and the table for parameters, and they can be well represented in similar ways. Indeed, the number of uses already is available in the first matrix for users. The percentage of uses requiring a given user facility can be represented by another distribution matrix, and the service hours by additions to the parameters table.

This part is represented by the following matrix:

User Facilities Factors	Minutes per Use	Sq. Ft. per Unit
Seating	60.00	30
Carrels	60.00	30
Terminals	6.00	30
Photocopy Machines	5.00	30
Circulation Chargeouts	2.00	30
Reference Stations	6.67	60

The second is that involved in describing and reflecting the queuing problem. As a first cut on representing that, *LPM* uses the total time involved in use of each kind of facility during a year, divides that by number of hours in a service year, and multiplies the result by a factor to reflect peak load demands. The result is an approximation to the number of service points for the given service.

The one service for which there is no identified workload or workload factor is seating. For that *LPM* relates the workload to the number of in-house uses and reserve materials uses (but with a portion of circulation uses).

Queuing

The numbers of facilities in the library, especially of user facilities, must be determined based on estimates of anticipated demand but subject to economic constraints. One parameter included in *LPM*, "Peak Load/Average Load," is used to deal with part of that decision—namely, what the anticipated demand is—since adequate service requires that the numbers of facilities be commensurate with the peak load rather than just the average load.

However, having said that, the fact remains that it is uneconomic to provide more facilities than really are needed to meet the needs. As a result, the number is likely to be such that users may need to wait for some period of time for a needed facility to become available. This is a classic "queuing problem" which is experienced by everyone in every context of service to the public, whether in grocery stores, banks, gasoline stations, or telephone calls.

The solution to the queuing problem in the library should involve balancing the effects on the user for waiting in line against the costs to the library for adding a facility to reduce that wait. Currently, *LPM* does not attempt to determine the latter, but it does provide means to see what the effects on the user for a given number of facilities will be.

The basis for *LPM* calculation of queuing statistics is a set of equations.[5] The variables represented in those equations are:

c: number of service facilities provided

K: average number of persons involved with the facilities

Kq: average number of persons in the queue (i.e., waiting for service)

W: average time for users

Wq: average time waiting in a queue

L: average arrival rate, per minute, of users

M: average service rate, per minute

t: average minutes per service (equals $1/M$)

T: total service time for arrival rate (equals $L*t$)

The equations are:

$$p(0) = 1/\{ T^{\wedge}c/(c!*(1 - T/c) + \overset{(c-1)}{\underset{n=0}{\text{Sum}}} (T^{\wedge}n/n!)\}$$

$$p(n) = p(0)*T^{\wedge}n/n! \qquad \text{for } n = 0, 1, \ldots, c$$
$$p(n) = p(0)*T^{\wedge}n*c^{\wedge}(c - n)/c! \qquad \text{for } n > c$$
$$Kq = p(0)*T^{\wedge}c*(T/c)/(c!*(1 - T/c))^{\wedge}2$$
$$Wq = Kq/L$$
$$W = Wq + 1/M$$
$$K = W*L$$

---

[5] Zwillinger, Daniel (ed.), *Standard Mathematical Tables and Formulae,* 30th ed. New York: Chemical Rubber Company, 1996, pp. 587–588.

LPM provides means for you to see the effects of these statistics for various traffic loads (expressed as a ratio to the average traffic load).

Standard Values for Number of Facilities

Determining the appropriate number of facilities, *C,* to be provided for any given type of facility is a tactical decision for library management. Given them, the number to be staffed or otherwise made available at any given time for expected workloads in use by patrons is an operational decision. *LPM* provides means to assist in the assessments needed to support those decisions.

LPM provides a standard estimate for the number of facilities required to serve the identified maximum workload. It is calculated from the total workload, multiplied by its distribution over service functions involving use of a given type of facility, then multiplied by the expected minutes for an average use of the facility divided by the number of minutes per service year, and finally multiplied by the parameter for ratio of peak load traffic to average traffic. Basically, it reflects the necessary total number of minutes of service required to meet the maximum workload. These values are automatically generated by *LPM* as the starting point for generating queuing statistics.

Of course, the underlying queuing problem is the fact that, even given the ability to handle the maximum workload, patrons will arrive at times that cause queues to develop, so the service statistic that is most crucial in making those decisions is the length of queues—the number of persons that are in line waiting for one of the facilities to become available. The equations shown above provide that statistic, among others.

Alternative Numbers of Facilities

To deal with that, *LPM* allows you to modify any of these values to test the effect of alternatives, although they will be restored to the standard estimate whenever you call for the Queuing menu. This is the simplest means to evaluate alternatives. You need merely enter alternative values for the number of service facilities to be provided and then see the effect they have on the length of the queue for that particular type of facility. That is easy to do, and the results are immediately available. Just enter the alternative value into the column for *C,* "Number of Facilities," in the table for queuing variables. The resulting length of the queue will appear in the column for *"Kq,"* "Length of Queue," in the table for queuing statistics.

This approach would be of special value in determining how many facilities should be staffed for a given workload. You need merely enter your guess as to the appropriate number and then see what the expected length of the queue would be.

To assist in making such guesses, *LPM* provides another means for determining alternative values. You may also use the "Solve?" button to have *LPM* directly calculate the number of facilities required to limit the expected length of the queue for a given type of user service. If you click on the "Solve?" button, you will be presented with a dialog box that will allow you to identify the type of facility and then the value for the length of queue that you wish to plan for. *LPM* will then generate a value for the number of facilities of the given type needed to provide that desired value for length of queue. The means for estimation is an iterative process, and you might want to repeat it in order to see how the estimation may change from one cycle of iterations to another.

5.4.2 Staff Facilities Models

The estimation of staff facilities is quite straightforward. For each type of function for staff and for each level of staff, there are standard areas required for work, and the space requirements for them can be easily determined. There are some details in the calculations that need to be recognized, of course. The most important of them is the degree of efficiency in use of office space. For example, for high-level staff there will be larger offices than for lower-level staff, and for good reasons as well as perquisites.

Despite those matters of detail, there are well-established figures for the net square feet required for each type of function and level of staff involved. Those figures need merely be multiplied by the number of staff of each type to obtain the estimate for net square feet.

To that, of course, must be added estimates for the overhead space, such as corridors for access, ancillary facilities, and so on.

Among the staff facilities are "working spaces." The number of them is a function not so much of the number of staff as of the workload. Therefore, similar to the means for handling service facilities, the number of working spaces of a given kind is calculated by multiplying the workload by the associated workload factor and dividing the result by the number of days in a working year. Of course this is simply an approximation to the answer to the queuing problem involved.

5.4.3 Library Location Models

It Chapter 2, it was pointed out that the location of a library facility should be based upon assessment of the effect of distance on the users. As was said there, it is well known that the use of a library or other information resource is inversely related to the distance that the user must travel in order to get to it, and there is a classic model which has been applied to just this kind of location and traffic analysis problem—the gravity model of market potential.

Essentially, it draws an analogy between the attraction of a user to a facility, on the one hand, and the attraction due to the force of gravity, on the other. Using that analogy, we could represent the library as one mass (perhaps proportional to its collection size) and the use population as a set of individual masses distributed about the city each equal to the expected level of utilization (books borrowed) each user might make of the library.[6]

In that model, the attraction of a user to the library, and therefore presumably the degree of utilization made, is inversely proportional to the square of the distance between the two:

$$\text{Use} = M(m/d^2)$$

In general, the gravity model appears to be applicable when the cost of travel is a linear function of distance (as might be the case for walking or bicycling). However, when the cost of travel is other than linear, different models must apply. For example, if the cost of travel is a logarithmic function of distance, the model is inversely proportional to the power of the 2:

$$\text{Use} = M(m/2^d)$$

A near-logarithmic function might be represented by automobile travel, in which there is an initial satartup time followed by a nearly linear travel time.

The consequences of either model might lead to decisions to establish a larger number of smaller branch libraries which would be geographically closer to the users and especially to users with a relatively low level of attraction (i.e., low mass m).

Bibliography

References to General Methods for Study of Library Use

Activity Statistics for a Large Biomedical Library. Part 2 of the Final Report on the Organization of Large Files. Sherman Oaks, CA: Advanced Information Systems Division, Hughes Dynamics, Inc., April 30, 1964.

Baker, Sharon L., and Lancaster, F. Wilfrid. *The Measurement and Evaluation of Library Services,* 2nd ed. Arlington, VA: Information Resources Press, 1991.

Bookstein, Abraham, "Questionnaire Research in a Library Setting," *Journal of Academic Librarianship* 1, 1, pp. 24–28.

Butler, Meredith, and Gratch, Bonnie. "Planning a User Study: The Process Defined," *College and Research Libraries* 43, 4, pp. 320–330.

[6] Koontz, Christine M., *Library Facility Siting and Location Handbook.* Westport, CT: Greenwood Press, 1997.

Colin, K., Lindsey, George N., and Callahan, Daniel. "Toward Usable User Studies," *Journal of the American Society for Information Science* 31, (1980), pp. 347–356.

Harris, Colin. "Surveying the User and User Studies," *Information and Library Manager* 5, 3 (1985), pp. 9–14.

Kidston, James S. "The Validity of Questionnaire Responses," *Library Quarterly* 55, 2 (1985), pp. 133–150.

Lancaster, F. Wilfrid. *If You Want to Evaluate Your Library.* Champaign, IL: University of Illinois, Graduate School of Library and Information Science, 1955.

Martin, Lowell. "User Studies and Library Planning," *Library Trends* 24, pp. 483–495.

Moran, Barbara B. "Construction of the Questionnaire in Survey Research," *Public Libraries* 24, 2 (1985), pp. 75–76.

Morse, Philip McCord. *Measures of Library Effectiveness.* Cambridge, MA: M.I.T., 1972.

NCLIS. *Conference on the Needs of Occupational, Ethnic, and Other Groups in the United States, University of Denver, 1973. Library and Information Service Needs of the Nation: Proceedings of a Conference on the Needs of Occupational, Ethnic, and Other Groups in the United States.* Washington, DC: Supt. of Docs., U.S. GPO, 1974.

OUTPUTM: Version 2. Center for the Study of Rural Librarianship. Clarion University of Pennsylvania, College of Library Science.

Powell, Ronald R. *The Relationship of Library User Studies to Performance Measures: A Review of the Literature.* Chicago: University of Illinois, 1985.

Ralli, Tony. "Performance Measures for Academic Libraries," *Australian Academic and Research Libraries* 18, 1 (1987), pp. 1–9.

Schwarz Kungl. tekniska högskolan. Biblioteket. Library Services in Transition: A Presentation of Current Activities at the Royal Institute of Technology Library. Edited by Stephan Schwarz, Gunnar Carlsson, and Gudmund Fröberg. Stockholm: The Library, 1978.

User Surveys and Evaluation of Library Services. SPEC Kit 71. Washington, DC: Association of Research Libraries, Office of Management Studies, Systems Procedures and Exchange Center, 1981.

User Surveys in ARL Libraries. SPEC Kit 101. Washington, DC: Association of Research Libraries, Office of Management Studies, Systems Procedures and Exchange Center, 1984.

User Surveys. SPEC Kit 148. Washington, DC: Association of Research Libraries, Office of Management Studies, Systems and Procedures Exchange Center, 1988.

Zweizig, Donald L. "With Our Eye on the User: Needed Research for Information and Referral in the Public Library," *Drexel Library Quarterly* 12, 1 (1976), pp. 48–58.

Zweizig, Douglas, and Eleanor Jo Roger. *Output Measures for Public Libraries: A Manual of Standardized Procedures.* Chicago: American Library Association, 1982.

References on General Library Use

American Library Association. *Student Use of Libraries: An Inquiry into the Needs of Students, Libraries and the Educational Process.* Chicago: 1964. I must confess that, aside from the relevance of the subject matter, this book has personal interest to me since it contains a commentary that I made in response to a paper presented by Ralph Shaw. In those remarks I dealt with several of the issues that in subsequent years have continued to be foci of my attention. But these comments were all very early on in that process.

Broadus. Robert. "Use Studies of Library Collections," *Library Resources and Technical Services* 24, 4 (1980), pp. 317–324.

Burns. Robert W., Jr. "Library Use as a Performance Measure: Its Background and Rationale," *Journal of Academic Librarianship* 4, 1 (1978), pp. 4–11.

Church, Steven S. "User Criteria for Evaluation of Library Services," *Journal of Library Administration* 2, 1 (1981), pp. 35–46.

Drott, M. Carl, and Mancall, Jacqueline C. "Magazines as Information Sources: Patterns of Student Use," *School Media Quarterly* 8, 4 (1980), pp. 240–250.

Gates, Jean Key. *Guide to the Use of Libraries and Information Sources,* 6th ed. New York: McGraw-Hill, 1989.

Hayes, Robert M. "Mathematical Models of Information System Use" (with H. Borko), *Information Processing and Management* 19, 3 (1983), pp. 173–186.

Hayes, Robert M., and Reilly, Kevin D. "The Effect of Response Time Upon the Utilization of an Information Retrieval System," *ORSA Annual Meeting* (June 1, 1967).

Hayes, Robert Mayo. *Mathematical Models of Information System Use.* Los Angeles, CA: UCLA, School of Library and Information Science, 1982.

Hindle, Anthony, and Michael Buckland. "In-library Usage in Relation to Circulation," *Collection Management* 2, 4 (Winter 1978), pp. 265–277. Hindle and Buckland discuss the relationship between different kinds of uses. Of greatest import is the recognition that, while materials that have heavy in-house use tend to have heavy circulation use, there still are large numbers of items used in-house that have low, even zero circulation. The results presented should be compared with those from Fussler and from Kent's study at Pittsburgh.

Humanists at Work. Papers presented at a symposium held at the University of Illinois at Chicago, April 27–28, 1989. Chicago: University of Illinois at Chicago, 1989. The title says it all. It focuses on the use of libraries by humanists.

King, Donald Ward, *The Evaluation of Information Services and Products.* Washington, DC: Information Resources Press, 1971.

Willard, Patricia. *An Exploratory Study of the Staffing of Reference Services in Public Libraries in the Sydney Metropolitan Area.* Kensington, N.S.W.: School of Librarianship, University of New South Wales, 1979.

Willard, Patricia. *People and Libraries: A Study of Why People Visit a Public Library and the Library's Response.* Kensington, N.S.W.: School of Librarianship, University of New South Wales, 1981.

Willard, Patricia. *Public Libraries and Automation: Four Case Studies.* Kensington, N.S.W.: School of Librarianship, University of New South Wales, 1983.

References on Use of Collections

Aguailar, William. "The Application of Relative Use and Interlibrary Demand in Collection Development," *Collection Management* 8, 1 (1986), pp. 15–24.

Bookstein, Abraham. "Comments on the Morse-Chen Discussion of Non-circulating Books," *Library Quarterly* 45, 2 (1975), pp. 195–198.

Bowen, Alice. *Nonrecorded Use of Books and Browsing in the Stacks of a Research Library.* MA Thesis. University of Chicago, 1961.

Buckland, Michael Keeble. *Book Availability and the Library User.* New York, Pergamon Press, 1975. Buckland discusses a wide range of issues involved in management of the collection. They include the effect of time on use of a title, the variations among titles, the use of lists and peer comparisons in selection, the effect of circulation policies. It draws heavily upon models and provides data on which to illustrate their use.

Bulick, Stephen, and others. "Circulation and In-house Use of Books," Chapter II of Kent, Allen, and others.

Chen, Ching-Chih. *A Case Study of the Use of Monographs in the Francis Countway Library of Medicine, Harvard University.* Cambridge: MIT Press, 1976. This is a superb example of modeling, providing both theoretical coverage and quantitative data within the theories.

Christiansen, Dorothy E., Davis, C. Roger, and Reed-Scott, Jutta. "Guide to Collection Evaluation Through Use and User Studies," *Library Resources and Technical Services* 27, 14 (1983), pp. 432–440.

Fussler, Herman H., and Simon, Julian L. *Patterns in the Use of Books in Large University Research Libraries.* Chicago: University of Chicago, 1961. This book is a crucial reference. It deals with a critical problem and uses mathematical models in doing so. It exemplifies both the methods and the pitfalls.

Harris, C. "A Comparison of Issues and In-library Use of Books," *Aslib Proceedings* 29, 3 (Mar. 1977), pp. 118–126.

Hayes, Robert M. "The Distribution of Use of Library Materials," *Library Research* 3 (Fall 1981), pp. 215–260.

Hindle, A., and Worthington, D. "Simple Stochastic Models for Library Loan," *Journal of Documentation* 36, 3 (Sep. 1980), pp. 209–213.

Intner, Sheila S. *Circulation Policy in Academic, Public, and School Libraries.* New York: Greenwood Press, 1987. Intner reviews and compares circulation policies across academic, public, and school libraries.

Jain, A. K. *A Statistical Study of Book Use.* Ph.D. Thesis. Layfette, IN: Purdue, 1967. NTIS PB176525.

Jain, A.K., and others. "A Statistical Model of Book Use and its Application to the Book Storage Problem," *Journal of the American Statistical Association* 64 (Dec. 1969), pp. 1211–1224.

Kaske, N.K. "Evaluation of Current Collection Utilization Methodologies and Findings," *Collection Management* 3, 2–3 (1979), pp. 197–199.

Katzer, Jeffrey, et al. *Evaluating Information: A Guide for Users of Social Science Research.* Reading, MA: Addison-Wesley, 1978.

Kent, Allen, et al. *Use of Library Materials: The University of Pittsburgh Study.* New York: Marcel Dekker, 1979. This study is of great importance for several reasons. First, it deals with a problem of critical importance: second, it clearly exemplifies the use of quantitative models; third, it equally demonstrates some of the pitfalls.

Kilgour, Frederick G. "Recorded Use of Books in the Yale Medical Library," *American Documentation* 12, 4 (October 1961), pp. 266–269.

Kilgour, Frederick, "Use of Medical and Biological Journals in the Yale Medical Library," *Bulletin of the Medical Library Association* 50, 3 (July 1962).

Konopasek, Katherine, and O'Brien, Nancy Patricia. "Undergraduate Periodical Usage: A Model of Measurement," *Serials Librarian* 9, 2 (1984), pp. 65–74.

Krummel, D.W. (ed.). *Trends in the Scholarly Use of Library Resources.* Urbana, IL: University of Illinois Graduate School of Library Science, 1977. While almost completely descriptive in content, this journal issue provides important insight into the nature of scholarly use of academic library materials.

Lancaster, F. Wilfrid. "Evaluating Collections by Their Use," *Collection Management* 4, 1-2 (1982), pp. 15–43.

Lazorick, Gerald J. "Patterns of Book Use Using the Binomial Distribution," *Library Research* 1 (1979), pp. 171–188.

Millson-Martula, Christopher. "Use Studies and Serials Rationalization: A Review," *Serials Librarian* 15, 1–2 (1988), pp. 121–136.

Moore, Carolyn M., and Mielke, Linda. "Taking the Measure: Applying Reference Outputs to Collection Development," *Public Libraries* 25, 3 (1986), pp. 108–111.

Morse, Philip M., and Chen, Ching-chih. "Using Circulation Data to Obtain Unbiased Estimates of Book Use," *Library Quarterly* 45, 2 (1975), pp. 179–194.

Obert, Beverly. "Collection Development Through Student Surveys and Collection Analysis," *Illinois Libraries* 70, 1 (1988), pp. 46–53.

Osbern, Charles B. "Non-use and Loser Studies in Collection Development," *Collection Management* 4, 1–2, pp. 45–53.

Reader Failure at the Shelf. Loughborough, Leicestershire: Centre for Library and Information Management, Department of Library and Information Studies, Loughborough University, 1982.

Rubin, Richard. "Measuring the In-house Use of Materials in Public Libraries," *Public Libraries* 25, 4 (1986), pp. 137–138.

The Senate Library Committee. *Report on The Study of Library Use at Pitt by Professor Allen Kent, et al.* University of Pittsburgh, July 1979.

Thompson, Donald D. *In-house Use and Immediacy of Need: The Riverside Pilot Studies* Berkeley: University of California, November 1978.

Wiemers, Eugene, Jr. *Materials Availability in Small Libraries: A Survey Handbook.* Urbana, IL: University of Illinois Graduate School of Library Science.

References Related to Queuing Theory

Bartlett, Maurice Stevenson. *An Introduction to Stochastic Processes: With Special Reference to Methods and Applications.* Cambridge: Cambridge University Press, 1956.

Bookstein, Abraham. *Congestion at Card and Book Catalogs. A Queuing Theory Approach.* Library Quarterly, 42(3) July 1972, 316–328 (also ERIC Document ED 054-793).

Cox, D.R. *Queues.* Boca Raton, FL: Chapman & Hall, 1999.

Hubbard, Charles L., et al. *Minimum Cost Decision Model for Additional Copies of Library Books Based on Multichannel Queuing Theory.* Tallahassee: Florida State University, 1968.

Khinchin, Aleksandr IAkovlevich. *Mathematical Methods in the Theory of Queuing.* Translated by D.M. Andrews and M.H. Quenouille. New York, Hafner, 1960.

Lee. Alec Miller. *Applied Queuing Theory.* New York: Macmillan, St Martin's Press, 1966.

Morse, Philip McCord. *A Queuing Theory, Bayesian Model for the Circulation of Books in a Library.* Cambridge, MA: Operations Research Center, Massachusetts Institute of Technology, 1977.

Morse, Philip McCord. *Queues, Inventories, and Maintenance. The Analysis of Operational System with Variable Demand and Supply.* New York: Wiley, 1958.

Panico, Joseph A. *Queuing Theory: A Study of Waiting Lines for Business, Economics, and Science.* Eglewood Cliffs, NJ: Prentice-Hall, 1969.

Queuing Theory. London: English Universities, 1967.

Riordan, John. *Stochastic Service Systems.* New York: Wiley, 1962.

Zwillinger, Daniel (ed.). *Standard Mathematical Tables and Formulae,* 30th ed. New York: Chemical Rubber Company, 1996, pp. 587–588.

6

Processing of Library Materials

Introduction

This chapter presents models for representing data about library acquisitions and technical processing (i.e., selection, acquisition, cataloging, and processing) of them in a form that permits generation of estimates for workloads on technical services based on readily available data about the populations of materials to be acquired and library-derived data about historical patterns of technical processing.

6.1

Populations of Materials

This section discusses various different kinds of populations of materials (e.g., books, journals, digital formats, media, etc.) and the means for measuring their characteristics. It then discusses relevant data on numbers of items in each relevant type of material.

The matrix for populations of materials is in two parts, one related to current holdings and the status of cataloging of them and the second related to planned acquisitions and the planned cataloging of them:

Holdings of Materials	Units of Measure	Total Holdings	Catalog Backlog	Planned Catalog	Remaining Backlog
Monographs	Volumes	642,822	6,000	2,000	4,000
Monographic Series	Volumes				
Periodicals	Vols/Titles	138,912			
Microforms	Linear Feet	15,275	100	100	
Special Collections	Linear Feet	515	10	10	
Documents	Linear Feet	3,377	50	50	10
Media (AV, Digital)	Items	55,988	500	300	200

Addition to Materials	Units of Measure	Annual Additions	Planned Status of Cataloging			
			None	Descriptive	Subject	Complete
Monographs	Volumes	19,338		2,000		19,338
Monographic Series	Volumes	6,000				6,000
Periodicals	Vols/Titles	7,498				
Microforms	Linear Feet	1,384		100		200
Special Collections	Linear Feet	19		10		9
Documents	Linear Feet	154	10	40		104
Media (AV, Digital)	Items	4,588		100		4,488

Note that cataloging has been divided into two pieces, descriptive cataloging and subject cataloging. This permits separate planning for each and separate estimation of the workload factors for each. This is of special value in cases where the need is not so much for a user-oriented catalog as for a collection management tool.

6.1.1 Distribution Among Types of Materials

The relative mix of types of materials, especially between monographs and journals, has become an issue of increasing concern. The exponential increases in prices of journals, averaging 15% to 20% per annum for those in the sciences and technology, have led to commitment of increasing portions of acquisitions budgets to journals, with a consequential decrease in acquisitions of monographs. Some institutions have adopted a policy of maintaining the commitment to monographs at a level of 40% of the total budget. To do so, they have had to adopt a program of deacquisition of journals. Later in this chapter, a model for making such decisions will be presented. Here the important point to recognize is the fact that the distribution of acquisitions among types of materials will change over time. The resulting workloads and associated staffing will therefore also change.

Before discussing specific allocations among formats, it is worth discussing the economic aspects of acquisition policies. Current acquisitions typically represent about 33% of total academic library budgets. Given an estimated annual income for academic libraries of $5 billion, that implies purchases of about $1.5 billion. In current acquisition practice, it is divided between monographs and journals in the ratio of about 34%/66% so, given that, $500 million goes to monographs and $1,000 million to periodicals. In passing, it is worth looking at the expenditures for materials by academic libraries in the context of the income to publishers. From prior studies, that income was $15 billion for books. However, scholarly, reference, and professional books (which are the bulk of acquisitions by academic libraries) represent only 20% of the total, or $3 billion.[1] Thus, the income from academic libraries to the publishers of scholarly, reference, and professional books would be about 20% of their total income (i.e., 0.6 billion/3 billion). In a study of some 25 years ago, examining the sales from two publishers of professional books to special and public as well as academic libraries, libraries in general represented 40% of their total sales, so the figure of 20% for academic libraries is reasonably consistent with that result.[2]

In 1996, for the average ARL library these figures translate into 30K monographs acquired, at a cost of $1.74 million, and 11K serials purchased (of a total of 29K current serials acquired, the remainder being through means other than purchase) at a cost of $3.4 million.

There is no reason to expect a significant change in that distribution of expenditures between monographs and journals, but there is likely to be a significant change in the distribution in both the means of access and the format. Specifically, take the monograph budget as continuing much as it now is and assume that it will be spent on the acquisition of print form books. But assume the journals budget will be distributed quite differently. The following (assuming constant dollars) are hypothetical values used to illustrate a possible pattern on which other kinds of estimates can be based:

	Percent	Dollars
Purchase of Print Monographs	34%	$500 million
Purchase of Print Journals	30%	$450 million
Purchase of Digital Journals	30%	$450 million
Document Delivery of Journals	6%	$100 million

For the average ARL library that would imply a purchase of 5K titles in print form (at say $1.5 million) and of 5K titles in digital form (again at $1.5 million) with dependence on document delivery services for the remaining 1K titles (at a cost of $0.4 million). Assuming a charge of $15 per document delivery request filled, that would imply nearly 27K requests. The current level of interlibrary borrowing at the average ARL library is 16K, of which half is for document delivery. So the effect of these hypothetical values would be to more

---

[1] Rubin, Michael Rogers, and Huber, Mary Taylor, *The Knowledge Industry in the United States, 1960–1980.* Princeton: Princeton University Press, 1986, p. 125.

[2] This was a personal study conducted in 1975, the results of which were not published. The methodology determined the extent to which 300 titles (150 from each of two publishers) were held by a group of 72 libraries (41 academic, 18 public, and 13 special), 12 in each of 6 cities. Based on that stratified sample, estimates were made of national sales to libraries and compared with actual total sales.

than triple the use of document delivery. Given the role that Internet access would play, that is not irrational.

One of the most significant effects of digital libraries will be on space requirements, since the digital media occupy dramatically less space than the print media. Of course, they do require equipment for their use, so already there have been substantial increases in the number of carrels with full multimedia capabilities in every academic library, but the space required for the equipment is orders of magnitude less than that for the storage. Taking the hypothetical figures in the table above as an illustration, future growth in space requirements would be 64%, less than 2/3, of what they would be for purely print acquisitions.

The existing print collections of academic libraries will continue to be important. While it is true that the use of library materials is highly skewed over their age, with current materials being much more heavily used than older materials, there still is a substantial amount of need for access to the older materials. In a very real sense, it is precisely this fact that makes the library important to society; by assuring the continued availability of older materials, despite a low level of use, we preserve the past for use in the future.

Of course, from the standpoint of "good business," that may make little economic sense. Why waste resources in preserving what is being little used when the resources could provide better access to the current information which is of greater immediate value? Indeed, for the individual person or company, such an investment is probably not worthwhile. But for society it is, and it is that which makes the library an essential institution. It is an investment by society at large to assure that individuals and companies will have access to information from the past without needing to make uneconomic and duplicative investments themselves. And the academic library or, more to the point perhaps, the research library is our primary means for doing so, in part because use of prior records is central to the academic functions of teaching, research, and public service.

Will print materials continue to be published and acquired? The printed book is still a remarkably effective means for publication and distribution, and the likelihood is that it will continue to be so for the foreseeable future.

Of course, electronic technology advances rapidly. There is no doubt that an "electronic book" is already in the works; indeed, there are announcements each year of the potential if not the reality of its development. Such an electronic book would be the size and weight of a printed book, even of a paperback, and could be easily held in the hand. It would contain high-density digital storage, with text and images on call from potentially hundreds of books, instantly available for reading and replaceable with other collections. It would have a display with all the resolution and appearance of the printed page. It would have functionalities that will permit the user to read the text and view the images exactly as though it were a printed book, but it would have additional functionalities (such as searching, annotating, and processing) that are impossible with just the printed page. It is likely that the cost for such a unit will be such that prices can be set to generate a reasonable market. Already we see hand-held DVD players selling at well less that $1,000.[3]

Why, then, the unequivocal view that print publication will continue? The economics of publishing, of the associated packaging decisions, of the mechanisms for distribution and sale, of the nature of the market, and of the orientation of the consumers all support that view, at least with respect to monographs (i.e., books) and popular journals. Assuming, then, that print publication will continue, libraries will also need to continue to acquire materials in that form. But the types of materials acquired in print form will increasingly be focused on monographs and popular journals.

It is interesting to note that few libraries have as yet made substantial investments in digitally formatted materials. There are, it is true, collections of CD-ROM reference databases, usually on a subscription basis, but very few collections of other kinds of materials, despite the increasing numbers of CD-ROM publications. It is especially surprising that few, if any, libraries acquire databases, software, or media in digital formats, despite the ease of use they provide.

But the current situation will change dramatically during the coming five years. First, the U.S. Census for 2000 is likely to be distributed primarily in electronic format, and that will add great impetus to distribution of other databases in similar form.[4] Second, there are rapidly increasing numbers of packages based on computer-mediated instruction, and academic libraries will of necessity need to acquire them. Third, software distribution must be in digital form, and libraries should at least consider acquisition of packages for use by students and faculty.

Of course, the significant acquisition in digital form is expected to be of scholarly journals. Here, there are substantial advantages to the digital formats, optical and online, to both the publishers and the users. For the publisher, the costs of printing and mailing are dramatically reduced. For the user, the journal issue is replaced by access to the journal article of specific interest or to tailored combinations of articles that match the needs of the individual user; these fit the real patterns of use far better than the current means for packaging and distribution.

If we take the hypothetical figures given above as a basis for estimate, there would be purchases by academic libraries of as much as $405 million of journals in digital format.

---

[3] Holmes, Stanley, "Making E-books Easier on the Eyes," *Los Angeles Times,* March 20, 2000. Reports on two products, Rocket eBooks by Nuvo Media and SoftBooks by SoftBook Press, each of which is claimed to have sold 20,000 copies. A prediction is reported that within five years sales will grow to 6.5 million e-book devices.

[4] "U.S. Counting on Web to Be Census Source; Bureau Plans to Post Most of its 2000 Enumeration Data on the Internet. Switch from Paper to Hypertext Raises Information Issues," *Los Angeles Times,* Sunday, November 15, 1998, Home Edition, Section A.

While preservation of the record of the past may be the primary imperative for the library, providing access to that record and assistance in its use is of virtually equal importance. These are the services provided by the library. The traditional services include circulation, in-house use, photocopying, and similar uses of the materials. They include reference, interlibrary borrowing and lending, access to means for document delivery, consulting and information analysis, assessment of quality and value and selection of the most appropriate information resources, and instruction and guidance in the use of them.

The effect of digital libraries and especially of online access to them will surely be a shifting of the workloads on these services from those involved in use of materials to those involved in substantive aspects. Already academic libraries have expanded their roles in providing substantive information services, in particular in bibliographic instruction. As part of that, though, the need for assessment of quality, of reliability, of accuracy is becoming even more important. The Internet and World Wide Web are overwhelming in the sheer magnitude of information available through them, and the user must carefully assess those issues of quality. Even in the context of journalism, despite its historic commitment to assurance of accuracy, there have recently been too many instances in which information was taken from the Internet as though it were valid that yet turned out to be false or even fradulent. Therefore, perhaps the most significant service that the library can provide is that in selection and quality control, in assessment of accuracy, reliability, and value.

Another service that is becoming increasingly important as a result of digital libraries is more technical perhaps but still vital. It is the creation of what is being called "meta-data" (i.e., "data describing data"). Historically, it is represented by cataloging, by indexing and abstracting, by bibliography, and by reference databases. Today, we see need for this service for digital libraries, again as exemplified in the overwhelming magnitude of what is available on the Internet.

One of the great potentials for a dramatic increase in the role of academic libraries is the production of digital libraries. Already there are a number of cooperative efforts to create state and regional "digital libraries." Just to consider one in 1997, the University of California announced the founding of the "California Digital Library ... a service that will make it possible to bring to computer screens statewide the holdings of UC libraries and others throughout the world." In the announcement, it was stated that, "UC libraries have already taken major steps towards digitizing parts of their collections, some of which are already available over the World Wide Web. For example, UC Berkeley had digitized much of the Bancroft Library's historical photos of California, UC Santa Barbara has put its vast map collection on the Web and the California Museum of Photography at UC Riverside also displays its rich store of photographs on-line."

Clearly, the existing print collections of academic libraries—books and especially rare books, journals, manuscripts, maps, photographs, and the rich array of other special collections—are a primary source for materials needed to create the vision of broad-scale digital libraries of the kind envisioned. Whether they are distributed online, as the description of the California digital library clearly implies, or in optical formats is not a significant issue. The important point is that academic libraries have a vital role to play in the future of digital libraries, beyond merely acquiring them and providing access to them. They will be the sources for much of what goes into them.

6.1.2 Growth in Populations of Materials

A crucial need in planning for the future is to recognize the potential that there will be growth in the number of materials acquired and held. Underlying such growth is the fact that publication in the world at large and in the sciences in particular has been growing exponentially for decades.

It is therefore necessary to establish a basis for estimating the expected future growth in acquisitions and collections held by the library. One easy means for doing so is to examine historic data to determine whether there has been a pattern of growth that can then serve as the basis for projecting continuation into the future. Another is to obtain external data, such as data on rates of publication, from which more fundamental factors determining future growth can be determined.

There are several models that have been used as the basis for projecting future growth.

Exponential Growth Models

This issue was recognized by librarians, at a very early time, as one susceptible to quantitative treatment. Fremont Rider applied a mathematical model to this issue in strategic planning when he fitted an exponential curve to the past data on research library collections.[5]

The model can be described very simply: "Libraries grow by a more or less fixed percentage each year, which results in a doubling in their size every 10 to 20 years (the period being different from one kind of library to another)." Such a growth model is a common one, particularly applicable to biological phenomena during their stages of early development. It is in fact the basis of projections of human population growth and predictions that population would outpace the capabilities to produce sufficient food to maintain it.[6]

---

[5] Rider, Fremont, *The Scholar and the Future of the Research Library.* New York: Hadham, 1944.

[6] Malthus, Thomas, *An Essay on the Principle of Population, as it Affects the Future Improvement of Society.* London: 1798.

Since Rider first suggested this exponential growth model some 50 years ago, the growth rates of libraries have equaled and even exceeded its predictions. In 1951, Louis Ridenour restated the same model in a now-classic volume, *Bibliography in an Age of Science*.[7] Later, extensive calculations were made, fitting exponential growth curves to the past histories of libraries in educational institutions of many sizes. The resulting curves, published in the report by Oliver Dunn and others, provide a statistical picture of such growth, at least up to 1970.[8]

Some efforts have been made to provide justifications for this apparent exponential growth on grounds other than simply fitting curves to historical data. In particular, the growth of libraries has been attributed to the more basic growth in publication rate, especially in the sciences and technology, in large part as the result of the increasing numbers of scientists and engineers publishing reports.[9]

These exponential growth models will be considered in detail in Chapter 8, in the context of institutional policies concerning acquisitions.

Linear Growth Models

Despite the evidence of exponential growth that was exhibited in those historic studies, though, something quite remarkable happened in academic libraries starting at about 1970. It appeared in the study by Oliver Dunn and was briefly commented on in that study; it appeared again in the study by Anthony M. Cummings and others, but little if any direct comment was made about it.[10] Suddenly, virtually overnight, the growth changed from exponential to linear.

Now, to see such a change from exponential growth to mere linear growth is really quite remarkable. When it happens it represents a very fundamental shift in the underlying forces. In the case of growth of academic libraries, the cause of that shift is evident. As the Cummings report says, "Generally speaking, the 1970s and most of the 1980s were years of retrenchment for both graduate programs and libraries."[11] It goes on to say, "other factors—including the increasingly severe fiscal problems of universities and the

---

[7] Ridenour, Louis, Shaw, Ralph R., and Hill, A.G., *Bibliography in an Age of Science*. Illinois: 1951.

[8] Dunn, Oliver, Seibert, W.F., and Scheuneman, Janice A. *The Past and Likely Future of 58 Research Libraries, 1951–1980s: A Statistical Study of Growth and Change*. Lafayette, IN: University Libraries and Audio Visual Center, Purdue University, 1968.

[9] Machlup, Fritz, *The Production and Distribution of Knowledge in the United States*. Princeton: University Press, 1962, pp. 155–156. Machlup reports that expenditures for research and development increased at an annual growth rate of nearly 20% per annum.

[10] Cummings, Anthony M., Witte, Marcia L., Bowen, William G., Lazarus, Laura O., and Ekman, Richard H., *University Libraries and Scholarly Communication*. Washington, DC: Association of Research Libraries, November 1992, pp. 17–21.

[11] op cit, p. 16.

rapidly rising prices of serials—were important in determining the rates at which collections were augmented."[12]

The evidence is that linear growth has continued to be the pattern for the major academic libraries during the three decades since 1970. The likelihood is that it will so continue into the future, especially given the potential for a shift from print publication to electronic publication of journals.

It is important to recognize that linear growth still implies growth, of course, but at a fixed rate rather than an increasing rate. Instead of doubling every ten to twenty years, though, as was the case with exponential growth, the doubling will occur at longer and longer intervals.

Steady-State Growth Models

However, there is the potential that library collections may even arrive at a steady state, with discards equalling acquisitions. Indeed, sone of the effects of increasing costs of journals has been the practice of deacquisition, with therefore declining rates of addition. At the same time, many institutions have replaced their bound volumes of journals by microform copies.

In fact, for certain types of collections, such a steady-state is almost to be expected. For example, reference collections by their nature could well be steady-state, with new editions simply replacing older ones. Of course, typically, the older editions of reference work are then transferred to the main collections, but there is no inherent reason for that to continue to be the case. As another example, special libraries in business are very likely to be steady-state collections, again with new editions simply replacing older ones.

Logistic Curve Growth

Underlying the behavior exhibited in the apparent historic transition of library acquisition rates from exponential growth to linear growth to steady state is a model called the "logistic curve." It represents a schedule of growth that is characterized by initial exponential increase followed by a leveling off—an s-shaped curve of growth. It appears to characterize population growth in the context of eventual limits due to the constraint of fixed resources. The equation for the logistic curve is

$$Y = K/(1 + a \star e^{(- b \star N)})$$

where K is the maximum value, N is the number of years, and a and b are parameters to be determined based on estimated or expected rates of growth.

To illustrate, consider a project to digitize a collection of materials. To do so may require a process of negotiation with the sources of that collection to

---

[12] op cit, p. 17.

obtain permission to do so. For some materials, agreement may already be at hand, and for others, the pace at which it can be obtained typically is represented by initial exponential growth, as the sources that are inherently willing to agree do so. Eventually, though, the process becomes increasingly difficult, with longer delays, and even in the long run for some portion agreement may never be obtained. The logistic curve is a model for representing this phenomenon. In year N (with a starting year being year 0), the percentage of a collection that can be available for digitization as a result of negotiation could be described by the following logistic curve:

$$Y = 0.9/(1 + 8 \star e^{(-0.20 \star N)})$$

The following are the percentages of the total collection of materials for which agreement has been obtained for each decade as implied by that logistic curve:

N	Percentage
0	0.10
10	0.43
20	0.78
30	0.88
40	0.90

Note that, in the equation for Y, the value for $N = 0$ is $1/(1 + a)$, which in the example is 0.10. The value for b represents the initial rate of exponential increase. Graphically, this logistic curve looks as follows and, in doing so, represents the typical s-shaped curve that characterizes the logistic curve:

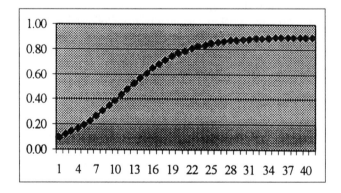

Note that the curve grows exponentially at the beginning (in this case, until about the year 15), grows linearly through the midpoint, and then begins to level off, becoming asymptotic to the value 0.90 as time goes on. The cause of the leveling and the asymptotic behavior is the constraint of the total population to be considered. In other cases, the constraint could be fixed resources. The latter may well be the cause of transition of library acquisition rates from exponential, to linear, to a leveling off, and even to a steady state during the past three decades.

Program-Related Growth Models

A somewhat different and even more basic approach was taken by Verner Clapp and his associate Robert Jordan in their study of the library collections of the institutions of higher education in the State of Ohio.[13] Their premise was that library growth is a result not of a simple exponential growth formula, even as a result of publication patterns. Rather, it was the result of the needs of the educational programs of the institutions themselves. This model will be explored in detail in Chapter 7 as part of the discussion of institutional objectives.

In summary, though, they adopted a "linear model"—a model which derives growth from a number of separate parameters (each characterizing some feature of the institution's academic programs) which are multiplied by corresponding coefficients for a number of volumes and then summed. Typical characterizing parameters might include number of students, number of faculty, number of doctoral programs, and so on. Library growth is then predicated upon the more fundamental growth pattern of increased numbers of students, faculty, doctoral programs, and so on. On the basis of this approach, the historical pattern of library growth could be interpreted as a result of the exponential growth in student population together with a continual fragmentation of areas of research.

Several institutions applying the Clapp-Jordan formula to their own specific situation then modified the coefficients to reflect their own judgment of the importance of various parameters. For example, the State University of New York developed a variation of the Clapp-Jordan formula which increased the size of the basic college collection and the allocation for master's-level study.[14]

A most important variant of the Clapp-Jordan model was developed by Melvin Voigt. It shifted the focus from the size of the collection to the level of acquisitions and, by doing so, directly related growth to the underlying parameters of academic program. The model, slightly modified and called the Voigt-Susskind model, became the basis for allocation of acquisition budgets within the University of California.[15]

---

[13] Clapp, Verner W., and Jordan, Robert T., "Quantitative Criteria for Adequacy of Academic Library Collections," *College and Research Libraries* 26, (September 1965), pp. 371–380.

[14] New York State.

[15] Voigt, Melvin, "Acquisition Rates in University Libraries," *College & Research Libraries* (July 1975), pp. 263–271.

Now, the point is not that one model or another really describes the growth pattern for libraries. In fact, the likelihood is that libraries actually grow for a number of reasons having little to do with quantitative models—a university chancellor is especially aware of the value of a research library, a donor provides funds for special acquisitions, an area of research becomes of worldwide renown and attracts researchers and resources, the librarian is especially astute in his or her collecting policies, or there are existing interinstitutional cooperative arrangements.

But it is also likely that on the average these effects balance out and that the librarian can use a rational model to lay out a long-range growth program. At least, a model lays bare those factors that must be considered in doing so—whether new program areas are involved, or increased publication rates, or other as-yet-unidentified aspects. Furthermore, a quantitative model may provide the justification necessary to support the librarian's long-range projections.

6.2
Distributions of Technical Processing

This section discusses the various kinds of technical processing (as listed above). It then discusses the differences in the relative distribution of such technical processing for various types of materials.

6.2.1 Workloads

The following matrix shows the distribution of workloads for various kinds of technical processing:

Acquisition of Units of Materials	Measure	Materials Ordering Originated	Standing	Gifts and Exchanges	Acquire	Serials	Receive Handle
Monographs	Volumes	50%	50%		100%		100%
Monographic Series	Volumes					100%	100%
Periodicals	Vols/Titles					100%	100%
Microforms	Linear Feet	10%			10%	90%	100%
Special Collections	Linear Feet	100%			100%		100%
Documents	Linear Feet					100%	100%
Media (AV, Digital)	Items	50%	50%		100%		100%

Cataloging of Materials	Descriptive Catalog		Subject Catalog		Authority Files	Retrocon	Catalog Handle
	Original	Copy	Original	Copy			
Monographs	7%	93%	7%	93%	5%		
Monographic Series		100%		100%	5%		
Periodicals					5%		
Microforms		100%		100%	5%		
Special Collections	100%		100%		5%		
Documents		100%		100%	5%		
Media (AV, Digital)	15%	85%	15%	85%	5%		

Conservation of Additions	Binding Prepare	Conserve		Reproduce Content	Conserve Handle	Binding
		Repair	Full			
Monographs						
Monographic Series						
Periodicals	100%					
Microforms						
Special Collections		5%				
Documents						
Media (AV, Digital)						

Conservation of Holdings	Binding Prepare	Conserve		Reproduce Content	Conserve Handle	Binding
		Repair	Full			
Monographs		0.01%				
Monographic Series						
Periodicals						
Microforms						
Special Collections						
Documents						
Media (AV, Digital)						

6.2.2 Effects of Future Developments

What is the likely future for library staffing, both for internal, technical services—the processing of materials acquired by academic libraries—and for services to the readers? Even in the current context, significant changes have occurred as a result of automation. Thirty years ago, the staff in technical services and reader services were virtually equal in numbers and, in technical services, those in acquisition and in cataloging were also virtually equal. To put it most simply, the division of operating staff was about 50% in reader services, 25% in selection and acquisition, and 25% in cataloging. Today, the division is about 60% in reader services, 25% in selection, and 15% in cataloging. The underlying cause, of course, is the growth of the bibliographic utilities and the resulting replacement of original cataloging by copy cataloging. In some libraries, the shift of staff was effected by retraining and reorientation, in others, by simply allowing retirement to do so.

A second significant change even today has been in the staff for central administration, again as a result of automation. It is in the addition of "systems staff," required to manage the computer-related equipment and software.

Those trends will continue as a result of digital libraries. There will be a continuing shift of staff from technical services into reader services and increasing requirements of systems staff in central administration. The following is a hypothetical distribution, say in a decade, compared with that of today and of 30 years ago:

	30 Years Ago	Current	10 Years From Now
Central Administration	5%	7%	9%
Reader Services	47%	56%	65%
Selection	24%	23%	18%
Cataloging	24%	14%	8%

6.3
Workload Factors for Technical Processing

The following are the workload factors relevant to technical processing of materials.

	Workload Factors		
Acquisition Processes	Intellectual	Procedural	Physical
Develop Collections	100	2	
Approval Plan, Deposit	10	2	
Gifts and Exchange		2	
Acquire (Order, Invoice)		40	
Process Serials		10	10
Acquisition Handling			2

	Workload Factors		
Cataloging Processes	Intellectual	Procedural	Physical
Descriptive: Original	80		
Descriptive: Copy		20	
Subject: Original	80		
Subject: Copy		20	
Authority Files		25	
Retro Conversion		40	
Catalog Handling		2	3

	Workload Factors		
Conservation Processes	Intellectual	Procedural	Physical
Binding Preparation	10	6	
Minor Repairs		15	
Full Conservation	250	250	
Reproduce (Micro, Photo, Digital)			
Conservation Handling		2	2
Binding			30

6.4
Materials Storage and Access

This section discusses the various means for storage of materials (open stack, closed stack, compact shelving, remote storage facilities, mechanized storage facilities, electronic, etc.). It then discusses the differences in the effect of each means for storage upon the use of materials. It concludes with discussion of the means for estimating the requirements for storage and access.

6.4.1 Storage Facilities

The estimation of storage facilities is quite straightforward. For each type of materials held by a library, there are standard means for storage, and the space requirements per unit of holdings can be easily determined. There are some details in the calculations that need to be recognized, of course. The most important of them is the degree of efficiency in use of storage. For example, in open-stack book shelving, books that are sequenced by classification code (which is the usual sequence in U.S. libraries) usually occupy less than 80% of each shelf; this is to provide space for insertion of new items into the collection without needing to move existing items. In closed-stack shelving, books that are sequenced by accession number (which is quite typical in libraries of Central Europe) can occupy as much as 100% of each shelf. Microfiche frequently are stored in sequences that make possible close to 100% efficiency. Manuscripts, archives, and similar special collections typically are stored in boxes, with each box devoted to a particular entity of the collection. The result is that boxes will to varying degrees be only partially full. Efficiency of about 50% may well be the resulting average.

Another matter of detail is the space required for access to the collection, such as the space between shelving stacks. In the United States, there are specifications resulting from the Americans with Disabilities Act (ADA) that require accessibility for persons in wheelchairs, and those add greatly to the space required. Another is the height of shelving, for which again the ADA has created specifications.

Despite those matters of detail, there are well-established figures for the net square feet required per unit of storage for the various kinds of materials. Those figures need merely be multiplied by the number of holdings of each type of material to obtain the estimate for net square feet. To that, of course, must be added estimates for the overhead space, such as corridors for access, ancillary facilities, and so on.

6.4.2 Alternative Places for Storage

There are a number of alternatives for storage that need to be considered:

1. Central libraries versus branch libraries
2. Open-stack shelving versus compact shelving
3. On-campus versus depository

Central Libraries vs. Branch Libraries

The choice between storing materials in central libraries versus branch libraries depends upon a complex combination of issues of cost and effectiveness. Usually, storage in a central library is cheaper and more efficient than storage at a branch, since a branch typically will be located in classroom and office building space, designed to accommodate people rather than books. So from the standpoint of costs, the central library will be cheaper, perhaps by half.

The effectiveness, as measured by user satisfaction, is much more difficult to assess. When the uses of materials are highly focused on the patrons of a branch, they are best satisfied if the materials are located at the branch. But as soon as there is diffusion of use to other groups, the total set of users will be more satisfied by location in the central library.

Open-Stack Shelving vs. Compact Shelving

There are at least three ways in which shelving can be made more compact. Most easily accomplished is to fill the shelves. Typically, open-stack shelves in a growing classified collection will be at most 80% filled because to exceed that percentage would then entail moving massive numbers of volumes to accommodate additions. If there are good reasons for expecting that there will be no growth in portions of the collection, they can be stored at 100% of shelf capacity.

A second means is to increase the number of shelves and decrease the access space between stacks. This can increase the density (per square foot, anyway) by as much as 20%. However, the ADA (Americans with Disabilities Act) regulations virtually prohibit this approach, except in highly specialized situations, since it limits access by wheelchairs and by those who are otherwise handicapped.

The third means is by use of movable stacks. This can nearly double the density of storage since the stacks share a single access row; by moving the stacks horizontally, the block of stacks can be separated at the deisred stack, opening up the access row for it. Of course, there are penalties. The floor loading capacity must be double, which increases costs of construction. And for heavily used materials there is likely to be conflict among persons wanting access within the same block of stacks at the same time.

On-Campus vs. Depository

Many universities, both individually and especially cooperatively, have adopted the use of depository facilities that are off-campus. The construction costs of such facilities can be half that of on-campus and they can be located in nonprime space.

Of course, again there are penalties. The library will incur costs in paging of the materials, and the patron will experience delays of as much as one or two days in getting access to wanted materials. Presumably, by using a depository facility for "rarely used" materials, those penalties will be reduced. The hope is that the materials will be so little used that there is really no penalty. Unfortunately, that hope is vain. The following data are specific to the Southern Regional Depository Facility (SRLF), used by the University of California, and to the use of materials from the facility by UCLA.[16] Since the SRLF is located on the UCLA campus, it is relatively more accessible than for any other of the institutions participating in it.

---

[16] Again, these results are based on the data so generously provided by the UCLA library.

Books allocated to SRLF in principle represent those of low "frequency of use," though probably that is measured not by frequency of use but by frequency of circulation. From current UCLA Library statistics, of the total holdings (1998/99) of 7.4M volumes, 2.0M (i.e., 27%) have been placed at SRLF. In 1999, there were 45,360 SRLF transactions. Assuming that each resulted in a circulation (which presumably is then included among the 662,471 charges), we can estimate the comparative use of SRLF materials with those from the general collection:

	Size	Charges	Ratio
General Collection	5,434,185	617,111	0.11
SRLF	1,967,595	45,360	0.02
Total	7,401,780	662,471	0.09

Clearly, this demonstrates the relatively lower level of use of SRLF materials (being about 20% of that for the general collection), but the use still is substantial and confirms that there is continuing interest even in materials that are regarded as "lesser used." Incidentally, the relative level of use for SRLF materials (20% of that for the general collection) in 1987/98 was the same at that for 1998/99, so there is reason to hypothesize that this is generally the case.

The total general collection can be divided into roughly equal portions, each of which represents additions to the UCLA catalog during one in a succession of time periods (in inverse order), as shown in the following table (all figures have been rounded to simplify the presentation):

	Size	Transactions	Ratio
Time Period 1	400,000	166,000	0.41
Time Period 2	400,000	99,000	0.25
Time Period 3	400,000	66,000	0.16
Time Period 4	400,000	66,000	0.16
Time Period 5	400,000	66,000	0.16
Time Period 6	400,000	66,000	0.16
Time Period 7	3,100,000	132,000	0.04
SRLF	2,000,000	45,000	0.02
Total	7,500,000	662,000	0.09

In this array, Time Period 7 is anomalous since it represents the initial conversion of catalog records, and thus includes materials covering the entire prior history of acquisitions and cataloging. It is interesting to note that the ratio of use to collection size for that group is quite similar to that for the SRLF materials.

Note that the uses for materials during the most recent time period is 25% of the total, for the next earlier time period, 15% and for each of the successive earlier periods (except number 7), 10%.

Let's consider the data for three primary categories of UCLA users (faculty, graduate, and undergraduate):

Category	Num.	SRLF	Total Charges	Non-SRLF	SRLF/ Num.	Non-SRLF/ Num.	SRLF/ Non-SRLF
Faculty	1,816	6,161	64,569	58,408	3.39	32.16	.26
Graduate	11,071	13,644	173,205	159,561	1.23	14.41	.09
Undergrad	22,567	4,692	221,217	216,525	0.21	9.59	.02

There are two points to make. First, note the steady decline in relative use of all materials (per person) as one goes from faculty to graduate to undergraduate. Second, that decline is substantially greater for SRLF materials than for non-SRLF materials, as shown in the final column. The implications are clear: The use of "little-used materials" is significantly greater as the user has research interests. This is at least some evidence in support of the view that research use depends on lesser-used materials which in many cases are probably older materials.

6.4.3 Frequency of Use Models

The choice among alternative storage locations, therefore, is an important tactical management decision.

Zipf's Law and Bradford's Law

One of the most important models that is applicable to that decision is called Zipf's law or Bradford's law. It was first applied, by Zipf, to the description of the frequency of use of words.[17] In its simplest form, the model says that the number of books that will be used n times is (k/n) of the number that will be used just once (where k is a constant parameter, usually very close to 2). Based on this model, books which are infrequently used can be allocated to remote or relatively inaccessible storage, without degrading the overall efficiency of operation and perhaps even improving it by making the frequently used material even more accessible.

Mixture of Poisson Distributions

An alternative model is a "mixture of Poisson distributions"—what might be called a "Bouillabaisse distribution." It is characterized by a set of parameters

[17] Zipf, G.K. *Human Behavior and the Principle of Least Effort.* Cambridge, MA: Addison-Wesley, 1949.

$<n(i), m(i)>$, where the value $n(i)$ is the number of volumes in component (i), and $m(i)$ is the "a priori expected frequency" with which a volume in component(i) will circulate during a given time period. This mixture leads to a frequency distribution based on the following formulation:

$$F(k) = \sum_{i=0}^{P} n(i)e^{(-m(i))}(m(i)^k)/k!$$

where $P + 1$ (i.e., 0 through P) is the number of components, and $F(k)$ is the number of volumes that the model predicts will circulate exactly k times in the given time period.

This model is presented as an alternative to those usually considered in attempting to represent frequency distributions of the kind involved here. As a model, it has a rationale dramatically different from those laws, even though superficially it may appear to have similar characteristics. The crucial point is that the other laws are predicated on the assumption of a concept of "contagion"—on the view that the use of an item increases the likelihood of future use, in an otherwise homogeneous population. In contrast, the mixture of Poisson distributions is predicated on the assumption that usage is determined by a priori probabilities so that actual use does not affect future use. As a result, the population is regarded as heterogeneous, so that items differ in their *a priori* expected frequency of use.

Of the two kinds of assumptions about the nature of the use of library materials, the assumption of a heterogeneous population of books seems far more realistic than the assumption that the use of a book increases the likelihood of future use. Admittedly, there are some kinds of use that might have that effect (a faculty member charging out the book with intent to determine whether it should be an assigned reading, for example), but such effects appear to be minor in comparison with the very evident differences in the nature of the types of books. Some books are "popular reading," likely to circulate frequently during their period of popularity; some books are classics, with a smaller but continuing level of use; some books are basic references, used whenever the subject area they relate to is active; some books are fundamentally research materials—of value to specific researchers or when their research importance is recognized, but of low use until then. For a research library to have only the first type, the popular material, might result in spectacular utilization levels and circulation averages, but such a policy would be a failure of responsibility to serve the basic, long-term research needs of the institution. That means that a diversity of *a priori* utilization levels is to be expected, even desired.

Unfortunately, the nature of long-tailed "J-shaped" curves is that many items in the long tail have effectively equal likelihood of being used. As a result, experience bears out the proverbial Murphy's Law that "If it can go wrong, it will." Whatever material may be put in remote storage all too frequently turns out to be exactly that which is next needed. Furthermore, the need for "browsability" varies widely from one subject to another. Mere frequency of use can completely fail to account for such differences. Finally, the issue of what constitutes efficiency in operation must be specified. Usually, the system analyst would use a cost/effectiveness measure, comparing the cost of storage with the average response time (that is, time to locate and deliver needed material. If the access time to remote storage is significantly long, it may be difficult to justify its use.

6.4.4 Date-Related Models

Total-frequency-of-use data has been at best difficult to accumulate. Furthermore, it is not at all clear that past frequency is a valid measure of future frequency. Therefore, in what is certainly a classic illustration of a quantitative model for library operational planning, Fussler and Simon studied patterns in the use of books in large research libraries.[18] Their aim was to evaluate several factors as both independent and joint determiners of future activity. These included "years since publication," "years since accession," and "years since last use" as well as "frequency of use." The data they used exhibited, with varying reliability, approximately the behavior one would have suspected.

Since Fussler's study, others have also related usage to publication date. Kilgour at Yale (on "Recorded Use of Books in the Yale Medical Library") showed curves which are also J-shaped for publications in increasing order of age.[19] At Purdue, Ferdinand Leimkuhler and a sequence of colleagues and students evaluated several quantitative models for allocating books to compact storage.[20] A discussion of the costs and benefits of various models of book storage was written by Ralph Ellsworth.[21]

6.4.5 Allocation Decisions Model

With that as background, this section presents a model for distribution of use of library materials and, based on it, derives a means for decision-making

[18] Fussler, Herman H., and Simon, J.L., *Patterns in the Use of Books in Large Research Libraries.* Chicago: University of Chicago Press, 1969.

[19] Kilgour, Frederick G. "Recorded use of books in the Yale Medical Library," American Documentation, 12(4) October 1961, pp. 266–269.

[20] Leimkuhler, Ferdinand F., *Storage Policies for Information Systems.* Lafayette, IN: School of Industrial Engineering, Purdue University, 1969.

Leimkuhler, Ferdinand F., and Cox, J.G., "Compact Book Storage in Libraries," *Operations Research* (May–June 1964).

[21] Ellsworth, Ralph E., *The Economics of Book Storage in College and University Libraries.* Metuchen, NJ: Scarecrow Press, 1969.

concerning allocation of them to various levels of access. The model is based on one already published, but significantly adds to it by dealing directly with the effects of alternatives for storage upon the levels of use.[22]

Relevant parameters are identified and hypothetical values are presented for them. The parameters included in the model are: Number of Volumes in the Collection Being Considered; Costs of the Collection; Kinds of Use; Amounts of Use; Distribution of Use; Effect of Alternatives on Use; Patron Needs and Costs in Access & Use, and Library Costs in Access & Use.

The model for distribution of use is based on an exponential J-shaped curve for frequency. The model for decision-making optimizes cost/effectiveness as measured by the "cost per use." Resulting allocation criteria are expressed as an equation involving the differences of costs for access and of those for storage. Application of the model is illustrated by evaluation of allocation alternatives including Open-Stack Shelving and Compact Shelving.

Parameters Encompassed by the Model for Decision-Making

The following subsections discuss each of a number of parameters that enter into the model. In the following summary list, those parameters represented by specific measures are identified by a code that will be used in equations:

V—Number of Volumes Being Considered
K—Scope of collection
N—Amount of Use
C—Costs of the Collection
F—Costs of Acquisition, Processing, and Storage
A—Operating Costs in Access & Use
P—Effects of Alternatives upon Use

Number of Volumes Being Considered.   Decisions on allocation of a collection to alternatives for storage obviously will depend upon the size of that collection, V. A related parameter is the scope, K, of the collection, intended to measure the range of academic disciplines, different breadths of coverage of them, and different time periods encompassed.

Clearly, any library will, through decisions made either internal to the library or by the institution, arrive at a balance of relative importance in the scope of coverage needed to meet objectives of research, instruction, and others. Of course, whatever the objectives may be, they must accommodate to the budgets that can be allocated to the library by the institution and by the library to the competing operational needs. The model assumes that the allocations are

---

[22] Hayes, Robert M., "Measurement of Use and Resulting Access Allocation Decisions," *Library & Information Science Research* 14, 4 (Oct.–Dec. 1992), pp. 361–378.

commensurate with the objectives and that scope of collection can be directly calculated from V, the holdings. The formula for doing so, as will be discussed, is $V/8$.

Kinds of Use.   In assessing the effectiveness of each alternative for storage, it is important to recognize differences among various kinds of use, two of which will be identified, though within each there are obviously more specific kinds with important differences. This parameter would normally be measured by a varying mix in the amount of usage among the two kinds, but hypothetically that mix will be taken as fixed in the ratio of one circulation to two in-house uses.

The first use is circulation use. The distinguishing characteristic is that this use requires that the book be taken from the library. The standard example, of course, is circulation in order to read the book over an extended period of time; another example might be extended reference use in which the book essentially becomes a part of a personal library.

The second use is in-house use. The distinguishing characteristic is that meeting the needs does not require that the book be taken from the library even though one might do so for practical purposes. Examples of such use include browsing with the intent of using the library's collection itself as a means of access and to identify material of interest; rejecting a book as not relevant; confirming a reference; acquiring specific data; photocopying specific pages; following a chain of references. The latter example illustrates a most significant aspect of in-house use; if a chain of references is to be pursued rapidly and effectively, it absolutely requires a large collection.

Amount of Use.   For any process of decision, there must be reasonably valid estimates of the level of use, both overall and in each category of use—circulation and in-house use. At the University of Pittsburgh, the circulation use of 36,892 volumes, representing acquisition in one year (1969), over a 7-year period was 144,000; in-house use was estimated to be 1.75 times circulation. In that same study circulation for the total Hillman Library collection of about 285,000 volumes during that 7-year period was 1,500,000; using the same ratio for in-house usage, the resulting yearly average would have been about one use per volume (that is, 2.75*1,500,000/7 divided by 553,000). That ratio of about 2/1 for in-house house use to circulation use appears to be typical.

Distribution of Use.   It is well established that books differ widely in the extent to which they will be used, both overall and by specific uses or for specific kinds of use. The model that will be used here for describing that distribution is Bradford's law: Let N be the total annual use over the entire set of books considered in the allocation decision; sequence the set of books in rank order of their expected level of use within the given library; divide the sequence of volumes into groups of K volumes each (K being the scope of the collection, as defined above). Then, the model says: The total annual use for volumes beyond the group with rank order X will be given by $N/2.^{(X)}$

Note that, in this model, the rank order X in the sequence of groups is expressed in "K volumes," K measuring the scope of the collection and reflecting the breadth of demand by the users of a given library. Presumably, the more diverse the needs and thus the wider the range of materials of interest, the larger K would be. It will be assumed that K is a linear function of V, the number of volumes being considered.

Costs of the Collection (i.e., Selection, Acquisition, and Processing).

Certainly the largest single capital investment for a major library is in its collections. That investment, though, is more than simply the cost in purchase of books and journals; it includes the costs of staff in selecting, acquiring, and cataloging them.

To illustrate costs, some hypothetical figures will be presented, most of them based on experience and previously published data. They include all elements of cost, and in particular library overhead, fully accounted for, as part of all costs presented.

Costs of acquisition are incurred by the library whenever it acquires the book instead of depending upon network availability. The average cost to acquire a volume obviously includes the purchase price (or for journals the present value of the continuing annual subscription, per volume), but it also includes the costs in selection, ordering, invoicing, and receipt. For illustration, the cost for purchase will be taken at $30 per volume, the costs of selection and ordering at $10 per volume.

The book, once received, must be cataloged and physically processed for shelving, and the costs will be taken at about $15 per title or $10 per volume.

Costs of Storage.

The cost of storage will be considered as a combination of the construction costs and acquisition of equipment (or shelving) and the "present value" of the future expenses in maintenance for the time period of storage. The present value calculation involves multiplying yearly figures by a factor for present value, as follows (with i being the interest rate and Y the number of years):

$$PV = [1 - 1/(1 + i)^Y]/i$$

For illustration, the interest rate, i, will be taken at 5% and the time period, Y, as 20 years. The value of PV is then 12.46.

Operating Costs in Access & Use. For use of materials already in the library, costs are incurred by the patron if we assume an open-access stack system or compact shelving organized seamlessly with open-stack shelves, so discussion of them will be deferred.

For access to closed-access compact storage, especially in depository facilities, the costs may involve staff time and some kind of accounting system (which is likely to be a counterpart of circulation control but additional to that for the patron's circulation).

Of course, the major costs in use are those of the patron but still there are some costs incurred by the library. For circulation use, the library must maintain records and must reshelve; for in-house use, the library will incur costs in reshelving.

Effects of Alternatives upon Use. The effect of alternative storage upon the kinds of use of books is an important parameter. It is best represented by the many kinds of in-house use that simply will not be satisfied through interlibrary loan access from other libraries and thus will not be requested; they may not be satisfied or even be requested from remote or closed-access compact storage or an automated facility.

To illustrate, browsing use clearly requires direct contact with the material; this is the reason that faculty are adamant about "browsing" of collections. The crucial point is that the reduction in such uses is not an unalloyed saving of the costs of access but instead is a reduction in the effectiveness of the total investment in the collection, as measured by use of it, as well as the effectiveness of the users (the ultimate measure of effectiveness).

Open-access shelving appears to have the best effect upon use, encouraging not only browsing but more active kinds of use, such as chained reference.

Data on the effect of compact shelving is mixed. It seems to be the case that when the material stored in compact shelving is less used overall, the effect is to limit the use even more. But when the compact shelving is used in a "seamless" fashion, well integrated with open-access shelving, there may be less of an effect. At the University of Illinois, the level of use of such integrated material appears to be about one-half to two-thirds that of the stack collection overall, but the data are not differentiated enough to be more accurate or specific than that.

User Needs and Costs in Access and Use. Aspects relevant to user needs and costs include financial costs (in cases in which the user must pay for the access), the effect of distance (an inverse function, either exponential or quadratic, depending upon the cost of travel), and response time. Each of those can be more or less measured. Less clear are the kinds of use (circulation versus in-house, in particular). Of special importance are the costs associated with unmet needs resulting from the effects of storage alternatives upon the amount of use made.

The model presented here can encompass two of these aspects. First, the costs incurred by the user can be added to those of the library. Second, the costs associated with unmet needs can be assigned to the effects of alternatives on use (i.e., if uses are lost because the material needed is not accessible enough, a "penalty cost" could be charged to it). However, there are no data available on which to estimate these values, so while they can in principle be dealt with they will not be illustrated.

Access Allocation Model

The access allocation model simply expresses total costs as a combination of costs for each alternative, weighted by the number of volumes stored at each alternative and recognizing the effects of distribution of use and of patron choices. It then calculates and optimizes two different criteria, first the total costs and second the cost/effectiveness as measured by the ratio: (Total Cost)/(Total Use).

Relevant Parameters.   Let the relevant parameters be symbolized as follows:

I—interest rate for present value calculation (taken at 0.05)
Y—years to be considered (taken at 20)
PV—present value factor (taken at 12.46, based on $I = 0.05$, $Y = 20$)
F_i—costs of storage (space, equipment, and present value of maintenance) for alternative (i)
A_i—present value of operating costs in access and use for alternative (i)
V—the total number of volumes in the collection being considered
C—collection costs (selection, acquisition, purchase, and processing)
N—the total desired usage (circulation and in-house) of the V volumes
P_i—the effect upon use of alternative (i)
K—the controlling parameter for distribution of use (taken as $0.125 \star V$)

Set of Volumes and Their Allocation.   Let the set of V volumes being considered be sequenced in rank order of expected frequency of use, and group them into successive groups of K volumes each. Assume that the total use for volumes in groups greater than or equal to group X is given by $N/2^{(X)}$, where N is the total annual use over all V volumes. Store volumes from group X_1 up to $X_i + 1$ at alternative i. The number of volumes stored there is $W_i = K \star (X_i + 1 - X_1)$. Total usage of the W_i volumes is $P_i \star N/2^{(X_i)} - P_i \star N/2^{(X_i + 1)}$.

Total Cost.   For the purposes of this section, consideration will be limited to the case of two alternatives, in which group $X = X_1$ (containing $W = K^\star X_1$ volumes) are stored at alternative 1 and the remainder at alternative 2. The total cost, S, for the access allocation decision will be given by:

(1) $$S = C + F_2^\star(V - K^\star X) + PV^\star A_2^\star P_2^\star N/2^{(X)} + F_1^\star K^\star X$$
$$PV^\star A_1^\star P_1^\star(N - N/2^{(X)})$$

$$= C + F_2^\star V + (F_1 - F_2)^\star K^\star X + PV^\star A_1^\star P_1^\star N +$$
$$PV^\star(A_2^\star P_2 - A_1^\star P_1)^\star N/2^{(X)}$$

Optimization on Total Cost.   Most simply, one can optimize the total cost. The calculation is simple. First, calculate the derivative of S as a function of X and set it to zero:

(2) $$dS/dX = (F_1 - F_2)^\star K - PV^\star(A_2^\star P_2 - A_1^\star P_1)^\star N^\star \ln_e 2/2^{(X)} = 0$$

The solution is

(3) $$X = \log_2[(N/K)^\star PV^\star(A_2^\star P_2 - A_1^\star P_1)/(F_1 - F_2)]$$

Effectively, the solution is determined by the ratio of differences between the total access costs and the total acquisitions costs. Of course, if $(A_2^\star P_2 - A_1^\star P_1) > 0$ and $(F_1 - F_2) < 0$, there is no solution, since we would face both greater access costs and greater capital costs for alternative 2.

Optimization on Cost/Effectiveness.   A more complicated criterion is to optimize cost/effectiveness, which will be taken here as the "cost per use." The total use is given by:

(4) $$U = P_1^\star N - (P_1 - P_2)^\star N/2^{(X)}$$

The optimum value for X is then given by taking the derivative of S/U with respect to X and setting it to zero:

(5) $$F = d(S/U)/dX = (U^\star dS/dX - S^\star dU/dX)/U^2 = 0$$

where

(6) $$dS/dX = (F_1 - F_2)^\star K - PV^\star(A_2^\star P_2 - A_1^\star P_1)^\star N^\star \ln_e 2/2^{(X)} \text{ and}$$
$$dU/dX = (1 - P_2)^\star N^\star \ln_e 2/2^{(X)}$$

The criterion condition then is equation (6). Newton's method is one means to solve that equation. It is an iterative procedure that requires calculating the derivative, dF, of F. Then, if X_0 is an approximation,

(7) $$X_1 = X_0 - F/dF$$

is a better approximation. The Newton iteration converges quadratically. Alternatively, one can use the "goal-seek" function of a spreadsheet program, and that has been incorporated into the *LPM* implementation of this model.

Illustrative Application for Allocation Decision. Simply to illustrate the application of equations (4) and (6), the allocation decision will be examined using assumed values for the parameters involved as shown below:

	Alternatives	
	$I = 1$ Open Stacks	$i = 2$ Compact Shelves
I	0.05	0.05
Y	20	20
F_i	$25	$15
A_i	$8	$12
V	1,200,000	1,200,000
C	$60,000,000	$60,000,000
N	1,500,000	1,500,000
P_i	1.00	0.80
K	150,000	150,000

Note that, for this illustration, the differences between the two alternatives have been limited just to the capital costs (i.e., $25 and $15, respectively), the access costs ($8 and $12, respectively), and the impact on use (1.0 and 0.8, respectively). Equation (4) is then:

(8) $$X = \log_2[(N/K) \star PV \star (A_2 \star P_2 - A_1 \star P_1)/$$
$$(F_1 - F_2)] = \log_2[(1.5 \star 8/1.2) \star 12.46 \star (0.8 \star 12 - 1 \star 8))/(10)]$$

$$= \log_2[19.9] = 4.3$$

That means that $X \star K = 4.3 \star 150,000 = 645,000$ of the total collection of 1,200,000 should be stored at alternative (1), the open-stack shelving:

$X = 4.3$	Collection	Use
Open Stack	645,000	1,139,000
Compact	555,000	49,000

Note that the cost per volume for storage in compact shelving is almost certain to be less that that for open-stack shelving so $(F_1 - F_2)$ should be greater than zero. However, there is a strong likelihood that the access costs $(A_2{\star}P_2 - A_1{\star}P_1)$ could be less than zero. That would make equation (4) completely invalid, since it would result in the logarithm of a negative number).

For example, if we limit ourselves just to the library's costs, the likelihood is that reshelving for compact storage costs the same as for open-stack shelves, $A_1 = A_2$. Then the reduced use of the compact shelves results in a negative total for access costs. While this may seem anomalous, it is a direct result of concentrating only on costs and ignoring effectiveness as represented by the use of the collection.

It is for that reason, plus the need to obtain the best use of the total investment in the collection, that the cost/effectiveness measure may be more appropriate.

The results from solution of equation (6) show that the optimum $X = 5.22$, and the number of volumes in open-stack shelving would be $X{\star}K = 5.22{\star}150{,}000 = 783{,}000$. The result is the following:

$X = 5.22$	Collection	Use
Open Stack	783,000	1,168,000
Compact	417,000	26,000

It is important to note that the cost/effectiveness ratio includes the cost of the total collection. Underlying that is the intent that the ratio should consider the maximum use of the total investment. To see the effect of different values for the magnitude of that investment, consider the case where $C = 0$ – that is, ignoring the investment in the collection. The result is a small but significant transfer of materials from open stack to compact:

$X = 4.91$	Collection	Use
Open Stack	737,000	1,161,000
Compact	463,000	31,000

Returning to the case where $C = \$60{,}000{,}000$, if the access costs, A_1 and A_2 are the same, say both are \$8, the results from equation (6) are:

$X = 3.31$	Collection	Use
Open Stack	497,000	1,079,000
Compact	703,000	97,000

Note that the decreased cost for compact reshelving (from $12 to $8) results in a substantial increase in the proportion of the collection going to compact shelving.

6.5
Choice Between Acquisition and Access

We turn now to a much more complex decision problem—the choice between acquisition and access (i.e., depending upon access from elsewhere to meet needs). Some have characterized the choice as "just in case" versus "just in time." Fundamentally, it is the choice between capital investment versus operating cost.

6.5.1 The Contexts for Acquisitions vs. Access Decisions

Alternatives for Access
There are several choices now available for providing access to materials from elsewhere. Of course, there is the traditional method of interlibrary borrowing, in which the source is another cooperating library. There is document delivery, with again the source being a cooperating library but now delivering a copy of the material instead of lending the original. Alternatively, document delivery can be from a commercial or quasi-commercial source.

The most exciting alternative for access is the Internet, of course. Online availability of full-text and images is now a reality. Sites such as J-Stor provide access to the images of pages from journal articles. Digital text for ever-increasing numbers of books as well as journals is now becoming readily available.

Implications for Acquisition Decisions
The choice between acquisition and access clearly has significance for the individual library, and in this section we will examine models on which to base that decision. But it also has implications for library cooperation in shared acquisition, as a means to ensure coverage of the materials and gain maximum benefit from the use of total budgets for acquisition. We will consider those implications in Chapter 9.

Implications for Deacquisition Decisions
There are also implications for deacquisition, as libraries face the problem of steadily increasing prices of journals. Any tactical management plan for journal acquisitions should balance the cost/effectiveness of acquiring a journal with that for access to articles, by electronic means or otherwise.

During the past ten years, there have been dramatic, continuing increases in prices for scholarly journals, especially among the most expensive ones in the fields of science and technology. They have averaged between 15% and 20% per annum, compounded, which has led to spectacular increases in the burden on the acquisitions budgets of academic libraries. Those increases continue.

The impact on academic institutions has been nearly catastrophic as their libraries face the difficulties in meeting the needs of the full range of disciplines they must serve, in maintaining an effective mix of monographs and journals, and in assuring a cost/effective balance between the capital costs in acquiring and the expenses in accessing.

Unfortunately, however, neither academic libraries nor the institutions they serve have any means to influence pricing decisions made by those publishers. The academic library market is minor for them in comparison with the commercial and industrial market, where the economic benefits of having the most current scientific and technical information can fully justify the costs being charged.

Each academic library therefore needs a plan for strategic management of its journal acquisitions program in a way that will resolve the difficulties.

6.5.2 Application of the Allocation Model to Acquisition vs. Access Decisions

We first turn to the application of the allocation model, as presented above, to the acquisition versus access decision.

Parameters for Application to Acquisitions vs. Access Decision

The model is essentially the same, but a few the parameters need to be reinterpreted. Recall the list of parameters for the allocation model:

V—Number of Volumes Being Considered
K—Scope of Collection
N—Amount of Use
C—Costs of the Collection
F—Costs of Acquisition, Processing, and Storage
A—Operating Costs in Access Use
P—Effects of Alternatives upon Use

Number of Volumes. In application to the storage problem, the total collection (or at least the total of the collection being considered for allocation) was the number of volumes. For acquisition, though, it is the population of publications that are potential acquisitions. Thus, in the case of application to storage, we are dealing with a well-defined population, one that the library already has under its control. For application to acquisition, the population is not well defined, either in principle or in application.

First, the definition of population to be considered is a function of the scope of collection. If that scope is worldwide and universal subject coverage, the population is very large, on the order of 200,000 new titles each year. If the scope is narrow, both geographically and in subject, the population may be quite focused, perhaps less than 1000 titles. This then is one of the roles of the parameter K, scope of collections. In general, in use of the allocation model, the approach has been to take the population as the broadest possible—"worldwide publication"—and then to use the parameter K as the means for determining the library's own focus within that large population. However, the model permits other definitions.

Second, whatever the population to be considered may be, there are difficulties in measuring the size of it. What is the worldwide production of publications? Fortunately, the nature of the J-shaped curve for distribution of use makes that question almost immaterial. If we have overestimated the size, the added items simply fall off the end.

Scope of Collection.   The parameter "Scope" is intended to measure the proportion of the population of information resources being considered which is required to support the institutional program. The scope could be measured in any one of several ways: by (1) the ratio of holdings to a maximum, (2) the ratio of library budget to a maximum, (3) the ratio of academic programs to a maximum, or perhaps others. The value for the maximum, in each case, is something to be determined. In the implementation of this model in *LPM,* the maximum is taken at 10,000,000 to represent a maximum collection size.

Amount of Use.   This is the same as for the application to storage allocation.

Cost of the Collection.   Currently, the existing capital investment in the collection is not included in the model for application to the acquisition versus access decision.

Costs of Acquisition, Processing, and Storage.   But these costs are crucial. In acquisition, that full array of costs is incurred. In access, none of them is incurred (at least by the borrowing library). It is this that makes the alternative of access appealing, of course.

Operating Costs in Access and Use.   And, of course, these are the counterbalancing costs. Access from elsewhere may entail costs by the borrowing library; it will involve costs incurred by the source, which may then involve charges by the source for the access services. It may result in costs to the user in delayed accessibility in getting the material from elsewhere.

Effects of Alternatives on Use.   It is self-evident that there is an effect of depending upon access from elsewhere upon the use of the materials. For example, browsing through the materials is not possible if they have not been acquired; the response time to get materials from elsewhere is likely to lead to substitution for them by other materials. Results from application of the allocation model to data for ARL libraries implies that interlibrary borrowing reduces the level of use to one-fifth what it would be if the materials had been acquired.

Illustrative Applications

Data from the 1998 ARL statistics will be used simply to illustrate the application. The following are the averages for relevant fields for the 111 ARL universities:

Total Volumes Held	3,516,353
Gross Volumes Added	86,262
Monographs Added	36,547
Serials Purchased	17,120
Serials Not Purchased	7,895
Current Serials	27,818
Expenses for Monographs	$1,865,144
Expenses for Serials	$3,937,441
Total Circulation	680,436
ILL Lending	34,462
ILL Borrowing	21,760

Monograph Acquisition vs. Access.   The following are the calculations for the parameters of the allocation model for application to monographs:

$V=$	100,000	as estimated worldwide production
$K=$	4,395	taken as V/8* Total Volumes/10,000,000
$N=$	1,361,000	3 times Total Circulation, assuming 2 in-house per circulation, 2/3 monographs
$C=$		Costs of the Collection will not be used
$F_1=$	$131	calculated as a combination of
		1 Expenses for Monograph/Monographs Added = $51.00
		2 Technical Processing selection, acquisition, cataloging, processing at $60,
		3 Storage at $20
$F_2=$	0	Cost of Acquisition, Processing, and Storage for access
$A_1=$	0	Operating Costs in Access & Use for Acquisition
$A_2=$	$30	Internal Operating costs and likely charges for Access
$P_1=$	1.0	Effects of Acquisition upon Use
$P_1=$	0.2	Effects of Access upon Use

Equation (4) yields a value of $X = 8.06$, so $K \star X = 35,414$ to be compared with the actual 36,547.

Serials Acquisitions vs. Access. The following are the calculations for the parameters of the allocation model for application to serials:

$V = 60,000$ (estimated worldwide production of serials)
$K = 2,637$
$C =$ Costs of the Collection will not be used
$N = 680,436$ (3 times Total Circulation, assuming 2 in-house use per circulation, with 1/3 of serials)
$F_1 = \$280$ (calculated as a combination of
    (1) Expenses for Serials/Serials Purchased $= \$230.00$
    (2) Technical Processing (receiving, records maintenance, binding) at \$20,
    (3) Storage at \$30
F_2, A_1, A_2, P_1, P_2 are as above

Equation (4) yields a value of $X = 6.59$, so $K \star X = 17,381$ to be compared with the actual 17,120 (not including the nonpurchased serials).

6.5.3 Application of the Allocation Model to Acquisition vs. Access Decisions

We now turn to application of the allocation model to the journal deacquisition decision. The approach to doing so is to develop an illustrative 5-year plan to accommodate assumed rates of increase in both the budget for journal acquisition (taken at 6%) and the average prices for journals (taken at 15%). Thus, it sets a "steady-state" budget objective, with year-to-year increases limited approximately to that for normal inflation. To accommodate the 15% anticipated inflation in the prices of journals, which is dramatically greater than normal inflation, the plan identifies a schedule for deacquisition based on continuing review of the cost/effectiveness of each journal and, especially, of those with the highest prices and highest rates of inflation.

The plan is based on use of the allocation model for the distribution of use of library materials, which serves as the means for assessment of the optimum balance between acquisition and access based on their respective costs. The data needed for that model are derived directly from the historical operating data for several libraries.

Historical Data and Status-Quo Projections

Table 6.1 shows illustrative historic data for academic years 1990/1991 through 1994/1995. They are derived from an actual library but are not equal

Table 6.1
Budgets and Expenditures (all dollar figures are in 1000s)

	Budgets			Expends				Pct
	Ser$	Mono$	Total$	Ser$	Mono$	Total$	Net$	Serials
Inflation	0.06	0.06						
90/1	657	375	1,032	571	398	969	63	0.59
91/2	696	398	1,094	595	421	1,016	78	0.59
92/3	738	421	1,160	674	447	1,121	39	0.60
93/4	782	447	1,229	764	473	1,238	−9	0.62
94/5	829	473	1,303	867	502	1,369	−66	0.63
95/6	879	502	1,381	984	532	1,516	−135	0.65
96/7	932	532	1,464	1,117	564	1,681	−217	0.66
97/8	988	564	1,552	1,268	598	1,866	−314	0.68
98/9	1,047	598	1,645	1,441	634	2,075	−430	0.69
99/0	1,110	634	1,744	1,638	672	2,310	−566	0.71

to the actuals, either for budgets or for expenditures. The actual data are highly variable due to differences between budgets and augmentations, differences in the timing of orders and receipts, differences in commitments of payments and the actual payments, and a variety of other sources of variance. Those differences have been averaged out to provide long-term patterns as the basis for projections.

Table 6.1 also shows anticipated future budgets and expenditures for academic years 1995/1996 through 1999/2000 based on projected inflation rates. Figures for budgets assume a steady 6% augmentation; figures for expenditures are derived from Table 6.2. The proportions in the final two columns show the ratio of expenditures for serials to totals and for journals to totals. The column labeled "NET$" is the difference between projected budget totals and those for expenditures; it clearly exhibits the problem created by the rate of inflation in journal prices, with a shortfall in 1999/2000 of $566,000 (nearly one-third of the projected budget).

Table 6.2 provides the basis for the projections of expenditures, based on projected rates for the three major types of print materials (journals, nonjournal serials, and monographs). The inflation rates assumed for each are shown under the price.

The inflation rate for journals as shown in Table 6.2 is derived from the data provided from the specific library for the distribution of titles and expenditures by price groups. Those data cover both the specific situation at that library and the average for academic libraries in general. Table 6.3 shows the distribution of titles by price group, and Table 6.4 those for expenditures. The price groups are "less than $50," "$50 to $100," "$100 to $200," "$200 to $600," "$600 to $1000," and "more than $1000").

Table 6.2

Bases for Projections of Expenditures (expenditures are in 1000s of dollars; prices are in dollars)

	Journals			Nonjournal serials			Monographs		
	Num	Price	Exp	Num	Price	Exp	Num	Price	Exp
Inflation		0.15			0.10			0.06	
90/1	2,609	150	391	1,500	120	180	7,500	53	398
91/2	2,300	173	397	1,500	132	198	7,500	56	421
92/3	2,300	198	456	1,500	145	218	7,500	60	447
93/4	2,300	228	525	1,500	160	240	7,500	63	473
94/5	2,300	262	603	1,500	176	264	7,500	67	502
95/6	2,300	302	694	1,500	193	290	7,500	71	532
96/7	2,300	347	798	1,500	213	319	7,500	75	564
97/8	2,300	399	918	1,500	234	351	7,500	80	598
98/9	2,300	459	1,055	1,500	257	386	7,500	84	634
99/0	2,300	528	1,214	1,500	283	424	7,500	90	672

Table 6.3

Distributions of Titles by Price Groups

	<50	100	200	600	1,000	>1,000	Total
			Specific Library Distribution of Titles				
90/91	0.341	0.246	0.172	0.153	0.040	0.048	1.000
91/92	0.376	0.236	0.156	0.144	0.042	0.046	1.000
92/93	0.322	0.244	0.178	0.152	0.040	0.063	0.999
			Average Distribution of Titles				
90/91	0.423	0.241	0.162	0.121	0.032	0.023	1.000
91/92	0.446	0.243	0.150	0.112	0.030	0.020	1.000

In Table 6.5 the percentages shown for the specific library in Tables 6.3 and 6.4 are applied to that library's data for total numbers of titles and total expenditures to derive absolute numbers of titles and dollars, respectively. From those absolute data, averages for title costs in each group can then be derived. The important point to note about these figures is the shift, year to year, of titles up from one group to the next higher group. Table 6.6 shows the data for that shift between 1991/1992 and 1992/1993; the row for "move" shows the number of titles that move up one group while that for "stay" shows the number that stay in a group. To estimate the inflation rates that underlie those moves, the price in 1991/92 for those that move are taken at the maximum for each group from which they move (which slightly underestimates the inflation rate for

Table 6.4
Distribution of Expenditures by Price Groups

	50	100	200	600	1,000	<1,000	Total
			Specific Library Distribution of Budgets				
90/91	0.047	0.07	0.093	0.203	0.141	0.446	1.00
91/92	0.044	0.072	0.101	0.214	0.132	0.437	1.00
92/93	0.036	0.062	0.089	0.183	0.113	0.517	1.00
			Average Distribution of Budgets				
90/91	0.086	0.117	0.142	0.25	0.157	0.247	1.00
91/92	0.077	0.108	0.142	0.249	0.148	0.275	1.00

Table 6.5
Absolute Numbers of Titles and Dollars

	50	100	200	600	1,000	<1,000	Total
			Specific Library Titles				
90/91	890	642	449	399	104	125	2609
91/92	865	543	359	331	97	106	2300
92/93	741	561	409	350	92	145	2298
			Specific Library Dollars (in 1,000 dollars)				
90/91	31	46	61	133	93	293	657
91/92	31	50	70	149	92	304	696
92/93	27	46	66	135	83	382	738
			Specific Library Title Average Cost				
90/91	35	72	136	334	888	2,340	
91/92	35	92	196	450	952	2,877	
92/93	36	82	160	386	907	2,634	

those titles that move and slightly overestimates that for titles that stay). The price for those that stay in a group can then be calculated directly, as can the resulting inflation rates for both sets (those that move and those that stay) in each group. The averages then provide the basis for the assumed rate of 15% used above.

Applying the Model for Allocation Decisions
As Table 6.1 shows, the projected growth in expenditures far exceeds the budget (even assuming normal increases to accommodate inflation). That requires that a strategic plan be established for deacquiring journals and shifting

Table 6.6

Estimated Inflation Rates

ranges	<50	100	200	600	1,000	>1,000	Total
91/92	865	543	359	331	97	106	2,300
92/93	741	561	409	350	92	145	2,298
Move	−124	−106	−55	−37	−41	−2	
Stay	741	437	304	294	55	104	
Move Price	50	100	200	600	1,000	3,000	
Stay Price	33	77	153	360	837	2,626	
Move inflate	0.15	0.15	0.16	0.22	0.22		
Stay inflate	0.09	0.15	0.15	0.16	0.22	0.22	
Avg inflate	0.10	0.15	0.15	0.17	0.22	0.22	0.15

Table 6.7

The Allocation Model

H = Holding	300,000	Purchase Price	$150
N = Uses	150,000	Tech Process	4
J = Jnl Pop	60,000	Bind	10
PV to Store	30		
A = Access Cost	$15 (taken as only fees for access)	C = Capital Cost	$194
K	$1,080 = .12*J*H/(2,000,000)$		
X	$2.37 = \log_2(A*N*LN_e2)/C*K))$		
K*X	2,560		
Lost uses	29,011	(Lost uses)/(Doc Del)	5

from acquisition to access by interlibrary borrowing and document delivery in a cost-effective way. Table 6.7 provides parameters and calculations related to the allocation model for making that decision.

The values shown for Purchase Price are those experienced at this small college library, so they are much less than those for the average ARL library.

Table 6.8 presents the results of applying the parameters in Table 6.7 to the data from the specific library. It shows, in successive columns, the following data: the academic year, the average price for a journal (based on 15% inflation), the optimum number of journals (according to the model), the status quo number, the difference between the two (as potential deacquisition), the cost savings due to that number of deacquisitions, the uses that would be lost through deacquisition, the level of ILL-borrowing or document delivery that would be generated from those lost uses (based on a ratio of 5 lost uses per request).

The calculation of cost saving (shown in the column "Cost Sav'g") assumes that distribution of deacquired titles across all acquired titles is proportional to that of total costs, as shown in Table 6.4. The result in 1991/92 would

Table 6.8

Application of Allocation Model to Specific Library

Year	Avg Price	Optimum Number	Status Quo	De-Acq	Cost Sav'g	Lost Uses	ILL& DocDel
90/1	150	2,560	2,609	−49	78	29,011	5,802
91/2	173	2,480	2,300	180	−62	30,543	6,109
92/3	198	2,395	2,300	95	−38	32,258	6,452
93/4	228	2,305	2,300	5	−2	34,168	6,834
94/5	262	2,211	2,300	−89	47	36,287	7,257
95/6	302	2,114	2,300	−186	112	38,631	7,726
96/7	347	2,013	2,300	−287	199	41,215	8,243
97/8	399	1,909	2,300	−391	312	44,058	8,812
98/9	459	1,802	2,300	−498	457	47,179	9,436
99/0	528	1,693	2,300	−607	640	50,601	10,120

have been that deacquired volumes would average $677 compared with the overall average of $321. For simplicity, the ratio is taken as 2/1 and applied to each year. The result of deacquisition not only is a reduction in total costs but also reduction in the average price to which inflation is applied. It should be noted that in years 1991/92 through 1993/94 there is a positive value for "De-Acq"; that reflects the actual deacquisitions in 1990/91 and suggests that the number (300 or so) at that time was not optimum, though appropriate, given the process. Of course, by 1993/94, the validity of the decisions made in 1990/91 is evident.

The column labeled "Lost uses" reports the results from the model for the total number of uses of journals that are not met because journals (among the total of 60000, it should be noted) are needed but not acquired, assuming that the journals implied in the "De-Acq" column are deacquired. The following column, "ILL& DocDel," is derived from that one simply by dividing it by 5; that figure reflects the overall experience in ARL libraries on the ratio between the lost uses and the actual ILL or document delivery requests and appears to be a realistic measure of the extent to which needs get translated into actions.

Table 6.9 shows the effects of using the results in Table 6.8 as the basis for a strategic plan for the specific library.

In this table, the column labeled "ILL" reflects the actual ILL borrowing for periodicals from 1990/91 through 1994/95; thereafter, it is assumed that it will be constant at the 1994/95 level, with any additional workload met through document delivery services. The column labeled "DocDel" is the difference between the estimated requests, from Table 6.8, and the number met through ILL. The next column is the estimated cost for document delivery, starting at $15 in 1994/94 and with inflation at 6%. The next column is the projected budget for document delivery, starting from $17,000 with inflation at 6%.

Table 6.9

A Strategic Plan for Optimum Mix of Acquisition and Access

	ILL	DocDel	Cost	Doc Deliver Budget	Expense	De-Acq Titles	Dollars	DocDel & Jnls Expense	Budget
Inflate			0.06	0.06					0.06
90/1	4,860	942	11.88	649	657				
91/2	4,876	1,233	12.59	657	696				
92/3	5,350	1,102	13.35	712	738				
93/4	5,975	859	14.15	767	782				
94/5	5,336	1,921	15.00	17	17				
95/6	5,300	2,155	15.90	18	34	−89	−47	849	847
96/7	5,300	2,226	16.85	19	38	−42	−29	868	898
97/8	5,300	2,251	17.87	21	40	−15	−15	929	951
98/9	5,300	2,261	18.94	22	43	−5	−10	997	1,008
99/0	5,300	2,267	20.07	23	46	−2	−9	1,072	1,069
						−1	−8	1,152	1,133

The column labeled "DocDel Expense" is then the product of the number "DocDel" by the cost. The columns labeled "De-Acq Title" and "De-Acq Dollars" are derived from the column "De-Acq" and "Cost" in Table 6.8. The column labeled "DocDel& Jnls Expense" is then the sum of the cost of journals and document delivery, less the savings from deacquisition as identified in the column "De-Acq Dollars." The final column repeats the budget column for journals from Table 6.2.

Bibliography

The following references provide a starting point for literature relevant to collection development and allocation:

References on Collection Development

American Library Association. *Guidelines for Collection Development,* Chicago; ALA, 1979.

American Library Association. *Planning and Role Settings for public libraries* Chicago: American Library Association, 1987.

Arthur, Anthony. "Collection Management: An Australian Project," *Australian Academic and Research Libraries* 17, 1 (1986), pp. 29–38.

Bryant, Edward C., et al. *Library Cost Models: Owning versus Borrowing Serial Publications.* Chicago: Center for Research Libraries, August 1968.

Buzzard, Marion L., and Whaley, John H. "Serials and Collection Development," *Drexel Library Quarterly* 21, 1 (1985), pp. 37–49.

Futas, Elizabeth, and Vidor, David L. "What Constitutes a 'Good' Collection?" *Library Journal* 112, 7 (1987), pp. 45–47.

Futas, Elizabeth. "Issues in Collection Development: Collection Evaluation," *Collection Building* 4, 1 (1982), pp. 54–55.

Futas, Elizabeth. "The Role of Public Services in Collection Evaluation," *Library Trends* 33, 3 (1985), pp. 397–416.

Grover, Mark L. "Collection Assessment in the 1980's," *Collection Building* 8, 4 (1988), pp. 23–26.

Hodge, Stanley P., and Ivins, Marilyn. "Current International Newspapers: Some Collection Management Implications," *College and Research Libraries* 48, 1 (1987), pp. 50–61.

Holt, M.I. "Collection Evaluation: A Managerial Tool," *Collection Management* 3 (Winter 1979), pp. 279–284.

Hyman, Ferne B. "Collection Evaluation in the Research Library," *Collection Building* 9, 3–4 (1989), pp. 33–37.

Katz, Bill. "A Way of Looking at Things," *Library Trends* 33, 3 (1985), pp. 367–384.

Laughlin, Mildred Knight. "Collection Development in Elementary School Library Media Centers," *Collection Management* 7, 3–4 (1985), pp. 85–86, 55–60.

Lopez, Manuel D. "The Lopez or Citation Technique of In-depth Collection Evaluation Explicated," *College and Research Libraries* 44, 3 (1983), pp. 251–255.

Magrill, Rose Mary. "Evaluation of Type of Library," *Library Trends* 3 (Winter, 1985), pp. 267–295.

Mancall, Jacqueline, and Christopher Swisher. "Developing Collections for the Eighties and Beyond," *School Library Media Annual* 1 (1983), p. 269.

McGrath, William E. "Collection Evaluation—Theory and Search for Structure," *Library Trends* 33, 3 (1985), pp. 241–266.

Miller, William, and Rockwood, Stephen D. "College Development from a College Perspective," *College and Research Libraries* 40, 4 (1979), pp. 318–324.

Mosher, Paul H. "A Natural Scheme for Collaboration in Collection Development: The RLG-NCIP Effort," *Resource Sharing and Information Networks* 2 (Spring/Summer 1985), pp. 21–35.

Nilsonger, Thomas E. "An Annotated Bibliography of Items Relating to Collection Evaluation in Academic Libraries, 1969–1981," *College and Research Libraries* 43, 4 (July 1982), pp. 300–311.

Nutter, Susan K. "Online Systems and the Management of Collections: Use and Implications," *Advances in Library Automation and Networking* 1, pp. 125–149.

Pitschmann, Louis A. *Collection Development Policy Statements: A Brief List of Publications Compiled for ALA/ALCTS Midwest Collection Management and Development Institute.* 1989.

Reed-Scott. Jutta. *Manual for the North American Inventory of Research Library Collections,* rev. ed. Washington, DC: Association of Research Libraries, Office of Management Services, September 1988.

Robbins-Carter, Jane, and Douglas L. Zweizig. "Are We There Yet?: Evaluating Library Collections, Reference Services, Programs and Personnel: Lesson Two: Evaluating Library Collections," *American Libraries* 16 (November 1985), pp. 724–727.

Trueswell, Richard W. "A Quantitative Measure of User Circulation Requirements and Its Possible Effect on Stack Thinning and Multiple Copy Determination," *American Documentation* 16(1), 20–25 (January 1965).

Guide to Evaluation of Library Collections. Chicago: American Library Association, 1989.

"Library Models and Empirical Findings," in Hamburg, Morris, and others, *Library Planning and Decision-Making Systems.* Cambridge, MA: MIT Press, 1974, Chapter 4, pp. 76–113.

References on Programmatic Criteria for Collection Development

Besson, Alain, and Sheriff, Ian. "Journal Collection Evaluation at the Medical College of St. Bartholomew's Hospital," *British Journal of Academic Librarianship* 1, 2 (1986), pp. 132–146.

Bland, Robert N. "The College Textbook as a Tool for Collection Evaluation, Analysis, and Retrospective Collection Development," *Library Acquisitions: Practice and Theory* 4, 3–4 (1980), pp. 193–197.

Clapp, Verner W., and Jordan, Robert T. "Quantitative Criteria for Adequacy of Academic Library Collections," *College and Research Libraries* 26 (September 1965), pp. 371–380.

Dowd, Sheila T. *The Formulation of a Collection Development Policy Statement*. Collection Development in Libraries: A Treatise. Greenwich, CT: JAI Press, 1980, pp. 67–87.

Faigel, Martin. "Methods and Issues in Collection Evaluation Today," *Library Acquisitions: Practice and Theory* 9, 1 (1985), pp. 21–35.

Hayes, Robert M. "Evaluation and Collection Development," a talk given at the *RTSD Collection Management and Developement Institute,* September 5, 1984.

Hayes, Robert M. *Project Status: An Approach to Methodology (Criteria and Goals for the Libraries of the University of California).* Los Angeles: Institute of Library Research, University of California, January 31, 1966.

Nilsonger, Thomas E. "A Test of Two Citation Checking Techniques for Evaluating Political Science Collections in University Libraries," *Library Resources and Technical Services* 27, 2 (1983), pp. 163–176.

Palais, Elliot. "Use of Course Analysis in Compiling a Collection Development Policy Statement for a University Library," *Journal of Academic Librarianship* 1 (March 1987), pp. 8–13.

Perrault, Anna H. "Humanities Collection Management—An Impressionistic/Realistic/Optimistic Appraisal of the State of the Art," *Collection Management* 5, 3–4 (1983), pp. 1–23.

Sarloe, Bart. "Achieving Client-Centered Collection Development in Small and Medium-Sized Academic Libraries," *College & Research Libraries.* 50 (May 1989), pp. 344–353.

Terwiliger, Gloria. "Evaluating the Role of the Learning Resource Centre," *Community and Junior College Libraries* 1, 4, pp. 23–32.

Trueswell, Richarci W. *Determining the Optimal Number of Volumes for Library Holdings.* Amherst: School of Engineering, University of Massachusetts, October 1964.

Voigt, Melvin. "Acquisition Rates in University Libraries," *College & Research Libraries* (July 1975), pp. 263–271.

Voos, Henry. "Collection Evaluation," *Collection Building* 3, 1 (1981), pp. 5–11.

Warwick, J.P. "Duplication of Texts in Academic Libraries: A Behavioral Model for Library Management," *Journal of Librarianship* 19, 1, pp. 41–52.

Whaley, John H. "An Approach to Collection Analysis," *Library Resources and Technical Services* 25, 4 (1981), pp. 330–338.

References for Peer Comparison Criteria

Armbrister, Ann. "Library Marc Tapes as a Resource for Collection Analysis: The AMIGOS Service," *Advances In Library Automation and Networking* 2 (1988), pp. 119–135.

Branin, Joseph J., Farrell, David, and Tibdin, Marriann. "The National Shelflist Count Project: Its History, Limitations, and Usefulness," *Library Resources and Technical Services* 29, (Oct./Dec. 1985), pp. 333–342.

Christiansen, Dorothy E., Davis, C. Roger, and Reed-Scott, Jutta. "Guidelines to Collection Evaluation through Use and User Studies," *Library Resources and Technical Services* 27, 4 (Oct./Dec.), pp. 432–440.

Dannelly, Gay N. "The National Shelflist Count: A Tool for Collection Management," paper presented at *Collection Development in Action,* Toledo, October 28, 1988.

Dillon, Martin, and Crook, Mark. "A Prototype Automated Collection Analysis Tool for Libraries," *OCLC Research Review* (July 1987), pp. 3–4.

Farrell, David. "The NCIP Option for Coordinated Collection Management," *Library Resources and Technical Services* 30 (Jan–Mar. 1986), pp. 47–56.

Farrell, David. "The North American Inventory Project (NCIP): Phase II Results in Indiana," *Resource Sharing and Information Networks* 2 (Spring/Summer 1985), pp. 37–48.

Ferguson, Anthony W., Grant, Joan, and Rutstein, Joel S. "The RLG Conspectus: Its Uses and Benefits," *College and Research Libraries* 49 (Mar. 1989), pp. 197–206.

Gwinn, Nancy E., and Mosher, Paul H. "Coordinating Collection Development: The RLG Conspectus," *College and Research Libraries* 44 (Mar. 1983), pp. 128–140.

MacEwan, Bonnie. "The North American Inventory Project: A Tool for Selection, Education and Communication," *Library Acquisitions: Practice and Theory* 13 (1989), pp. 45–50.

Manual for the North American Inventory of Research Collections, prepared by Jutta Reed-Scott. Washington, DC: Association of Research Libraries. Office of Management Studies, 1988.

Oberg, Larry R. "Evaluating the Conspectus Approach for Smaller Library Collections," *College and Research Libraries* 49 (May 1988), pp. 187–196.

Ortopan, Leroy D. "National Shelflist Count: A Historical Introduction," *Library Resources and Technical Services* 29 (Oct./Dec. 1985), pp. 328–332.

"Project: Implications for the Future of Coordinated Management of Research Collections," *Library Resources and Technical Services* 33 (Jan. 1989), pp. 15–28.

Qualitative Collection Analysis: The Conspectus Methodology. SPEC Kit 151. Washington, DC: Association of Research Libraries. Office of Management Studies, 1989.

Sanders, Nancy P., O'Neill, Edward T. and Weibe, Stuart L. "Automated Collection Analysis Using the OCLC and RLG Bibliographic Databases," *College and Research Libraries* 49 (July 1985), pp. 305–315.

References for Growth Rates

Dunn, Oliver C., Seibert, W. F., and Scheuneman, Janice A., *The Past and Likely Future of 58 Research Libraries, 1951–1980: A Statistical Study of Growth and Change.* Lafayette: Indiana University Libraries, 1965.

Hacken, Richard D. "Statistical Assumption-Making in Library Collection Assessment: Peccadilloes and Pitfalls," *Collection Management* 7, 2 (1985), pp. 17–32.

Rider, Fremont, *The Scholar and the Future of the Research Library.* New York: Hadham, 1944. "This book exploded like a bomb in the library profession." (See the review by Herman Henkle and Seymour Lubetzky, *Classical Journal,* xli (3), December 1945). The mathematical model presented is one of exponential growth (see Malthus) applied to library collections. The solution? Use "microcards."

Sandler, Mark. "Quantitative Approaches to Qualitative Collection Assessment," *Collection Building* S, 4 (1988), pp. 12–17.

Seibert, Warren, and others. *Research Library Trends, 1951–1980 and Beyond.* Bethesda, MD: Lister Hill Center for Biomedical Communications, March 1987.

Seibert, Warren, and others. *Research Library Trends II: 35 Libraries in the 1970s and Beyond.* Bethesda, MD: Lister Hill Center for Biomedical Communications, January 1990.

References on Storage Allocation

Axford, H.W. "Collection Management: A New Dimension," *Journal of Academic Librarianship* 6 (1981), pp. 324–329.

Bradford, S.C. "Sources of Information on Specific Subjects," *Engineering* 137, 3549 (1934), pp. 85–86.

Buckland, M.K. and Hindle, A. "Acquisitions, Growth, and Performance Control Through Systems Analysis," in Gore, D. *Farewell to Alexandria.* Westport, CT: Greenwood Press, 1976, pp. 44–61.

Burrell, Q. "A Simple Stochastic Model for Library Loans," *Journal of Documentation,* 36 (1980), pp. 115–132.

Burrell, Q. "Alternative Models for Library Circulation Data," *Journal of Documentation* 38 (1982), pp. 1–13.

Ellsworth, Ralph E., *The Economics of Book Storage in College and University Libraries.* Metuchen, NJ: Scarecrow Press, 1969.

Fussler, Herman H., and Simon, J.L. *Patterns in the Use of Books in Large Research Libraries.* Chicago: University of Chicago Press, 1969.

Hayes, Robert M. *Handbook of Data Processing for Libraries,* 2nd ed. New York: Wiley, 1972, Chapter 4.

Hayes, Robert M. "The Distribution of Use of Library Materials: Analysis of Data from the University of Pittsburgh," *Library Research* 3 (Fall 1981), pp. 215–260.

Hayes, Robert M. "Measurement of Use and Resulting Access Allocation Decisions," *Library & Information Science Research* 14, 4 (Oct–Dec 1992), pp. 361–378.

Hayes, Robert M. "Application of a Mixture of Poisson Distributions to Data on the Use of Library Materials," *Proceedings of the Annual Conference of ASIS,* Oct. 1981. 22–30. Washington, DC: ASIS, 1981, pp. 295–297.

Hayes, Robert M. *Strategic Management for Academic Libraries.* Westport, CT: Greenwood Press, 1993, pp. 169–188, Chapter 10, "Making Allocation Decisions."

Hindle, Anthony, and Buckland, Michael. "In-library Book Usage in Relation to Circulation," *Collection Management* 2, 4 (Winter 1978), pp. 265–277.

Jain, A.K. *A Statistical Study of Book Use.* Ph. D. Thesis, Purdue University, 1967.

Kent, Allen, and others. *Use of Library Materials: The University of Pittsburgh Study.* New York: Marcel Dekker, 1979.

Lawrence, Gary S. "A Cost Model for Storage and Weeding Programs," *College and Research Libraries* 42 (1981), pp. 138–147.

Lawrence, Gary S., and Oja, Anne R. *The Use of the General Collections at the University of California.* Berkeley: University of California, Library. Studies and Research Division, January 30, 1980.

Leimkuhler, Ferdinand F. *Storage Policies for Information Systems* Lafayette, IN: School of Industrial Engineering, Purdue University, 1969.

Leimkuhler, Ferdinand F., and Cox, J.G., "Compact Book Storage in Libraries," *Operations Research* (May–June 1964).

Line, M.B., and Sandison, A. "Obsolescence and Changes in the Use of Literature with Time," *Journal of Documentation* 30 (1974), pp. 283–350.

Lister, W.C. *Least-Cost Decision Rules for the Selection of Library Materials for Compact Storage.* Purdue University, Ph.D. Thesis, 1967.

Morse, P.M. and Elston, C. "A Probabilistic Model for Obsolescence," *Operations Research* 17, 1 (1969), pp. 36–47.

Muller, R.H., "Economics of Compact Book Shelving," *Library Trends* (April 1965).

Olsen. Wallace C. *Digital Storage of an Academic Library Book Collection: Nontechnological Information to Aid Consideration.* Boston: EDUCOM, April 1969.

Orne, J. "Book Review of 'Optimum Storage of Library Material,'" *College and Research Libraries* (May 1965).

Stayner, Richard A., and Richardson, Valerie E. *The Cost-effectiveness of Alternative Library Storage Programs.* Melbourne, Australia: Graduate School of Librarianship, Monash University, 1983.

Thompson, Donald. *In-house Use and Immediacy of Need: The Riverside Pilot Studies.* University of California Library Studies and Research Division. Nov. 1978.

Zipf, G.K. *Human Behavior and the Principle of Least Effort.* Cambridge, MA: Addison-Wesley, 1949.

7

Institutional Requirements

Introduction

Library planning must deal with the effects of various strategic contexts. Probably the most important of them relates to the nature of the users and their needs, and that one has been incorporated into the structure of *LPM*. Others, though are much more complex and the means for representing them are more speculative. They include: (1) institutional requirements, (2) sources of information, (3) information technology. (4) cooperative arrangements among libraries, (5) bibliographic utilities, and (6) national information policies. Preliminary means have been included in *LPM* to deal with some of them, and this chapter and the next two will describe those means along with other aspects of these strategic contexts.

The flowchart on page 164 shows the relationship of the first two of those contexts to the elements that are specific to the library:

This chapter deals with institutional objectives for the impact they have on library operations. A most evident element of the institutional context is the allocation of budgets, representing the level of commitment of the institution to information resources (libraries, computing facilities, and telecomm) in support of instruction, research, and public service. That commitment is exhibited both in the absolute magnitude of the budget for information resources and in the relative percentage of overall institutional budget it represents. It affects a wide range of strategic, tactical, and operational decisions in the library.

7.1
The Context: Universities in the Coming Decades

First, let's look at the context. Universities in the United States indeed will face a number of needs and critical problems during the coming decades, all of them affecting decisions concerning libraries and information resources.

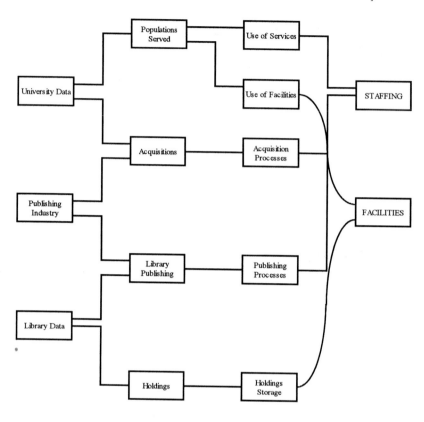

Several issues are paramount as determinants of future development: changes in the economics of universities, effects of technology, changes in the academic enterprise, and changes in patterns of publication.

7.1.1 Economics

For most of the past two decades there has been a steady erosion in the basis of financial support for academic institutions. In the early 1990s, it reached crisis proportions as state budgets throughout the country were decimated by the recession. The perception at that time was that universities would face even more decades of decreased resources.

Then came the dramatic economic upturn of the most recent five years or so. Today, support for universities has begun to increase. But, whether up or down, there are dramatic changes occurring in the basis for funding of universities and of libraries within them—an increasing shift from public funding to private (even for the public universities), an increasing shift from federal funding to industrial funding of research. How do we fit strategic management of information resources into such fundamental changes in funding patterns?

Special problems arise with respect to capital needs, as buildings are aging and as academic programs generate new requirements for information processing equipment. Since information resources generally and libraries especially are capital-intensive operations, requiring both buildings and equipment, this becomes a critical factor in predicting their progress during the coming decades. Furthermore, library automation, academic computing, and telecommunications equipment each represent not just onetime capital demands but ongoing commitments in operation, maintenance, and replacement.

7.1.2 Effects of Technology

The effects of technology are dramatic. The continuing increases in functional capabilities, capacities, and speeds of computers, combined with equally spectacular decreases in cost, have revolutionized our entire society, the university as much as any other institution. The effects of microcomputers and supercomputers; the capabilities for data acquisition, data storage, data display; the development of optical disk formats and the expansion of telecommunications as means for data distribution—all of that technological development clearly is affecting universities, both in what faculty and students will do and in what administrators and librarians must do.

7.1.3 Faculty Renewal

There is a strange ambivalence today with respect to faculty. On the one hand, recruitment and retention of faculty is perhaps the most crucial problem faced by universities, both currently and for the coming decade, especially for the humanities and social sciences; it is exacerbated by the decreased production of Ph.D.s during the 1970s and 1980s. On the other hand, there were increasing incentives during the early 1990s for early retirement of faculty as one response to the fiscal crisis then endemic in universities. Together, though, they add up to the fact that universities are facing dramatic changes in faculty.

Since libraries, computer facilities, and other kinds of information resources are primary among the means for attracting faculty, the implications are clear. Those institutions that commit resources to collection development, to service staff, to access services, and to information equipment are the ones that will be successful, but the tension between these demands and others in the context of decreased resources will be difficult to reconcile.

7.1.4 Student Diversity

There is increasing diversity of students—in age, cultural and ethnic background, and quality of preacademic preparation. Cultural and ethnic diversity is increasingly important, and universities must deal with it as a major and critical instrument in response to social change. Certainly, as universities respond to this need, new and different demands will be placed on their libraries and other information resources. They will require new kinds of materials and services.

7.1.5 Academic Priorities

In the decades following the end of World War II, universities placed steadily increasing emphasis upon research, especially funded research. The result was a shift of institutional priorities from undergraduate teaching to graduate, from teaching at whatever level into research, and from individual research into organized research.

But that emphasis in academic programs now is undergoing dramatic change. There has been a reduction in governmental funding of research which has not been totally replaced by industrial funding. There are concerns about the quality of undergraduate work and about incorporation of diversity into curricula. As a result, universities face internal pressures in setting priorities among levels of education—undergraduate and graduate—and between them and research. Indeed, one question is whether graduate education and research will be as intertwined as they have been in the past. But today, the proper balance between undergraduate and graduate education is especially complex, raising questions about what the university is responsible for and what values there are in what it provides.

These tensions are exhibited especially in the reward system for faculty. The almost overwhelming emphasis that has been placed upon published research in tenure and promotion decisions is now being questioned, and institutions throughout the country are trying to find means to recognize and reward excellence in teaching.

7.1.6 Means for Scholarly Communication

Primarily as a result of the impact of technology on publishing but also in part as a result of changes in the disciplines themselves, there are changes occurring in patterns of publication. The new media—computer databases, online access to them, electronic mail and facsimile, distribution of data and images in optical disk formats, desk-top publishing—all provide new means for communication of scholarly information. In this context, some university administrators have argued that electronic means for distribution make it possible for the university to take back the control of scholarly publication.

7.1.7 Information Needs of Academic Programs

Print is still the essential medium for scholarship and scholarly communication, though clearly the information technologies and the new media must be considered, not only in their own right but as essential adjuncts and supplements to the printed formats. It must be said, though, that this view is not supported by the enthusiasts who have proclaimed, loudly and persuasively, what wonderful changes electronic information will bring, what great new capabilities it will provide, and what an important opportunity it means for the librarian. An article published in *Scribner's Magazine* entitled "The End of Books" has said, "Printing, which since 1436 has reigned despotically over the mind of man, is in my opinion threatened with death by the various devices which have lately been invented and which little by little will go on to perfection." It concludes, "Either the books must go, or they must swallow us up." Of course, the date of that article was August 1894.[1]

But even recognizing the immediate impact of the information technologies in the United States and other developed countries, academic programs involve research and education with respect to developing countries— language and literature, society and economy, agriculture and industry, medicine and health, and the arts and the sciences. Furthermore, we should anticipate that the developing countries will become important sources of scientific and technical information, certainly by the end of the decade. The examples of countries like Taiwan and Korea surely represent what can be expected elsewhere. But whatever may be the pace in development of a national "electronic library" in the United States, it surely will take decades longer in those countries because they lack the necessary infrastructure in telecommunications, logistical support, and skills in use and management of the technologies.

Among the most exciting promises, and not just for the enthusiast, are those related to the potentials for use of computers in scholarly work and teaching. The ability to retrieve, to analyze, to compare and to combine, to process and to manipulate, to communicate, is a promise far more important than mere access to information. It is the potential to *use* it. This, in the long-run, is the most important promise. It opens up new ways of thinking, of conceptualizing, of dealing with needs and with problems. It provides researchers and students with means for stretching the mind, for seeing new relationships,

---

[1] Uzanne, Octave. "The End of Books," *Scribner's Magazine* (August 1894), pp. 221–232 (see p. 224).

for comprehending dimensions far beyond the three or four of our immediate sense of space and time through the use of color, windowing, and multidimensional matrices.

From the standpoint of scholarship, this process clearly facilitates communication among a small peer group. A similar effort was carried out by NIH from 1961 through 1967 to establish what they called "information exchange groups" (IEGs) as formalizations of invisible colleges to facilitate rapid communication within those groups. Over 3600 researchers participated in seven groups, and over 2500 preprints were distributed among them during the six-year program. However, controversy arose around the program, as many scientists argued that the improved effectiveness in communication is heavily outweighed by the inherent limitations. The peer group is by no means the only or even the most appropriate context for research progress and especially evaluation. Research should be of importance beyond the limits of the peer group; it should be subject to evaluation and assessment by other minds, other tests of validity. The cold, clear light of day needs to enter, but the invisible college, by its very mode of operation, prevents that kind of "sunshine" effect.

7.1.8 Investment in Information Activities

Virtually every academic administrator has, at one time or another, seen the library as a fiscal black hole—growing exponentially, needing more and more resources, needing new, ever-larger buildings. And now appears the answer to every academic administrator's dream—the promise of electronic distribution of information! Instead of acquiring more and more books and journals—so many of which appear never to be used—we can get them when we need them, by electronic access. No more acquisitions budgets; no more unused, dusty old volumes taking up valuable space; no more library buildings which are so expensive to build.

The fact, though, is that investments in technological infrastructure are at least as great as those in the library. Wiring the campus, installing mainframe computers and legions of microcomputers, dealing with external communications—during the past two decades, these have represented massive investments. Of even greater importance, though, are two further facts. First, the investment in the equipment must be repeated, at about five-year intervals, as it rapidly becomes obsolescent if not obsolete; manufacturers cease to provide spare parts or adequate maintenance for equipment that no longer is in widespread use. Second, the investment in equipment is now only a small percentage of the total costs it engenders, perhaps as little as 20%; the remaining 80% of costs arise from staff, from maintenance, from software, from applications, from space and supporting facilities. And, in sharp contrast to the university library, which serves as a central manager of these expenditures, the information technology equipment is so dispersed throughout the university that there is almost no means for even identifying what costs are being incurred.

Certainly a primary concern of university management must be the effect of libraries and information resources upon allocation of resources, especially budgets. The proportion of the instructional budget for any given university that historically has been allocated to libraries varies, of course, but percentages around 5% to 6% of the instructional budget appear to be typical for public universities in the United States. For the broader context of general information resources, though, estimation is far more diffuse since it is not clear what will be included within it; whatever may be included, the actual scope will vary much more widely among universities than it does for libraries; and the budget allocations are not delineated as clearly as they typically are for libraries.

What, then, is likely to happen with the percentage of the university budget that will be allocated to information resources during the coming decade? First, with respect to libraries, it seems unlikely that there will be any significant increases. The budgets are clearly delineated, easy to see (frequently showing up as the line item second in size only to faculty salaries!), and historically subject to tight management control. Even in the face of dramatic inflation in journal prices during the past decade, library budgets have remained at a fairly constant percentage of total budget.

But with respect to information resources broadly defined, the pressures have become so great that substantial increases are likely during the coming decade. They all imply substantial increases in commitments of university budgets to information resources. How much of an increase? That's even more problematic; but increases, from the present level of say 10% (for libraries and information technologies combined) of the university budget, to as much as 12% are likely. Assuming that the library's budget remains at a constant proportion, that would imply about a 50% increase in the percentages for expenditures for the non-library components.

7.1.9 Other Effects

Other effects of the institutional context may be important but as yet they are not dealt with in *LPM*. For example, the allocation of institutional budgets among the three primary roles of the university—instruction, research, and public service—might affect the populations served, the distributions of acquisition budgets, and the allocations of staff. A more fundamental effect might come from the institution's administrative structure if it includes a high-level position with responsibility for management of all information facilities of the university. That would imply that the decisions concerning allocation of resources—budgets, staff, acquisitions of information materials, purchases of equipment and services, buildings and other capital investments—would need to deal with the entire range of facilities and not just with those of the library.

7.2
Institutional Needs for Information Services

In the earlier chapters of this book, the focus has been on libraries. Information services, as covered both by the text and by *LPM*, were primarily within that focus. Specifically, Chapter 5 dealt with the workloads and the distribution of them across the services provided by the library. However, in the context of this chapter, it is important to note that the institutional needs are the driving force for those workloads and for the distribution of them. Therefore, we will here reexamine the nature of the populations served and of their needs for information services, doing so from the institution's perspective rather than the library's.

Beyond that, it should be noted that information technologies are also important in providing information services and, from the standpoint of library management, there is need to coordinate library operations, tactical decision-making, and planning with the comparable management issues for the information technologies. Therefore, we will review some of the elements in that coordination as they relate to library management.

7.2.1 Populations Served

First, in Chapter 5 the data in the model for population served were considered as given. The simplest effect of the institutional context is in determining those data. The primary constituencies are the faculties, students, and researchers associated with the array of academic programs in the institution. To represent this effect, *LPM* identifies categories of programs (humanities, social sciences, biological sciences, natural sciences, professions) and provides means for entering data for the numbers of programs (departments, research institutes, or similar activities) and for the numbers of faculty members, students, and researchers within each category. The sums for each type of population across the categories for programs can be used as input to the "Populations Matrix." To do so, the display for academic programs includes a button labeled "Replace?" by which you can initiate that input.

7.2.2 Information Services Required

In Chapter 5, the distributions of uses across the information services of the library, including the uses of materials, were measured by expected frequency of use by each type of population. Again, while in Chapter 5 those data were taken as given, in principle they can be derived from underlying, more fundamental characteristics of the institutional objectives. While *LPM* does not currently include means for doing so, it could be expanded to incorporate such means.

Specifically, the use of "reserve book collections" is largely determined not by the library but by the faculty. Measures of the relative intensity of faculty interest in such assigned readings could serve as the basis for determining those uses. Of immediate significance in this respect is the potential role of electronic reserve and the delivery of materials from faculty members for inclusion in it.

The workloads on use of the collection for instructional purposes are totally a function of the requirements placed on students by faculty in their assignments. There is substantial difference among institutions in the extent to which faculty place emphasis on independent study and on use of library resources. Therefore, in principle, the workload on use of materials could be derived from parameters reflecting the institutional objectives in this respect.

7.2.3 Coordination of Libraries and Information Technologies

Access to Computing Within Libraries

In many institutions, the library serves as one of the primary locations for use of computers, not so much for library purposes as for computational use. The allocation of space for this purpose is significant and clearly requires coordination between the management of libraries and information technologies.

Automated Systems for Libraries

Of special concern in the coordination of libraries and information technologies is the fact that today library operations and services absolutely depend upon the information technologies. As will be discussed later in this chapter, it is very appropriate and even necessary for there to be overall policy management of the automated systems at a university, covering all uses of computers and telecommunications—academic computing, administrative computing, the integrated library system, and doubtless others (such as medical imaging or the use of supercomputers).

For the library in particular, management responsibility for technology aspects, such as the hardware and software for an integrated library system, might well lie with the campus computing staff, not the library staff. Alternatively, of course, it certainly can be managed by the library, especially if it is a dedicated facility. Clearly the choice is a matter of local priorities, capabilities, and interests.

7.3
Institutional Needs for Information Materials

This section discusses the role of library acquisitions in meeting institutional objectives. It discusses the relationship between information materials and academic productivity with respect to research, education, and public service. It discusses alternative means for measuring institutional requirements for materials. They include the use of formulas (Clapp-Jordan, for holdings, and Voigt-Susskind, for acquisitions, in particular), of "standards" (such as those of ACRL or ALA), and of comparisons with peer institutions. Parameters are presented for measuring or estimating the levels of uses resulting from various levels of institutional objectives or aspirations. The effect of these institutional decisions upon the workload faced by the library in providing services are discussed and translated into input to the *Library Planning Model*.

7.3.1 Program-Based Acquisitions Decisions

In program-based acquisitions decisions, the numbers of programs, faculty members, students, and researchers serve as part of the basis for determining the number of acquisitions needed both to serve each category of program and, accumulated, to serve the institution at large. The most well-tested model for doing so is the Voigt-Susskind model, which has been used for over twenty years as the basis for allocation among the campuses of the University of California, and which was used as a starting point for the model used in *LPM* (see Melvin Voigt, "Acquisition Rates in University Libraries," *College & Research Libraries*, July 1975, pp. 263–271). Two changes have been made from the Voigt-Susskind model, though. First, the values proposed by Voigt have been separated into two groups, one for acquisitions of books and the other for acquisitions of journals. Second, the values used by Voigt have been simplified and changed to reflect the categories used in *LPM*.

The structure of the model used in *LPM* is shown in the table below, which includes the default values used in *LPM*. Of course, as throughout *LPM*, the default values may be modified as appropriate to represent specific assessments, priorities, and experience. The model simply multiplies the number of programs in each category (row) by the values in "acquisitions per program" for the category. The results can then serve as input to the "Acquisitions Matrix."

Hypothetical numbers are included in the column for "Number of Programs" simply to illustrate the calculation in the model; they are for a representative ARL university, with one campus, 16 fields of doctoral research, two professional schools, 14,000 undergraduate students, and $75 Million in sponsored research.

| | Number of Programs | | Acquisitions Per Program | | Product of Columns 2 & 3 | |
Programmatic Element			Books	Journals	Books	Journals
Basic Acquisitions	Campuses	1	35,000	5,000	35,000	5,000
Humanities	Grad Fields	4	1,500	500	6,000	2,000
Social Sciences	Grad Fields	4	1,000	1,000	4,000	4,000
Biological Sciences	Grad Fields	4	500	1,500	2,000	6,000
Physical Sciences	Grad Fields	4	500	1,500	2,000	6,000
Professions	Grad Fields	2	3,000	3,000	6,000	6,000
Undergrad Students	Per 2,000	7	1,000		7,000	
Sponsored Research	Per $15M	5	200	800	1,000	4,000
Total					63,000	33,000

The total for volumes of journals needs to be divided by the ratio of "volumes per journal title" to get the total number of subscriptions; using the default value of 1.5, that implies about 22K journal subscriptions per annum.

7.3.2 Budget-Based Allocation Decisions

The allocation of budgets within the university is a significant measure of institutional objectives. So it can be built into both the formula model (used for acquisition decisions) and the allocation model (used for storage and acquisition versus access decisions). In the formula model, the number of academic programs is a measure of institutional objectives. In fact it is the underlying structure for the formula approach, since the number of programs in each category is the primary determinant of the results (given that the weighting factors are intended to be generic). Within the allocation model, it is represented by the parameter for "scope of collection." Currently that is measured by the ratio of library holdings to a specified standard value, but it could be measured either by the ratio of numbers of programs to some standard value or by the ratio of institutional budget to some standard value.

So, one means for incorporating budget into the formula approach is to base the number of programs that can be launched on the institutional budget and assume some percentage (like say 5%) of that institutional budget as the generic value for the library's proportion, making that percentage a parameter. And it could be incorporated into the allocation model by making it the basis for calculating scope of collection.

Given that such means can deal with incorporating the budget into the two models, the question then is how those two interrelate. One way might be to have the allocation model determine the weights to be assigned in the formula approach. The following schematic shows what this looks like:

		Publishing Statistics
		∨
	>>>>>	Allocation Model
Budget		∨
	>>>>>	Formula Approach
		∨
		Acquisitions Data Entry

The connecting lines show the possible effects that each module or source of data has on other modules. In particular, the budget module (from institutional data) can affect both the allocation model and the formula approach. In the allocation model, it affects the "scope of collection(s)" and sets a budgetary boundary condition on the total of acquisitions and access. In the formula approach, the budget module may also be used to determine the number of academic programs.

As a generic context for viewing this approach, the following table is derived from HEGIS/IPEDS data from the National Center for Educational Statistics, U.S. Department of Education.[2] It provides average data for financial variables that would seem especially relevant to the issue of institutional commitment. To produce this table, the institutions were grouped by Carnegie category, as shown in column 1.[3] The number of institutions in each category is shown in column 2. All financial figures are in "thousands of dollars." The ratios

---

[2] ICPSR Inter-university Consortium for Political and Social Research, *Integrated Postsecondary Education Data System: Higher Education Finance Data*. Washington, DC: U.S. Department of Education, National Center for Education Statistics. (ICPSR 2738A-8, yearly).

[3] The 1994 classifications of the Carnegie Foundation for the Advancement of Teaching are included in the IPEDS data files. The categories and coding for them as used in this file are as follows:

11—RESEARCH UNIVERSITIES I. These institutions offer a full range of baccalaureate programs, are committed to graduate education through the doctorate, and give high priority to research. They award 50 or more doctoral degrees each year. In addition, they receive annually $40 million or more in federal support.

12—RESEARCH UNIVERSITIES II. These institutions offer a full range of baccalaureate programs, are committed to graduate education through the doctorate, and give high priority to research. They award 50 or more doctoral degrees each year. In addition, they receive annually between $15.5 million and $40 million in federal support.

13—DOCTORAL UNIVERSITIES I. These institutions offer a full range of baccalaureate programs and are committed to graduate education through the doctorate. They award at least 40 doctoral degrees annually in five or more disciplines.

14—DOCTORAL UNIVERSITIES II. These institutions offer a full range of baccalaureate programs and are committed to graduate education through the doctorate. They award annually at least 10 doctoral degrees (in three or more disciplines), or 20 or more doctoral degrees in one or more disciplines.

(Footnote Continues)

of library expenditures, both in total and for acquisitions, to the total institutional expenditures vary only slightly from one Carnegie category to another with the exception of the schools of medicine (category 52) for which they are substantially greater.

Carnegie No.	Instruction Total	Instruction Salary	Research Total	Research Salary	Public Service Total	Public Service Salary	Academic Support Total	Academic Support Salary
11	88	$204,995	$136,561	$139,065	$69,396	$35,921	$18,874	$53,753	$28,097
12	37	$92,131	$62,886	$38,692	$20,069	$14,118	$7,806	$24,060	$11,416
13	51	$57,411	$39,930	$8,613	$4,360	$4,950	$2,254	$13,408	$7,006
14	60	$50,399	$34,279	$15,627	$7,360	$7,949	$4,403	$13,573	$6,693
21	435	$22,777	$16,292	$1,358	$612	$1,459	$637	$4,813	$2,516
22	94	$8,855	$6,166	$507	$221	$419	$186	$2,022	$992
31	166	$11,148	$7,081	$526	$180	$271	$102	$2,679	$1,166
32	467	$4,902	$3,481	$103	$41	$211	$93	$1,079	$550
40	1383	$7,570	$5,500	$18	$10	$328	$153	$1,574	$995
52	50	$62,368	$40,789	$28,691	$14,211	$20,119	$12,586	$9,234	$4,641
Library %		9.37%	13.70%						
Acquis %		3.69%	5.41%						

21—MASTER'S (COMPREHENSIVE) UNIVERSITIES AND COLLEGES I. These institutions offer a full range of baccalaureate programs and are committed to graduate education through the master's degree. They award 40 or more master's degrees annually in three or more disciplines.

22—MASTER'S (COMPREHENSIVE) UNIVERSITIES AND COLLEGES II. These institutions offer a full range of baccalaureate programs and are committed to graduate education through the master's degree. They award 20 or more master's degrees annually in one or more disciplines.

31—BACCALAUREATE (LIBERAL ARTS) COLLEGES I. These institutions are primarily undergraduate colleges with major emphasis on baccalaureate degree programs. They award 40 percent or more of their baccalaureate degrees in liberal arts fields and are restrictive in admissions.

32—BACCALAUREATE COLLEGES II. These institutions are primarily undergraduate colleges with major emphasis on baccalaureate degree programs. They award less than 40 percent of their baccalaureate degrees in liberal arts fields or are less restrictive in admissions.

40—ASSOCIATE OF ARTS COLLEGES. These institutions offer associate of arts certificate or degree programs and, with few exceptions, offer no baccalaureate degrees.

50, 60—SPECIALIZED INSTITUTIONS. These institutions offer degrees ranging from the baccalaureate to the doctorate. At least 50 percent of the degrees awarded by these institutions are in a single discipline. They include: 51—Theological seminaries, Bible colleges, and other institutions offering degrees in religion; 52—Medical schools and medical centers; 53—Other separate health profession schools; 54—Schools of engineering and technology; 55—Schools of business and management; 56—Schools of art, music, and design; 57—Schools of law; 58—Teachers colleges; 59—Other specialized institutions; 60—Tribal colleges.

Carnegie	No.	Total Expenditures		Library		
		Total	Salary & Wages	Total	Acquis.	Salary
11	88	$612,566	$373,826	$16,938	$5,684	$11,254
12	37	$255,724	$157,000	$8,253	$3,509	$4,744
13	51	$143,949	$86,333	$5,208	$2,374	$2,834
14	60	$137,818	$81,839	$4,263	$1,755	$2,508
21	435	$57,047	$33,492	$1,773	$636	$1,137
22	94	$26,118	$14,027	$745	$260	$485
31	166	$36,061	$17,472	$1,263	$539	$724
32	467	$16,186	$7,946	$402	$150	$252
40	1,383	$18,127	$11,731	$343	$91	$252
52	20	$234,071	$100,532	$1,788	$793	$995
Library %		3.69%	5.41%	100.00%		
Acquis %		1.18%	2.58%	38.81%	100.00%	

7.3.3 Comparison with Peer Institutions

Another means for assessing the appropriate level of expenditures for acquisitions is by comparison with peer institutions. In principle, there are three contexts for such comparison: (1) one reflecting past academic objectives, (2) one representing future academic aspirations, and (3) one reflecting the current academic program. The first two are likely to involve the identification of a small set, perhaps 10 to 12, of institutions that are regarded as similar to the institution of focus with respect to their academic programs. The third is perhaps best represented by the relative position (based on total expenditures for education and research) of the institution of focus within the Carnegie Classification in which it falls.

In each case, data for making these comparisons can be found in the IPEDS database.

7.4

Institutional Governance of Information Activities

In this section, "governance" is intended to refer to the means for determination of policies, and "information resources" is intended to refer to libraries, to computers used in support of academic programs, to computers used in support of administrative activities, to instructional media and related equipment, and to telecommunications. As a result of the increasing importance of information resources in academic institutions, the issue of governance for them has become one of increasing concern. Some have argued that information resources should be dealt with in a unified governance structure, usually with the view that they are substitutable for each other (fungible, as the economists say) or at the least that they are now so interrelated that they must be dealt with as a totality. Others have argued that each of these is operationally different and that to combine them into a single governance structure will impose a bureaucratic burden that is unwarranted by the presumed gains, which would be at best ephemeral.

The purpose of this section is to identify the current models for governance of information resources in U.S. academic institutions to the extent that they can be identified from published information. The objective in doing so is to provide a starting point for more detailed and complete assessment based on other methodology that would obtain data directly from institutions. The focus on U.S. institutions is solely because the relevant data for them are readily accessible.

The data presented in this paper relate to the U.S. institutions whose libraries are members of the Association of Research Libraries (the major academic libraries of the U.S.). They are derived from "Higher Education Directory" (HED).[4] The library adminstrator titles from HED have been compared with those in a recent (February 1997) "ARL Membership Roster," and the two are reasonably consistent.

Among other things, HED lists the titles and names for officials in each institution of higher education in the United States. The order of listing appears to be that of administrative precedence, sequenced in an order of relative ranking with the highest-ranking officers listed first; then typically follow various administrative officers (in which, although no relative ranking is directly implied by the titles, it is likely there is an order of hierarchy underlying the sequence); then follow deans (i.e., the officers responsible for specific schools, colleges, or other academic activities).

With respect to the sequence, it is relevant to note that the position of library administrators on the average is earlier in the sequence than that of administrators of either academic computing or administrative computing. Relatively few of the institutions identify a position related to instructional media and, even for those that do, they are far down in the sequence.

7.4.1 Commentary on Terminology

Titles for Academic Administrators

Terms used in the United States for the chief administrative officer (CAO) can be any of the following: president (overwhelmingly the most frequent),

---

[4] *Higher Education Directory,* published yearly by Higher Education Publications, Falls Church, Virginia

chancellor, executive officer, director, superintendent, or virtually any combination of those (e.g., president/director). To an extent, use of terms other than "president" reflects the fact that some institutions are part of a larger entity (such as the nine campuses of the University of California). In such cases, sometimes the term "president" is used for the CAO of the larger entity, and another term is then used for the constituent institution (in the case of UC, "president" being used for its CAO and "chancellor" for the CAO of each of the nine campuses). But that is by no means necessarily the case. For the campuses of the California State University and College System, the CAO for the system is called "chancellor" and the CAO for each campus is called "president"!

For other levels of administrative position, the titles become much more diffuse. In some cases, they will be variations of the CAO's title with some qualifier attached—for example, "vice-president." Thus there will be titles such as "Academic Vice-Chancellor" or "Vice-President for Administration and Finance." In some cases, the term "provost" will be used, especially for a high academic administrative position. The terms "director," "superintendent," and "officer" are also used, again with qualifiers. In some cases the term "dean" is used for what are clearly administrative positions—such as "Dean of Students." Of course, the usual terms for hierarchy—associate and assistant, in particular—can be used with any of those titles.

Titles Relating to Information Resources

For the titles of position of administrative responsibility for various information resource activities, there are terms that can be ambiguous. The terms "Information Services" and "Information Resources" usually will refer to library-related responsibilities or activities when used in a librarian's frame of reference. However, when computer applications are involved, they tend to be assigned to administrative computer contexts. All of the terms "Information Systems and Computing," "Information Technology," "Information Systems," "Information and Technology" and so on usually refer to technology contexts.

7.4.2 Governance Patterns

The governance patterns for libraries, computing, telecommunication, and media will be discussed by reviewing the titles for administrators and the governance patterns for each type of information activity.

Summary of Titles for Library Administrators

The titles for library administrators occur with frequencies as follows (the numbers being the number of institutions using that title, for the total of 95 institutions):

1 Associate Provost, Information Services/Technology
1 Associate Vice-President, University Libraries
  Vice-Provost, Director of Libraries
1 Vice Provost, University Libraries
1 Vice-President, Director of Libraries
1 Vice-President of Library/Information Resources
1 Vice-President and University Librarian
7 Dean of Libraries
2 Dean of Library
1 Dean of Library Affairs
2 Dean of Library Services
5 Dean of University Libraries
1 Dean of the University Library

1 Dean and Director of Libraries
1 Dean and University Librarian
1 Director of General Libraries
19 Director of Libraries
3 Director of the Library
8 Director of University Libraries
1 Director and Dean of Libraries
7 Librarian
1 Librarian of the University
1 Library Director
25 University Librarian
1 University Library Director

Note that in 21 cases the term "dean" appears in the title, and that is consistent with the perception that almost universally the administrative officer for the library functions at the level of academic deans (i.e., positions that are responsible for major academic programs, such as schools and colleges—the equivalents of "faculties" at universities based on a European and Latin American model of development). Beyond that, in seven cases, they function at the vice-CAO level, which presumably puts them at least on a par with deans. This reflects the fact that at most if not all of the ARL institutions, the library directors and, indeed, the professional library staff are regarded as part of the academic community. The University of California, in particular, specifically identifies professional librarians as "academic" appointments.

In 34 cases, the term is one or another variant of "librarian," and in 37 cases, the title is one or another variant of "director."

In the listing above, seven titles have been set at the beginning of the list. They each imply administrative responsibilities other than just for the library—associate provost, associate vice-president, vice-provost, vice-president. In most of those cases, the title is clearly focused on library responsibility. But two cases—"Associate Provost, Information Services/Technology" and "Vice-President of Library-Information Resources"—imply something more or different, and in one of the cases where the apparent focus is the library (i.e., "Vice President, Director of Libraries" at Columbia) actual responsibilities are in fact greater, encompassing the campus academic computer system as well.

Looking at those three cases, in all of them the position is in fact filled by a professional librarian. Indeed, about a dozen of the library administrators have been assigned administrative responsibility for academic computing at their institutions, though their titles may not reflect such broadened scope.

Considering the entire set of 95 institutions, in all but one case positions of responsibility for administration of the library are filled by professional librarians. The unique case is Harvard, where the identified position of responsibility is focused completely on the library but is filled by a faculty member, not by a professional librarian; even there, however, the person actually responsible for operations of the library is a librarian and reports not to the identified faculty person but to the CAO for Harvard College.

It is to be noted that in absolutely none of the listings is there more than one position identified that is related to the library. Only the position of chief responsibility is ever included. Even in cases where the title implies wider responsibilities (such as at Stanford or Columbia), there is no separate position of "library director." The implication is clear: The director of libraries, whatever the title may be, is regarded as responsible for library operations and policies.

Before discussing issues related to governance, there is one terminological issue implied by the titles for library administrators on which to comment. Note that the terms "library" and "libraries" appear with almost equal frequency. Where the term "library" is used, the implication is that the library is seen as a single administrative entity; where the term "libraries" is used, the library is seen as an array of branch libraries. The term used at the University of Texas, Austin ("Director of General Libraries") is specifically revealing in this respect. In either case, though, there can be two libraries—medicine and law— at the institution that may or may not be included in the responsibilities of the general library director position; if they are at the institution but not under the general librarian, the directors of them usually will report to the respective faculty deans.

Governance Structure for Academic Libraries

Turning to the issue of patterns of governance for libraries, it is relevant to note that, as described above, the library administrative officer is almost universally operating at a level equivalent to that of deans, as directors of major academic units. In over 20% of the cases the title is indeed "dean," but beyond that, whatever the title they function at that level. The crucial point is that deans generally report directly to the CAO for the institution or at the least to the "Executive Vice-CAO" or to the "Academic Vice-CAO," and in all cases the executive vice-CAO or academic vice-CAO are functionally equivalent to the CAO itself. In other words, for virtually every ARL institution, the library director (whatever the title) reports directly to the institution's CAO (or functionally equivalent "Executive Vice-CAO" or "Academic Vice-CAO").

The role of "committees" is even more evident. At no ARL library is there any "committee" functioning between the campus administrative officer and the library director, whatever the title. There is no case in which the policies of the library are determined by a committee. In all cases, they are determined by the interaction between CAO (or equivalent) and library director.

Now, having said that, committees play exceptionally important roles at every ARL institution—as advisors to the library director and/or to the CAO and/or to the faculty (i.e., academic teaching and research staff). In those roles, they can serve as a support to the library director by assuring the faculty that the views of the academic program are represented in library decisions; they can provide means for advising the CAO and/or the faculty about problems.

Summary of Titles for Computer-Related Administrators

The situation with respect to computer-related administration is much more complicated than that for library administration. Most significant is the fact that on many, if not most, campuses there is a division between "academic computing" and "administrative computing." Another is the fact that today computers are simply one among the array of information technologies; telecommunications in particular is another crucial one of them.

Although the respective roles of each are probably evident, to be specific, "administrative computing" covers those facilities and operations involved in support to campus administration and, to some degree, departmental administration. That typically includes budget and finance, payroll, student records, class registration, nonacademic services, grant and contract administration. In contrast, "academic computing" covers those facilities and operations that support the use of computing in research and instruction, by both faculty and students.

The division of the two reflects quite different priorities as well as differences in the needs of people served, the software needed to serve them, the operations needed for control of data. Administrative computing is driven by established schedules and is very patterned. Academic computing is driven by ad hoc demands and is completely unpatterned.

It also reflects the historic differences in the staff who established and have operated the two facilities. Administrative computing arose from data processing centers (in the early days, all based on use of punched cards). Academic computing arose out of computer science departments and the use of computers in numerical analysis—number crunching, as it was called.

As a result, in many cases there are two and, in some cases, more positions of responsibility for computing. In other cases, that division may or may not be reflected in the enumerated titles because administrative computing may be treated as the responsibility of a vice-CAO for administration and thus not be separately identified. Finally, in still other cases the two kinds of computing operations may be combined, using a single central computing facility.

Anyway, there are the following distributions of titles related to administration of information technologies:

9 No position
17 Vice-CAO position (presumably both academic and administrative)

10 Assoc Vice-CAO (presumably both academic and administrative)

2 Asst Vice-CAO (presumably both academic and administrative)

29 Director (presumably both academic and administrative)

5 Vice-CAO and Director of Academic Computing

8 Academic Computing only

2 Administrative Computing only

2 Vice-CAO, Director of Academic, and Director of Administrative, separate

11 Director of Academic and Director of Administrative, separate

In this listing, the parenthetical comment "presumably both academic and administrative" is made when nothing in the title clearly reveals that there is anything limiting about the responsibilities. However, in many of those cases, the position is focused on academic computing, with administrative computing being the responsibility of a vice-CAO for administration. It is likely that such is the situation in as many as half the cases so qualified.

With that caveat, the great majority (58) of institutions have established a single position and it is possible that it is responsible for all aspects of computing, telecomm, network development, and so forth on the campus. That makes sense and reflects good management policy. It is likely that there may still be separate computing facilities for the two kinds of service (academic and administrative), and they would probably have "directors," but the policy responsibility for both is still highly focused.

It is surprising that in nine cases there are no positions identified in the listing; however, recall that in about a dozen cases the library administrator has been assigned responsibility for academic computing. That may account for cases with no positions identified.

For the remaining 18 institutions, there are multiple positions, probably reflecting a difference between policy responsibility and operational responsibility.

Governance of Telecommunications

In the table presented above for titles related to administration of information technologies, there are no titles specific to telecommunications.

Governance of Instructional Media and Technology

These activities are largely procedural, involving the scheduling for delivery of equipment to classrooms, and the maintenance of that equipment, both in the classrooms and centrally stored. Only 13 of the 95 ARL institutions clearly identify a separate administrative position responsible for instructional media, and for those that do, the position is quite far down the sequence in hierarchy.

Titles for Administrators of Instructional Media and Technology	
Director of Educational Media	Director, Instructional Media Technology
Director, Academic Support Systems	Director, Instructional Services Center
Director, Audio-Visual Department	Director, Instructional Technology Systems
Director, Audio-Visual Service	Director, Media Services
Director, Instructional Development	Director, Media Technology Services
Director, Instructional Media	Director, Teaching & Learning Center
Director, Instructional Media Center	

There is nothing in the titles that implies anything about the governance structure for instructional technology. In some of the ARL institutions, the media (i.e., the disks, video tapes, records, etc.) are stored in the library and are therefore subject to the governance patterns of the library. In general, though, the equipment-related activities appear to be treated as an administrative function, reporting to the appropriate person in the office of the CAO, but without further policy control.

7.4.3 Centralized Management

An issue in institutional management is whether management of information activities, both individually and as a whole, should be centralized or decentralized.

Library Management

Historically, libraries in U.S. academic institutions have been centrally managed in the respect that the director of the library generally reports directly to the CAO. Both policy and operations are the responsibility of the director of libraries, and committees are essentially advisory to the institution's CAO and the director of libraries.

A question of continuing debate is whether there should be similar centralized management of policy for information technologies in academic institutions—an "information technology czar." As the listing presented above exhibits, there are some institutions in which such centralized management has been implemented, although in most of them the several information activities still function independently in policy decisions, administration, and operations.

A subsidiary question is whether such centralized management should encompass operations as well.

A related question is whether such centralized management of policy should combine all information activities—libraries as well as the information technologies—within a single structure. Again, some institutions, though relatively few, have done so.

In the following sections, the issues related to the relative merits of centralized management will be discussed, first with respect to policies and operations of information technology, and second with respect to whether libraries should be combined with information technology in such centralized management of policy and operations.

Information Technology Management

Historically (prior to 20 years ago), management of computers was universally highly centralized. They were large machines and decisions were governed by "Grosch's law."[5] Then came the microcomputer revolution of 20 years ago and suddenly everything changed. Today, academic computing tends to be a mix of centralized management (of the mainframe equipment still needed for massive "number cruching" and, especially, image processing) and decentralized management (with departments controlling their own microcomputer installations).

In contrast to academic computing, administrative computing is still usually highly centralized, though frequently with distributed input and output so that academic departments can use the centralized data for local management.

In either event, but especially if there is significant decentralization, there would be great value in having a high-level policy committee covering all aspects of automated information systems—responsible for policy regarding computing systems that support academic programs (research and instruction), administrative data processing, library operations and services, medical diagnosis and hospital records, and for policy regarding telecommunication systems to interconnect the computer systems as necessary and to communicate with remote sources (such as among several campuses, with Internet, etc.). It would include policy responsibility for the entire array of computer and telecomm equipment within the institution—central mainframes, client-server systems,

---

[5] Grosch, H.R.J. "High Speed Arithmetic: The Digital Computer as a Research Tool," *Journal of the Optical Society of America* 43, 4 (April 1953). Herbert R.J. Grosch, during his time as an IBM employee, said "computing power increases with the square of its costs," or to put it succinctly, "bigger is better"—a beautiful marketing strategy!

standalone PCs, supercomputers—and for other policy issues such as staffing patterns.

Let's call that committee the "Autmoated Information Systems Policy Committee." The membership of that committee should consist of representation of all operational activities that depend upon the use of automated systems. That would include the vice-CAO for Budget and Finance, the director of the library, and representatives of the several faculties that most critically depend upon computing.

Note that representation on that committee does not imply that the committee controls policy for those represented on it. Quite to the contrary, it means that *they* control the policies of the automated systems that they depend upon to meet their operational needs. This is vitally important, so that the needs of the library system or of academic computing, for example, with respect to services provided by the automated systems, will be recognized in policy decisions.

Total Information Resource Management

However, even assuming that such an information technology policy committee were established, an independent question is whether there should be centralized management of operational responsibilities. At least a few institutions have established a position of central management responsibility for all information resources, libraries, and computer technologies combined. This may reflect the view that there needs to be not only policy coordination among them but perhaps also centralized management of them.

Frankly, given the effectiveness of distributed computing systems today, there is no need for there to be centralized control of operations, even if there were a single central server for all kinds of computing. Operational needs in academic computing, administrative computing, instructional media use, and medical services are all substantially different. And telecommunications, while it must be well integrated with computing, has its own independent operational imperatives. To attempt to centralize operational management for all of these is likely to be catastrophic rather than efficient.

Furthermore, while it is conceivable that a single central facility might be an efficient server for the full range of computing requirements, the operational needs are almost certainly better met by independent servers for each major type of user.

In this context, as was indicated in the earlier discussion in this chapter concerning coordination between management of libraries and management of information technology, responsibility for an integrated library system hardware and software might appropriately be assigned to the information technology manager. Having said that, it must also be said that the policy needs for the library system are totally different from those required for computing and telecommunications. The view that, in some abstract sense, the library and the computer are both "information resources," though conceptually appealing, becomes meaningless when it is used to lump totally different management requirements under one policy committee. Virtually every issue of policy decision—the requirements in staffing, the nature of services, the management of operations, the uses of funds, the relationship to other institutions—is totally different in the two contexts of the library, on the one hand, and of the automated systems, on the other.

To put the library under an "Automated Systems Management Committee" simply "because it is an information resource and uses an automated system" makes as little sense as it would to put the Office of Budget and Finance under such a committee "because it is an information resource and uses an automated system." Why not put all of the faculties of the University under such a committee "because they are all information resources and use an automated system" (in instruction and research)?

The important point is what is needed to manage academic libraries wherever they may be. In that respect, it is essential to recognize that the crucial need for libraries and the institutions they serve is that policy-making relate to their operational responsibilities, not to their use of an automated integrated library system. The fact that it is automated is immaterial; it is simply a tool as far as library responsibilities and operations are concerned. To put the library system under the policy guidance of a committee whose concern is with automated information systems would be disastrous in regard to those operational responsibilities.

In particular, the crucial operational aspects relate to the services provided by the library, for which the automated system is simply a tool, and to the quality of the data which is provided by the library, whether through automated systems or otherwise, and that is determined by the staff of the libraries, not by the automated system. All of those are responsibilities of library staff that require policy guidance that will directly reflect the needs of faculty and of the academic program. None of them is concerned with the operation of the automated system except as it may facilitate or interfere with them, and in that respect they should not be under the policy management of a committee focused on automated systems but should instead be external to it so that the library's needs can be brought as pressure on that committee, not the reverse.

They relate to policies in acquisition of materials, and those decisions are not determined by automation but by the needs of users of the library with respect to the full range of materials. Those decisions require careful balancing of needs with the alternative range of forms of publication; those include auto-mated forms (such as CD-ROM as well as online) but for the foreseeable future they will continue to be predominantly print forms (especially mono-graphs but also journals).

The services include the full range of information services, nonautomat-ed as well as automated, instructional and consulting services, and publication services.

In other words, the real needs for policy decisions concerning the library are not at all driven by or determined by issues related to automated systems. They are driven by the imperatives of library operations.

Bibliography

References for Carnegie Classification

A Classification of Institutions of Higher Education, with a foreword by Ernest L. Boyer, 1987 ed. Princeton, NJ: Carnegie Foundation for the Advancement of Teaching, c1987. Series title: Original edition: A Carnegie Foundation Technical Report, Carnegie Foundation Technical Report.

A Classification of Institutions of Higher Education, 1994 ed. Princeton, NJ: Carnegie Foundation for the Advancement of Teaching, 1994. 1 computer disk; 3 1/2 in. System requirements: IBM com-patible PC.

A Classification of Institutions of Higher Education. Princeton, NJ: Carnegie Foundation for the Advancement of Teaching. Began with 1973? Series title: <1987>: Carnegie Foundation Technical Report, 1994-: Technical Report/Carnegie Foundation for the Advancement of Teaching,

A Classification of Institutions of Higher Education, with a foreword by Ernest L. Boyer, 1994 ed. Princeton, NJ: Carnegie Foundation for the Advancement of Teaching, c1994. Series title: A Technical Report, Technical Report (Carnegie Foundation for the Advancement of Teaching).

A Classification of Institutions of Higher Education, with a foreword by Ernest L. Boyer, 1987 ed. Princeton, NJ: Carnegie Foundation for the Advancement of Teaching, c1987. Series title: A Carnegie Foundation Technical Report. Language: English.

References for Economics of Libraries

Baumol, William J. *Economics of Academic Libraries.* Prepared for Council on Library Resources by Mathematica, Inc. Washington, DC: American Council on Education, 1973.

Bergman, Jed I. *Managing Change in the Nonprofit Sector: Lessons from the Evolution of Five Independent Research Libraries.* San Francisco: Jossey-Bass, 1996.

Cummings, Martin Marc. *The Economics of Research Libraries.* Washington, DC: Council on Library Resources, 1986.

Duffus, R.L. *Our Starving Libraries: Studies in Ten American Communities During the Depression Years.* Boston; New York: Houghton Mifflin, 1933.

Pasadena (CA). *Pasadena Public Library Future Funding Task Force. Recommendations for Financing the Pasadena Public Library System. Presented to the Pasadena Public Library Commission by the Citizen's Task Force on Alternative Financing.* Pasadena, CA: Task Force, February 16, 1993.

Prentice, Ann E. *Financial Planning for Libraries,* 2nd ed. Lanham, MD: Scarecrow Press, 1996. This is an excellent coverage of the issues related to library budgeting. Chapter IV, on Data Gathering Methodologies, includes discussion of unit costing, cost accounting, cost/benefit analysis, cost effectiveness, and model building.

The Economic of Academic Libraries. Allen Kent, Jacob Cohen, and K. Leon Montgomery, issue editors. *Library Trends* 28, 1 (Summer 1979). Urbana, I: University of Illinois Graduate School of Library Science, 1979. The articles in this issue of *Library Trends* provide excellent examples of modeling, including not only applications but pitfalls.

8

Information Production and Distribution

Introduction

This chapter deals with a crucial strategic context for a library, the sources for the information it contains, the processes in production of that information, and the impact of decisions by the information publication and distribution industry upon library acquisitions and services.

8.1
The Production of Information

8.1.1 Authorship

Authorship is one means for creation of information materials. In general, the costs incurred in authorship appear to be substantially greater than the typical return to the author, as represented by royalties on sales. For example, a professor on the average might have two articles a year accepted for publication, each of about 10 to 20 pages in length. The cost of authorship is likely to reflect 25% of the yearly salary (taking that as the commitment of time in research), amounting to say $20K (including benefits). For those articles, the professor usually receives no royalties and in some cases may even need to pay page charges to cover some of the costs of publication. Of course, the benefit to the professor in publication is tangible, in the form of tenure and promotion.

For authors in general, the picture is not much different. For the few best sellers, there are innumerable books that sell just a few thousand copies and some that sell virtually none. In technical and professional fields, break even for the publisher is likely to occur at the level of a few thousand copies, and the royalty income to the author might be on the order of $5,000 to $10,000. Yet it is likely to have taken years to write the book.

8.1.2 Processing

Processing is a second means by which information materials can be produced. It is represented by the production of databases, by the organization of data for presentation, and by the selection of material to be acquired and distributed. For this means of production of information, there are potential means for measurement of the information produced, one of which has been established as valid and useful.[1]

The following is a definition of the term "information" that is appropriate for assessment of processing as a means for production of information:

> Information is that property of data (i.e., recorded symbols) which represents (and measures) effects of processing of them.

At least the following four levels of processes are covered by that definition:

1. Data Transfer (e.g., communication by the telephone)
2. Data Selection (e.g., retrieval from a file)
3. Data Analysis (e.g., sequencing and formatting)
4. Data Reduction (e.g., replacement of data by a surrogate)

For the first, there is a well-established measure; for the other three, there are successive generalizations that will be presented that reflect the increasing complexity of information provided.

Measure for Communication of Information

The only formally recognized measure for information is called the "entropy measure." It was developed by Claude Shannon as the basis for "information theory" (for which read *communication* theory).[2] It measures the amount of information (but not its value) by the statistical properties of the signals transmitted. That is, let $X = (x_1, x_2, \ldots, x_M)$ be a set of signals and let $p_i = p(x_i)$ be the *a priori* probability that signal x_i will be transmitted; let $n_i = \log(1/p_i)$. Then, the amount of information conveyed by signal x_i is given by

$$H(x_i) = -\log(p_i) = \log(1/p_i) = n_i$$

[1] Hayes, Robert M., "Measurement of Information," in Vakkari, Pertti, and Cronin, Blaise (eds.), *Conceptions of Library and Information Science*. London: Taylor Graham, 1992, pp. 268–285.

Hayes, Robert M., "Measurement of Information," *Information Processing and Management* 29, 1 (1993), pp. 1–11.

[2] Shannon, Claude, and Weaver, Warren, *The Mathematical Theory of Communication*. Urbana: University of Illinois Press, 1949.

For the set of signals $X = (x_1, x_2, \ldots, x_M)$:

$$H(X) = -\Sigma p_i \star \log(p_i) = \Sigma p_i \star \log(1/p_i) = \Sigma p_i \star n_i$$

The following heuristic has been used to justify this measure. Consider two signals that are successively transmitted. Normally, one would want the measure of the amount of information provided by the two signals to be equal to the sum of the amount provided by each independently. That is, $H(x$ AND $y)$ is to equal $(H(x) + H(y))$. If information is to be a function of the probability of the signal, then the measure needs to recognize that the probability of the two statistically independent signals x AND y is the product of the independent probabilities $p(x)$ and $p(y)$. The logarithm is one function that does so.

As part of the basis for developing a heuristic justification for the generalizations of this measure that we will be presenting, it is valuable to examine a semantic interpretation of this measure. The recipient of a given signal needs to determine how to interpret it and, to do so, needs to perform some kind of "table look-up"; the amount of information provided by the signal is exactly the measure of the number of binary decisions that need to be made in that table look-up process (assuming a structure for the table that reflects the appropriate encoding of the signal). An underlying parameter is the size of the table (i.e., the number of entries in it), representing the size of the semantic vocabulary in the communication. Simply to illustrate, consider the case where signals are all equally probable; then for all i, $1/p_i = M$, the size of the file of signals. The entropy measure for information is then simply $\log_2(M)$ and represents exactly the number of decisions in binary search of such a file. And, typically, the amount of information conveyed by a signal is represented by the number of bits used in transmission of it (assuming appropriate encoding).

The entropy or Shannon measure has been of exceptional value in design of communication systems. In that context, a specific problem with which it deals is the effect of errors in transmission. The problem arises because there are finite probabilities that a signal in being communicated may be in error, as a result of "noise." The design requirement is to assure a desired level of accuracy, expressed as a low probability of error, and the question is how that is to be accomplished and what it costs to do so. The answer is the use of redundancy, usually in the form of "check digits" that reveal whether an error has occurred and that can even correct errors that do occur. What it costs to achieve a desired level of accuracy is expressed by one of the fundamental theorems of communication theory: An exponential decrease in the probability of error can be obtained with a linear increase in the length of the signal.

While the entropy measure has been exceptionally valuable in the context of communication theory where the only concern is with efficient transmission of signals, it has rarely if ever been successfully applied in contexts in which the value of the signal, measured in some way, is important.

Measure for Selection of Information

As a result, a generalization of Shannon's measure, called "weighted entropy," has been developed that indeed seems to provide means for recognizing both the statistical issues involved in efficient transmission and the importance of the signal to the user or recipient of it. This measure assigns to each signal, x_i, in addition to the *a priori* probability, another function $r_i = r(x_i)$, which measures that importance. Such a measure of importance can be illustrated by the "relevancy" of the signal, in the sense in which that term is used in retrieval system evaluation.[3] The resulting weighted entropy measure, which will be here called "significance," for a given signal is given by:

$$S(x_i) = r_i \star \log(1/p_i) = r_i \star n_i$$

For the set of signals $X = (x_1, x_2, \ldots, x_M)$: $S(X) = \Sigma r_i \star p_i \star \log(1/p_i) = \Sigma r_i \star p_i \star n_i$

Note that if all signals are equally important (which is the usual assumption for telecommunication system design), the weighted entropy measure reduces to the Shannon measure; if all signals are equally probable, it reduces to what is called the *relevancy* measure in the field of information storage and retrieval. Thus, it is a suitable generalization for each.

To provide a heuristic justification for this as a measure of information, consider a file of items from which we wish to retrieve (i.e., select) information. Let an item in the file consist of N bits, and let a request, Y, be matched against each item in the file in order to identify which of them matches the query on a specified set of n of the N bits. What is the amount of information provided by the file in response to such a query? As we have pointed out, Shannon's entropy measure considers only statistical probabilities, not measures of value (such as relevancy). Let the significance of a signal, say x_i, be regarded as a function of the two quantities, $p(x_i)$, the a priori probability, and $r(x_i)$, the relevance: $S(x_i) = S(p(x_i), r(x_i))$. For simplicity in describing the heuristic, suppose that each item is equally likely, and that $r(x_i)$ is measured by the proportion of the N bits on which x_i and the request y match. Then,

$$S(x_i) = S(1/2^N, (x_i \text{ AND } y)/N)$$

Consider now selecting a second item from the file. It is reasonable to expect that a measure of the amount of information from both should be treated as the sum of the amount from each, that is,

[3] Guiasu, Silviu, *Information Theory with Applications.* New York: McGraw-Hill, 1977. Hayes, Robert M., "The Measurement of Information from a File," in Stevens, Mary E., et al (eds.), *Statistical Association Methods for Mechanized Documentation, Proceedings of the Symposium, Washington, 1964.* Washington, DC: National Bureau of Standards Miscellaneous Publication 269, December 15, 1965, pp. 161–162.

$$S(x_i, x_j) = S(x_i) + S(x_j)$$

One solution to this functional equation is the proposed measure:

$$S(x_i) = r(x_i) \star \log(1/p(x_i))$$

Measure for Organization of Information

For the third level of processing—analysis and organization—a distinction will be made between the information conveyed by the content of a signal, which will be called "semantic information," and that by the structure, which will be called "syntactic information."[4]

To establish a measure for this division between syntactic and semantic information, consider a record of F fields. Let there be associated with each possible value in each field an *a priori* probability; thus for field j and value i_j, there is a probability $p(ji_j)$, where for each j, $\Sigma_i(p(ji_j)) = 1$. A given signal is then the combination of a specific set of values, one for each field. The probability of the particular combination, assuming independence, is then the product of the $p(ji_j)$ and the amount of information conveyed by the signal is the logarithm of that product.

That total amount of information, however, is divided between syntactic and semantic as follows:

Syntactic Information	Semantic Information
$\displaystyle\sum_{j=1}^{F} \log(1/p(ji_j)) - \log(\sum_{j=1}^{F} 1/p(ji_j))$	$\displaystyle\log(\sum_{j=1}^{F} 1/p(ji_j))$

Substituting $n(ij_j)$ for $\log(1/p(ij_j))$

$\displaystyle\sum_{j=1}^{F} n(ji_j) - \log(\sum_{j=1}^{F} 2^{n(ji_j)})$	$\displaystyle\log(\sum 2^{n(ji_j)})$

This can be interpreted in the following way: The semantic information is the number of bits that reflects the size of the database required to store the set of terms; that database is the means to translate the terms from each field into their meanings. The syntactic information is the total information, conveyed by the sum of the $n(ji_j)$, less the amount of semantic information.

As a rationale for this measure of the third level of processing—analysis and organization—we will examine the nature and effects of the structuring of data. The objective of structure is to establish "separability" of data into com-

---

[4] Hayes, Robert M., "A Theory for File Organization," in Karplus, Walter (ed.), *Online Computing: Time-Shared Man-Computer Systems.* New York: McGraw-Hill, 1967, pp. 264–289.

ponents, to reduce permutations to combinations, and to reduce the number of decisions required to identify a symbol by increasing the number of dimensions embodied in its structure.

To illustrate, consider a set of symbols. If each of them is treated as independent, with no structure or organization imposed, the recipient of one of them must match it against the entire set of symbols in order to determine what it means. However, suppose a structure has been imposed on the symbols. For simplicity in exposition, we will characterize that as "subdividing the symbol into fields." Just to provide a simple illustration, consider a symbol set that is used to identify people. Each of 16 persons could be uniquely identified by a four-bit array; one would need to have a table with 16 entries in order to determine which person was represented by a given four-bit code.

But now, let's impose a structure on that code:

(Male/Female) (Young/Old) (Rich/Poor) (Urban/Rural)

Suddenly, instead of needing to recognize 16 different things, we need recognize only 8 different things, the combination of which gives us the full set of 16. Receiving a signal, say 0110, we can easily identify the category as "male, old, poor, urban"; we have looked at four tables of just two entries each, yet we have identified one from 16 categories.

The imposition of a matrix upon a set of data accomplishes the same objective. One need deal only with $(N + M)$ things rather than $(N \times M)$ things (where N and M are the dimensions of the matrix).

Of course, there are two problems that must be recognized: Symbols may not be uniquely characterized by the structure (e.g., there may be more than one person in a category), and not all categories from the combination are necessarily represented. But while those effects may modify details of the illustration, they do not change the basic principles or the significance of the reduction of effort provided by imposition of a structure.

The measure identified above measures that effect. That is, let the source signal be N bits in length (so that we have 2^N symbols). Let's divide it into F fields of lengths $(n_1, n_2, \ldots n_F)$ bits, averaging N/F. Instead of looking among 2^N entries, we need look only among the sum of the (2^{n_i}). The content of the original N bits of information is conveyed by the logarithm of that sum. That has been called "semantic information," since it is that part of the total symbol that involves table look-up (which can be interpreted as "meaning") with the remainder being "syntactic information," conveyed by the structure. Note that, as F increases, the amount of semantic information rapidly decreases, and the syntactic information increases linearly.

This measure identifies the process of analysis and organization with the docomposition (i.e., analysis) of the original symbol into component fields and the resulting structure (i.e., organization) with the syntactic result. The information produced by the process is then the syntactic information.

Note that if there is only one field ($F = 1$), the syntactic information is zero and the semantic information is simply the original entropy measure. This means that the proposed measure is a consistent generalization of the entropy measure.

We will not here discuss the means for creating structures of for analyzing data as the basis for doing so except to comment that the several parameters identified in the proposed measures potentially play roles in analysis and in data reduction. For example, we can use r as the basis for clustering. We can use linkages (such as embodied in a "hypertext" structure or a citation structure) as a basis for decomposition and reduction.

Measure for Reduction of Information

We turn now to the final level of processing, data reduction. It can be exemplified by curve fitting, factor analysis, clustering, and similar means for reducing large amounts of data to a limited set of parameters. In general, these mathematical processes can be considered as transformations of the data, treated as a vector space, into alternative dimensional representations in which the original data have nearly zero values on a large number of the transformed dimensions.

To illustrate, consider data representing a set of F test scores (represented by a total of N bits) for a number, $M,$ of individuals (the classical example for factor analysis). Those data can be considered as an ($M \times N$) matrix. Methods such as factor analysis, eigenvector analysis, and clustering are means by which an alternative "basis" (i.e., dimensional transformation) can be determined. The original data, treated as vectors, can now be represented by their "projections" on the new basis. In virtually any realistic context, only a few of the new basis vectors contribute significantly to the representation of the original data.

The result is that much of the significant information from the original set of ($M \times N$) data can be communicated by sending just the weightings on the new dominant basis vectors (F scores, or N bits, for say G dominant basis vectors); the full content can be conveyed by also sending the G values for the projections of each individual on them. Thus, the significant content of ($M \times F$) items of data are communicated by ($G \star F$) values, the full content by ($G \star (M + F)$) values. Typically this might reduce data about 100 test scores for 1000 individuals to perhaps 5 factors; the substance of the original data could be transmitted by 5 values instead of 100 values.

How do we measure the amount of information conveyed by such a process of data reduction? At the moment, the suggested measures are too tentative to discuss here.

8.2
The Distribution of Information

8.2.1 Context and Overview

The distribution of information will be discussed in terms of the costs to the producers (i.e., the costs incurred by them in producing information and related products and services) and distributors and the values to the producers in derived income. For purposes of this book, some generic data concerning costs in various kinds of information activities are used; they are in part from standard statistical sources (such as *Statistical Abstract of the United States*[5]), in part from data available on the Internet, and in part from a prior review of the economics of information.[6]

There are a variety of forms for information products—books, journals, databases, software, media, and now digital libraries—and there are a variety of means for distribution—book distributor and retail outlets, libraries of all kinds, and online services (including the Internet and World Wide Web). The review of the economics of information provides estimates of the distribution of costs between capital investment and delivery expenses for most of these industries, and those estimates as shown in the following table will serve as the starting point for this discussion.[7] Gross estimates of the total income for all types of sales in the industries involved in distribution of information in the United States can be made based on reported data, projecting them to 2000:

Yearly Sales, Projected to 2000	
Forms of Publication	
Book Publishing	$15 billion[8]
Journal Publishing	$20 billion[9]
Database Publishing	$5 billion[10]
Software Publishing	$5 billion[11]
Means for Distribution	
Book Distribution & Retail Outlets	$10 billion[12]
Academic/Research Libraries	$5 billion[13]
Public Libraries	$5 billion[14]
Online Services (Internet & WWW)	$1 billion[15]

---

[5] U.S. Bureau of the Census, *Statistical Abstract of the United States: 1997* (118th ed.). Washington, DC, 1997 (downloaded from "http://www.census.gov/prod/www/abs/cc97stab.html").

[6] Hayes, Robert M., "Economics of Information," in Feather, John and Sturges, Paul, *International Encyclopedia of Information and Library Science*. London: Routledge, 1997, pp. 116–129.

[7] op cit, p. 124.

8.2.2 The Forms and Formats of Distribution

A major concern today is the likely future for each form and format of publication given the potentials for electronic, digitized distribution. What is going to happen?

Books

Of all of the forms of publication, that of books seems most likely to continue in print form distribution, and sales of the printed book itself will be the primary expected source of income. That means that any digital libraries

---

[8] *Bowker Annual of Library and Book Trade Information.* New York: R.R. Bowker, 1988.

[9] Ibid.

[10] Ibid.

[11] "Software scorecard," *Los Angeles Times,* Dec. 15, 1998, p. C15. "Software Sales Leaders, Measuring Retail Sales of All Computer Software, Excluding Sales of Software that Comes Loaded on New Computers, from November 1997 through October 1998 (source *PC Data*)."

Rank	Company	Retail Sales	Market Share
1	Microsoft	$1,200.0 million	22.9%
2	Learning Co.	592.8 million	11.7%
3	Cendant Software	419.5 million	8.3%
4	Intuit	296.3 million	5.8%
5	Symantec	216.2 million	4.3%
6	Electronic Arts	158.3 million	3.1%
7	Adobe Systems	155.4 million	3.1%
8	Network Associates	132.2 million	2.6%
9	GT Interactive	120.6 million	2.4%
10	Hasbro Interactive	102.7 million	2.0%
	Others	1,771.2 million	33.8%
	TOTAL	$5,240.2 million	100.0%

[12] Bowker, op cit.

[13] *Research Library Statistics.* Washington, DC: Association of Research Libraries (published yearly). Available online at http://www.arl.org/stats/arlstats.

Molyneux, Robert E, *ACRL Academic Library Statistics: 1978/79–1987/88.* Chicago: Association of College and Research Libraries, 1989.

National Center for Educational Statistics: *Academic Library Survey.* Available online at http://nces.ed.gov/surveys/academic data.

[14] National Center for Educational Statistics: *Public Library Survey.* Available online at http://nces.ed.gov/surveys/librarydata.

[15] The estimate for online services is based on applying the proportion of total national sales represented by publishing products (approximately 0.5% to 1%) to projections for total online sales made by *USA Today* (3 Aug. 98) which reported that Internet sales in 1997 were $200 million, in 1998 will be $500 million, and in 2000 will be $200 billion.

derived from current publications really represent marginal costs. The marketing problem is how to set the prices for the print and digital versions so as to maximize a combination of sales and profits; the underlying accounting problem is how to allocate the capital costs across the product lines.

It is relevant to note that today, throughout the world, a digital file is used at some stage in the production of virtually every form of print publication. Indeed, increasingly authors produce and submit manuscripts in digital form. It was for this reason that the Association of American Publishers established guidelines for encoding of manuscripts; based on SGML (Standard Generalized Markup Language), they are now embodied in HTLM and XML in the context of World Wide Web–based publication.[16] The implications are evident: Essentially everything now being published in print form can be included in digital libraries without the need for conversion to digital form. Of course, the conversion from one digital format to another is not a trivial task, but it can be programmed and, once that is done, carried out essentially automatically.

Popular Journals

It is likely that magazines and newspapers will, like books, continue to be published in print form, with the digital library formats used as add-on products combined with related services. Indeed, already the specialized trade publications and many newspapers have moved in this direction. A key point about magazines and newspapers, in contrast to books, is the role of advertising as a source of income. For some, like the "controlled" circulation trade magazines, in fact, advertising is the dominant source of revenue, since many of them are distributed free to the readers. In any event, the analysis with respect to costs as applied to books, as outlined above, is likely to apply to magazines and newspapers, with perhaps minor changes.

Scholarly Journals

For scholarly journals, however, the picture is likely to be quite different. The nature of scholarly journals and, especially, of their use is that the important thing is not the issues of the journal but the articles. The journal issue is simply a means for packaging the articles for efficient distribution. The online digital library environment provides an ideal means for making the individual

[16] *Author's Guide to Electronic Manuscript Preparation and Markup,* version 2.0, rev. ed. Washington, DC: Association of American Publishers, 1989. ("An SGML application conforming to international standard ISO 8879, Standard generalized markup language. This is a companion guide to the American national standard for electronic manuscript preparation and markup ANSI/NISO.")

Smith, Joan M., *SGML and Related Standards: Document Description and Processing Languages.* New York: Ellis Horwood, 1992.

Castro, Elizabeth, *HTML for the World Wide Web.* Berkeley, CA: Peachpit Press, 1997.

articles readily available. In addition, it permits the publisher to avoid all of the up-front costs incurred in printing and mailing multiple copies of each issue of a journal. It therefore seems very likely that online distribution will become the preferred mode for virtually every scholarly journal. Furthermore, the CD-ROM or DVD now becomes an excellent means for packaging a large number of articles—the equivalent of one or more years of the journal—for archival purposes and for continuing important but comparatively low levels of use that characterize the historic journal volumes.

It must be said that the several experiments, jointly among publishers of scholarly journals and academic libraries, such as the agreements with Elsevier, all require that the participating libraries continue to acquire print copies at their current number of subscriptions, for a time period such as five years. The transition to access purely from digital libraries is therefore certainly not imme-diate. However, within the coming decade, there is likely to be an almost com-plete transfer of scholarly journals to digital library formats (online for current articles and CD-ROM or DVD for retrospective).

Retrospective Books and Journals

A second source of digital libraries is retrospective conversion. While that task certainly is huge, there are many parallel ad hoc projects underway for such conversion in specific subject areas and in specific institutions. Among the ratio-nales for such conversion is the need for preservation of at least the information content of paper-based publications that literally are disintegrating in libraries throughout the world.[17] But, whatever may be the reasons, the result is that today there are hundreds of CD-ROM digital libraries that include full-text and images each covering an entire corpus of historic publication—such as the clas-sics of Greek philosophy, of American history, of genealogy, and so on. And vir-tually all of those corpi are available online, through the Internet and the World Wide Web.

The major cost in creating digital libraries of retrospective books clearly is in conversion of the originals into digitized form, either as images or as text. The functions involved include identifying and selecting materials to be converted, maintaining appropriate catalog data about them, preparing the materials for conversion, scanning them (either for creating images or for optical character recognition), and quality control. None of these tasks is by any means simple or cheap, and the total cost for them is likely to be on the order of $100 for an

---

[17] Council on Library Resources. Committee on Preservation and Access, *Brittle Books: Reports of the Committee on Preservation and Access*. Washington, DC: Council on Library Resources, 1986.

George, Gerald W., *Difficult Choices: How Can Scholars Help Save Endangered Research Resources?: A Report to the Commission on Preservation and Access*. Washington, DC: Commission on Preservation and Access, 1995.

average 300-page item. The storage requirements clearly are for the page images, so the typical 300-page book will require 30MB.

Databases

Database services, providing access to digitized text, numerical data files, images, reference and bibliographic databases are another widespread means for electronic publication. The U.S. Census for the year 2000, for example, may well be distributed primarily in electronic form, with print serving only archival purposes.[18]

Among the databases are the online catalogs of major academic/research libraries. And these illustrate the complexities in assessing the economics of digital libraries. The point is that each of these catalogs is created and maintained primarily for the needs of the clientele served by the given library. To support those needs, it must be mounted on a server and must be accessible through the Internet or, at the least, through the institutional server itself (whose connection to the Internet is virtually a marginal cost, given the array of uses already requiring it). The result is that the availability of these catalogs as digital libraries on the Internet is essentially at minimal, virtually zero marginal costs.

Parenthetically, the capital costs represented by those library catalogs are huge. They reflect decades of investment in establishing OCLC and RLIN as shared cataloging utilities, in retrospective conversion of at least 30 million primary catalog records, and in the copy cataloging of literally hundreds of millions of individual catalog records.

The size of a database, as a digital library, cannot be evaluated in such simple terms as books and journals. It is completely determined by the nature and scope of the data stored in it, not by the effects of packaging.

Software

This example of digital libraries includes those that provide software— operating systems, application programs, educational multimedia packages, games. The software industry as a whole is huge, but the issue at hand here concerns the role of digital libraries in the distribution of software in contrast to the sale of individual programs.

The nature of software digital libraries can be nicely represented by shareware libraries, since they are well established in exactly that way. They are readily available in both CD-ROM and online, with dozens of servers providing access to them. A typical such library will contain 5K programs, ranging from 10KB to 1MB and more, so it can be very effectively distributed on a CD-

---

[18] "U.S. Counting on Web to be Census Source; Bureau Plans to Post Most of its 2000 Enumeration Data on the Internet. Switch from Paper to Hypertext Raises Information Issues," *Los Angeles Times,* Sunday, Nov. 15, 1998, Home Edition, Section A.

ROM. Online distribution is equally effective, and the downloading of a single program takes only minutes.

Digital Libraries of Multimedia

The final example of digital libraries are those that include films, videos, and other images of all kinds; music, voice, and sounds of all kinds; and maps, graphs, and illustrations of all kinds. All of these forms of data require massive amounts of storage, so the related digital libraries, whether in CD-ROM or online, will be huge.

8.2.3 The Operating Costs in Distribution of Information

Distributors and Retail Outlets

These are the traditional means for book distribution that have become important means for software distribution. It is of interest to note, though, that retail stores as examples of this means for distribution are now facing severe competition from the online services and mail-order delivery houses.

As means for distribution in CD-ROM format, these are crucial agencies. They are likely to continue to represent the 40% cost (in the form of the discount to the distributor) that they do for print materials. They include stores that sell computer hardware and software and office equipment and supplies, mail-order houses, and online versions of each that continue to proliferate.

Academic, Research, and Public Libraries

An issue of current concern in libraries and in the institutions they serve is the role of digital libraries in their operations. The predominant view is that print will continue to be important and that the two forms of libraries—print libraries and digital libraries—are complementary rather than competitive. In this view, print materials will continue to be acquired by libraries, and digital libraries will be both acquired by them, usually in the form of optical media (i.e., CD-ROM and DVD), and accessed by them (through the online services). Printed books will continue to be acquired so as to fulfill the library's traditional imperatives of assuring preservation of the records of the past and providing economic access to them at minimal costs to the library's clientele. Optical media will be acquired for the same purposes, in this case of the digital records, and the online services will be used for reference services to the most current materials.

It is likely, though, that journals of whatever kind, even though some perhaps may be acquired in print form, may not be stored in print form. Already

many libraries have replaced their bound volumes of popular journals, magazines, newspapers, and scholarly journals by microforms, and the transition from
that to digital libraries in optical formats is almost certain.

The Internet and the World Wide Web

Turning now to that remarkable phenomenon, the Internet and the
World Wide Web, as the means for online distribution, not only are production
costs of digital libraries dramatically reduced, but distribution costs are possibly even more so. The cost of physical transport, whether of books or CD-
ROMs, is replaced by the cost of online storage and of digital transmission.
Mailing a book might cost $2.00; mailing a CD-ROM, the equivalent of say
20 to 30 books, perhaps a dollar; sending the text of the book at 28K baud,
perhaps 3 minutes of connect time at zero cost through almost any of the
online services.

Unfortunately, assessment of Internet costs clearly is very complex. Costs
occur at several stages in the chain of distribution, and funding them are mixtures of public funding, institutional funding, advertising funding, and individual funding. Many of the costs are subsidized and thus buried in other accounting categories. The costs for network access are largely independent of actual
use, being represented by connection charges that are a function of delivered
bandwidth, reflecting anticipated demand. The rate of growth of the Internet
and the World Wide Web is so great that it is virtually impossible to obtain data
that will be consistent; data on one component of operations, reported at one
point in time, cannot be compared with data for another component, reported
at another point in time.

Complicating the assessment of costs in distribution on the Internet is the
fact that many elements of costs are borne by the users instead of by the producers and/or distributors. In particular, the cost of printing is totally borne by
the user, and it is by no means negligible. And if binding is required, the costs
are a magnitude two or three times greater than experienced by the publisher.
Beyond that are the very real costs in users' time in all of the processes of acquisition, downloading, and managing of the digital files. Even in cases where the
Internet is used as means for ordering rather than downloading, many of the
distribution costs are shifted to the user. An example is "shipping and handling
costs," a set of costs that users apparently have become either oblivious to or
willing to pay, and the charges for them are now at a level that they represent
not recovery of costs but sources of profit. Presumably, shifting of costs to users
represents a decrease in the costs of distribution as far as publishers and/or inter-
mediaries are concerned and therefore either decreased prices to the users or
increased profits to the vendors.

The spectacular rate of growth of the Internet is well established.
Worldwide, the number of hosts has increased by nearly 50% from year to year.
Of course, the impact in this respect varies greatly from country to country.

Internet Sites Per 1 Million Population and Comparative Position					
	Jan 1998		Jan 1999		Jan 2000
U.S.	69,002	(2)	102,111	(2)	178,105	(1)
Finland	90,008	(1)	109,249	(1)	126,250	(2)
Taiwan	7,368	(22)	12,862	(23)	24,876	(16)
Brazil	586	(50)	1,075	(51)	2,232	(49)
Croatia	1,302	(38)	1,377	(47)	2,829	(45)
Guatemala	42	(96)	57	(103)	111	(99)

In the United States, the number of installations has recently (from 1999 to 2000) increased by nearly 100%. This reflects the extent to which personal use in the United States has so dramatically increased. The *Statistical Abstract of the United States*[19] reported that the number of persons with Internet access was as follows:

	Year	Home or Work	Home Only	Work Only	Total
Access	1997	46.3	25.5	22.9	94.7
	1998	62.3	37.0	29.8	129.1
	1999	83.7	53.7	38.9	176.3
	2000	112.9	77.6	50.5	241.0
Acess in Last 30 days	1997	28.1	19.8	13.9	61.8
	1998	43.6	27.6	20.4	91.6
	1999	64.1	44.9	31.1	140.1
	2000	86.3	65.5	40.4	192.2

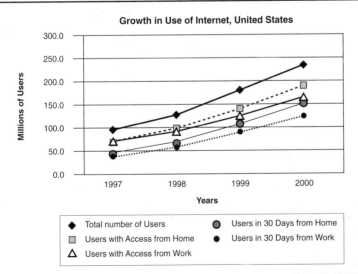

Growth in Use of Internet, United States

Total number of Users
Users in 30 Days from Home
Users with Access from Home
Users in 30 Days from Work
Users with Access from Work

[19] Statistical Abstract of the United States, 1997, Table 890 (p. 567), 1998, Table 917 (pl 574), 1999, Table 923 (p. 582), 2000, Table 913 (p. 568).

The number of corporate users (adding together "home or work" and "work only") grew from 70M in 1997 to 163M in 2000, a 132% increase, but the number of home users (adding together "home or work" and "home only") grew from 70M to 190M, a 171% increase. Even more dramatic is the increase in use within the past 30 days from home, increasing from 48M to 152M, more than tripling!

8.3
The Economics of Information

With that as background, we turn now to modeling the role of information as an economic entity in the sense that associated with it are both costs and values and that people differ in their perception of the balance between the two. Beyond that almost self-evident fact, though, information resources have more specific properties that directly affect decisions about them at both macroeconomic and microeconomic levels.

8.3.1 Context

Before presenting the substance of this section, it is valuable to set the context and motivation for it. Examination of the "economics" of information arose from a concern about the extent to which some persons viewed electronic media as replacing print forms of distribution. They also see the Internet as replacing libraries as we know them by electronic delivery. Those views have been expressed not only by the enthusiasts for electronic distribution as replacement for print but by academic administrators who hope that they will not need to continue erecting new library buildings and acquiring additional collections of dusty old books.

But the two forms of distribution (print and electronic) are not substitutable for each other but are complementary, serving substantially different functions and purposes. Indeed, instead of one substituting for the other, use of one increases the need for and use of the other.

Leaving that aside, though, the enthusiasts and the administrators have failed to recognize the economic facts in the costs involved in creation, distribution, and use of both media. They have not recognized the decisions by publishers about how they will distribute and when they will change the means for distribution. Those facts are by no means easy to obtain or to rationalize, especially as they relate to the Internet, which is growing at such a rate that data obtained at any given time cannot effectively be related to data obtained at other times.

8.3.2 Economic Properties

In a previously published review of the economics of information, the economic properties were discussed.[20] Among them, the following are of special relevance to this discussion:

Cheaply Shareable

Information is easily and cheaply transportable and shareable. The first copy is likely to represent most of the costs, with costs for reproduction and distribution relatively minor. As a result, the number of copies that can be produced without serious depletion of physical resources is great.

Value Increases with Accumulation

The value of information increases at more than a linear rate as it grows. This is perhaps one of the most distinctive and important features of information as a resource. As it grows and when it is combined with other information, it may be transformed, new relationships developed, and new insights gained as a result of the interconnections. As a result, indeed the value of an accumulation of information is far more than the total of the individual values.

Self-Generating

Information is expandable and self-generating. This is especially important because virtually an unlimited amount of intellectual goods can be created, and digital libraries have exponentially increased the ability to do so.

Costs Independent of Scale of Application

The cost of information is independent of the scale of application. Economists use the phrase "indivisible in use" to mean that, and information indeed is indivisible, so there are immense economies of scale. Putting this together with the value in accumulation provides strong incentives for large-scale users to acquire information. For the same reason, there is efficiency for shared rather than independent accumulation. As a result, joint consumption is likely because it is inefficient to exclude or withhold service from those who don't pay. This may well be the most significant contribution of the World Wide Web, as a digital library source.

8.3.3 The Capital Investment in Information

We now turn to a question that can be stated quite simply: How does one assess the value of the capital investment in information? This question was an

[20] Hayes, Robert M., "Economics of Information," in Feather, John, and Sturges, Paul, *International Encyclopedia of Information and Library Science*. London: Routledge, 1997, pp. 116–129.

issue of concern during the deliberations of the Public Sector/Private Sector Task Force of the NCLIS when some members of the panel were adamantly opposed to the suggestion that a database should be viewed as a capital resource. Their view was that to do so would give it undue importance since, as they saw it, a database really has value only as a tool in support of other activities. The counterargument was that, for an information company at the very least, its database was as much a capital investment as the manufacturing plant of an auto company. But that argument fell on deaf ears.

In the years since then, efforts to assess the impact of information upon national economies at both a macro level and a micro level repeatedly have shown evidence that increasingly important expenditures are incurred in developing databases and creating other forms of information. Those expenditures simply were not being recognized. The result has been serious mismeasurement of phenomena of fundamental economic importance. It appears even in such areas as the balance of international trade.

In principle, of course, the value of any company is a combination of tangible net assets and intangible ones, the latter usually being what euphemistically is called goodwill. The tangible net assets are directly derived from the books of the company as the difference between tangible assets and liabilities. Tangible assets include such items as accounts receivable, inventory, and fixed assets such as land, buildings, and machinery. The liabilities include accounts payable, loans and other financial obligations, and contingencies for possible losses.

Of course, there are subtleties in accounting for both tangible assets and liabilities, and in many cases they result in significant failures in properly representing the "true" value of a company. An example that comes to mind is of a company with substantial investments in real estate that are carried on the books at the costs of purchase but for which the current market value is far greater. Such a company is clearly the target for a hostile takeover with the intent of converting that real estate into immediate profit. But, recognizing those potentials for erroneous assessment of value, there are no fundamental difficulties with respect to the tangible assets and liabilities.

In contrast, though, assessment of the intangible assets is fraught with difficulties. They arise as a result of accounting practices that reflect consideration of tax implications rather than operational value. First, let's look at the definition of intangible assets: They are "assets having a life of one year or more but which lack physical substance." Classical examples include patents and copyrights and they clearly reveal the role of investment in information resources.

APB 17 of the AICPA (American Institute of Certified Public Accountants) covers accounting practices for intangible assets, whether purchased or internally developed. The costs of intangibles acquired from others are to be reported as tangible assets and are to reflect the cash or fair market value of the consideration given for them. That seems straightforward and surely will represent at least the value of such intangible assets as perceived at the time of acquisition. The book value of such assets will then be treated like that of tangible assets, typically with amortization over an expected period of benefit.

But the situation for intangible assets that are internally developed is significantly different. Their costs, for both developing them and maintaining them, are to be charged against earnings "if the assets are not specifically identifiable, or have indeterminate lives, or are inherent in the continuing business." Now, the reasons for this quite different treatment presumably reflect tax implications. The more that costs can be legitimately charged against earnings, the lower those earnings and hence the lower the taxes. It must be said, though, that the distinction between acquired intangibles and internally developed ones seems to be arbitrary, especially in the context of "outsourcing" in which increasing amounts of things are being acquired rather than internally developed.

8.3.4 Application to Database Companies

Leaving that aside, though, let's now consider a database. While it will always exist in some physical form and thus might be treated as a physical asset, the physical form is literally immaterial. The costs incurred in producing it have virtually nothing to do with production in that physical form but reflect instead the production of information content. It is almost certain that the database will be regarded as an intangible asset. Now, it clearly is "specifically identifiable," but it also is likely to have an "indeterminant life" and, for the database company, is "inherent in the continuing business." Hence, the costs in developing and in maintaining the database are to be charged against earnings. *Voila,* so be it, and *amen!*

In other words, given the accounting practices, in general any such intangible asset as a database will not be reflected on the books, so the problem in assessing the value of the company is how to treat such assets. Let's explore the issues involved in dealing with this problem. Aside from doing so with companies like ISI and OCLC, let's explore them as they relate to academic libraries. And there is a final context in which to do so as well—Internet companies for which their databases are the means for providing online services.

Aside from the database itself, there are also intangibles in the form of the software developed to process it for production of products and services from it. Again the costs in creation of that software typically are also expensed and do not appear as assets on the books (although there is a new potential change to which in that respect reference will be made shortly).

Of course, aside from these issues, which are specific to companies that depend upon a database, there are the more traditional elements of goodwill, including such things as the ability to penetrate a given market, or having significant skills in marketing and management, or owning a patent on a process or a copyright on a publication. Each of those is not in itself a tool for production, so they will not be of concern here. There would seem to no reason to expect there to be any difference in treatment of them for any particular type of company.

Institute for Scientific Information

The facts are that the database, with related software, is literally the machine tool from which products and services are produced in a company like ISI. At the time of first sale of the company, in 1971, the accumulated cost was probably about half of the sale price. The important point is not that amount per se but the fact that the costs of the database were not represented on the books, and from an accounting standpoint, it had no value in the assessment of the company for purchase, despite the magnitude of the expenditures.

OCLC

In the same vein, let's consider another company, OCLC, for which the database (WorldCat) is not only the machine tool but the very heart of its business, indeed the very reason for its existence. This is a fascinating example since the costs involved in creating the WorldCat are a complex combination of expenditures by OCLC, by the Library of Congress, and by the great array of libraries that cooperatively have contributed cataloging data to it. The file today contains over 30 million records. Any proper accounting would assign a cost of at least $30 to the work in creating just one of those records. Beyond the catalog records as such, WorldCat includes data for each record identifying the libraries holding that item; the result is a database of value not only for the cataloging data but as the tool for access. There are several hundred million entries for holdings, each of which entailed a cost by the library entering it. But looking only at the cost of the cataloging, that alone says that the cost of the WorldCat database is nearly $1 billion. The books of OCLC show a value of nothing for it. In fact, they do not show even the small part of the costs that OCLC itself incurred in creating the database.

An Academic Research Library

As another example, for an academic library, its database (as represented in its collection and its catalog) is the very reason for its existence. Of course, there is no real counterpart of a corporate balance sheet for an academic library, but leaving that aside, there is also no representation of the costs represented by the collection or by the catalog in any reporting about any library. At most there may be a value of the collection established for insurance purposes, but it will not usually reflect the costs in selecting the books, in acquiring and processing them, in cataloging them, or in maintaining them. In a very real sense those are all costs that could be regarded as creating the capital resource from which library services are derived.

An Internet Company

Finally, if we consider any company engaged in providing Internet products and services, a key portion of its means for doing so is its database and, for many, it is the only means. The fact that its investment in creating the database is not recorded on its books makes it almost impossible to assess the value of that company.

8.3.5 Determination of "Goodwill"

Let's start with the representation of the determination of the value of the database as part of "goodwill." One general and effective rule is that the total value of a company should reflect the present value of the expected future income stream to be derived from its operations. Within that, there are two means for determining goodwill: capitalization of earnings and capitalization of excess earnings, which are equivalent if the underlying estimations (for industry average rate of return, values of tangible assets, and average expected annual earnings) are equal. To illustrate, consider the following hypothetical data:

Estimated from Capitalization of Earnings	
Expected average annual earnings	$30M
Industry average rate of return on investment	20%
Imputed asset value ($30M/20%)	$150M
Estimated fair value of tangible assets	$100M
Estimated goodwill	$50M

Estimated from Capitalization of Excess Earnings	
Estimated fair value of tangible assets	$100M
Industry average rate of return on investment	20%
Implied earnings from tangible assets	$20M
Expected average annual earnings	$30M
Estimated goodwill ($30M-$20M)/.20	$50M

There is a variation that can result in a difference between the two calculations. Specifically, the approach using excess earnings permits one to demand a rate of return from goodwill different from that for tangible assets (typically, substantially greater so as to reflect relative uncertainty in the investment in goodwill). For example, if the rate of return from goodwill were chosen at 40% (instead of the 20% used for tangible assets), the goodwill estimated from the excess earnings would be only $25M. But for the purposes of this exploration, they will be taken as equivalent.

One reasonable means for assessing the significance of goodwill is by the ratio of it to tangible assets. In the example above, it would be one-half of the tangible asset value, one-third of the total value. On the surface, all of this is reasonable, even unquestionable. But consider a database company which, quite typically, might have *no* tangible assets. The ratio of goodwill to tangible assets would be infinite, since goodwill is 100% of the total value. The problem, of course, is that the database is not like what one would normally think of in considering "goodwill." It is clearly a means for production and, as such, is far more tangible than such things as the ability to penetrate a given market, or having skills in marketing and management, or even owning a patent on a process or a copyright on a publication.

The issue at hand, therefore, is how do we value a database as a means for production, indeed as a counterpart of a machine tool?

8.3.6 Evaluation of a Database as Means for Production

As a starting point, let's consider some contexts analogous to that of investment in databases. Three seem relevant:

1. Investment in research and development, leading to patents and copyrights
2. Investment in computer software, leading to publishable products
3. Investment in motion pictures, leading to distribution through a variety of markets

Each reflects substantial expenditures for information resources that serve as the means for producing products and services that generate income in a variety of ways from a variety of markets.

Research and Development
Unfortunately, the first analogy leads into the same dead end. Indeed, in its Statement of Accounting Standards No. 2. October 1974, the FASB ruled that all research and development costs must be charged to expense when incurred. (There are two exceptions. One is when the costs are incurred for others, under contractual arrangements; the second is for extractive industries, such as oil exploration.) The argument in favor of this policy (aside from the evident tax implications) is that to capitalize investments in research and devel-

opment would fail to recognize that future returns from them are uncertain. The problem, though, is that one of the most important elements of future growth in every industry is totally unrecognized in accounting, both for individual companies and for the nation as a whole. Beyond that, a patent or a copyright is not in itself a means for production, though it may give the right to engage in production.

Computer Software

The second analogy is much more promising, though only recently having become so. In a *Los Angeles Times* article of Friday, October 29, 1999, it was reported that, "As part of its periodic update of its methods, the Commerce Department redefined software as an investment, something of value in its own right and thus counts *(sic)* toward economic output." It went on to say, "For last year alone, the rejiggering added about $250 billion to estimates of total economic output. Fully two-thirds of that was due to the redefinition of software." Now, that is getting somewhere!

Incidentally, the current "update of methods" has much wider significance, since it involves restructuring of the national economic accounts, replacing the hoary SIC codes with new ones called NAICS (North American Industrial Classification System). This long-overdue overhaul begins to recognize the role of information industries in the national economy.

It must be said, though, that this step of the federal government by no means implies that there will be immediate changes in accounting policies or practices in individual companies. Nor it is clear what aspects of the investment in software are to be capitalized, those of the producers of the software or those of the purchasers of them. For the former, the software is indeed the basis for production of a variety of products; for the latter, with some exceptions, software is more of a supporting tool than a means for production. Incidentally, the latter point exactly reflects the position of those members of the Public Sector/Private Sector Task Force who objected to treating a database (or, analogously, software) as a capital resource, and one must essentially agree with them in that respect, except for the exceptional cases. There are those exceptions, though, for which software really is a means for production by the company acquiring it. An example that comes immediately to mind is imaging software, which is vital in the production of television advertising, in a variety of kinds of motion pictures, and in companies that depend on CAD-CAM software for engineering and architecture. For them, amortizing the imaging software makes eminent sense.

It is possible, at least, that the new federal policy concerning amortization of software may eventually provide a basis for analogous treatment of expenditures for databases. For the moment, however, there are no accounting policies that provide for doing so.

Motion Picture Production

The third analogy, though, is quite relevant and there appears to be some basis for application of it to database companies. FASB Statement of Financial Accounting Standards No. 53 relates to "Financial Reporting by Producers and Distributors of Motion Picture Films." The copy at hand is dated December 1981 and, while it may have changed in the years since then, it probably reflects current policy and practice. Paragraph 10 states, "Costs to produce a film (production costs) shall be capitalized as film cost inventory." It goes on to state that the costs shall be amortized "in the same ratio that current gross revenues bear to anticipated total gross revenues." It is evident that the film, once produced, provides the means for producing further products and even services, and the accounting should recognize that by capitalization of those costs.

In an earlier, 1979, report, the AICPA discussed the background that led to FASB Standard No. 53 and, among other things, considered "allocation of production costs to primary and secondary exploitation." It defines the primary market as that for which the film was principally produced, with the secondary market as all residual exploitation. It comments, "When a film is expected to be exploited in secondary markets, it is appropriate to allocate a portion of production costs to revenues to be realized from secondary exploitation."

8.3.7 Application of Standard No. 53 to Database Contexts

Institute for Scientific Information

This would appear to be highly relevant to a database company. For ISI, as an example, production costs are incurred in creating the database entries from which successive issues of their various citation indexes are published. The primary market for each index presumably is in the sale of those current issues to the libraries subscribing to it.

But there are substantial secondary markets for those indexes. Historically most evident were the five-year cumulations. Indeed, it seems that the operations of the ISI index products first became profitable with issuance of the first five-year cumulation of Science Citation Index. Today, though, there are innumerable secondary markets in the sale of online services, CD-ROMs, and a variety of other potential products and services.

OCLC

In the case of OCLC, the production costs are incurred as a combination of efforts at contributing libraries and OCLC itself. The primary market presumably is in the subsequent sale of records for copy-cataloging by other libraries. Historically, that was the purpose for both OCLC and RLIN and it is still the primary source of income for them.

But there are substantial secondary markets for those catalog records. Most evident are use of them as means for adding holdings data, which then serve as the basis for interlibrary loan services. Others are in the sale of subsidiary products (such as CD-ROMs) and other kinds of online services, such as reference services.

An Academic Research Library

Turning to the academic research library, the situation presumably is quite different. These are entities that do not function as though they were profit-making companies; they do not have balance sheets; they do not generally "market" their services; there is no reason to set a "value" on them, as there may be for a company being acquired. In other words, on the surface, there appears to be little basis for considering them in the context of the question of evaluating "database companies." Despite that, let's do so, with the following rationale.

Treat the budget of the academic research library as the equivalent of income from sales of services as represented and measured by circulation. (Measurement of library services by circulation alone is obviously simplistic but it will suffice for the purposes of this discussion and may even be rational if we assume that all other services are roughly proportional to it.) Thus, for the median ARL library, with a budget of $15M and circulation of 500K, the fee (i.e., cost) per circulation is $30. Considered as a company, the income and expenditures are in balance, so there is neither profit nor loss and taxes will be zero.

An academic research library spends a significant portion of its income in creating and maintaining the database, the collection of books, and the catalog that provides access to it. That database is its very reason for existence. The yearly costs for creating that database include those for purchase of the materials, of course, but they will also include the costs in technical processing (selection, acquisition, cataloging, physical processing, and preservation). For the median library, the costs for purchase of materials will be taken at $5.5M and for technical processing staff, at $2.5M for a total of $8M. The remaining $7M are in direct services (circulation, reference, etc.) to the using public.

It is the set of costs ($8M) for purchase and technical processing that is at issue. How are they to be treated? To answer that, we first must deal with an interesting question: What are the primary and secondary markets for delivery of services from the database? There are a variety of potential answers to that question. The markets could be segmented by type of customers (e.g., faculty, students, other libraries, etc.) or by type of usage (circulation use, in-house use, reference use, etc.). Either of those, however, becomes quite complex and probably difficult to measure. Beyond that, they do not provide ready generalization to other contexts.

Let's consider the time period of use as a relatively simple but provocative basis for segmentation. The primary market is defined as uses occurring within, say, the five-year period after acquisition of material, and the secondary market, as all subsequent uses. These are relatively easy to measure, at least for circulation uses. It is a fact of typical library operation that the great frequency of use of a given item occurs within that first five-year time period so, in that sense, it is the primary market. It is also the case, though, that the very purpose of the academic research library is to assure that uses of an item subsequent to that period of maximum frequency will also be met, and those uses can properly be considered as the secondary market.

Underlying these definitions of primary and secondary markets is the view that uses during the two time periods are fundamentally different. In particular, during the early five-year period, the uses are in the nature of environmental scanning, maintaining currency with what is going on today. Subsequent usage has more the nature of reference use, retrospective in nature.

For the median ARL library, the holdings are 3.5M volumes and yearly additions are 86K volumes. Thus the five-year period would represent a total of 430K volumes or about 12% of the collection. Let's conjecture that about 25% of the usage of the library in a given year will be to that 12% of the collection, the remaining 75% being scattered across the rest of the collection. Then, the primary market would represent 25% of the income and the secondary market, 75%.

Turning now to the issue of amortization, the capital costs (i.e., purchase and technical processing) should now be allocated in proportion to the anticipated income. That will be taken at the 25%/75% division implied by the conjectured division of markets. For the median ARL library, that would mean $2M allocated to the primary market and $6M to the secondary market. Clearly, the allocation to the primary market will be amortized over the assumed five-year period. The simplest rule for doing so would be linear, with the resulting amortization each year equaling the $2M so the books would show a steady state of about $10M for the capitalization account for the primary market. However, if the rules of Standard No. 53 were applied there would be a much more rapid amortization, since the general pattern is that use of materials drops exponentially during that initial five-year period.

But how should the amortization of the capitalization for the secondary market be treated? Aha! A very difficult question. It could be argued though that there should be no amortization of that capitalization and that therefore the capitalization for the secondary market, the long-term market, will steadily grow. The rationale is that the market for use beyond the first five-year period is essentially infinite so the income during any given year has a ratio of zero to the total market. Recognize, of course, that no library will have an infinite life, but the one at Harvard has been around for several hundred years and surely will be so for centuries to come. If one is uncomfortable with an infinite lifetime for a collection of books, we could amortize over three or four hundred years instead, with a result not dramatically different.

Now, in this description there are some conjectured values (five years as the period for the primary market, 25%/75% as the split between primary and secondary, and infinity as the time period for amortization of the secondary market, in particular). Those clearly can be whatever they need to be to reflect reality and policy. The point is that, whatever those values may be, there is a basis for reflecting the investment in the database that has some rationale.

Online Database Services

The same approach seems eminently applicable to segmenting the primary and secondary markets for online database services (although the infinite lifetime clearly is not at all appropriate). Typically, the primary market for such services represents immediacy of data and very current awareness. Stock market data are perhaps the characterizing example, with the value and therefore the fee that can be charged decaying literally within minutes if not seconds. But there is a secondary market for which immediacy is no longer significant but for which, instead, comprehensiveness is the crucial need.

That secondary market partakes of much of the characteristics of the secondary market for the academic research library. It is likely to be at a virtual steady-state indefinitely into the future. However, the analogy with the academic research library fails because there is an important marketing strategy currently operating. It reflects the fact that immediacy is worth money, so the online service wants to attract customers that will use and pay well for access to the most current data. To attract those customers, the secondary market services are likely to be made available at no cost. Thus, while there is a secondary market it is not likely to generate enough income to warrant the separate accounting.

8.3.8 The Combinatorial Effect of Database Size

Any rational rule for assigning value to a database will almost certainly be represented by a linear function of its size, and each of the examples presented above (ISI, OCLC, academic research libraries, and online database services) illustrates that fact. But, in all of those examples, the operational value of the database is actually not a linear function of its size. As a database grows, the number of combinations that can be made from the data within it increases. Indeed, the effect is combinatorial and, as a result, exponential. If the size of the database doubles, its value more than doubles and may even be as much as four times as great.

Just to illustrate, a real value of a major academic research library is evident when one must pursue a "chain of references," leading one after another through a succession of items from the collection. Only in a very large collection can such a chain of references be continued for very long. Clearly there is value in being able to relate, in this way as well as others, a number of items from the collection. As the size of the database grows, the ability to make such connections grows combinatorially.

There appears to be no rational means for representing this combinatorial effect in a simple accounting process, and it is doubtful that there will be any formal recognition of it in assessments of the value of database companies. However, despite that, it is important to recognize the phenomenon, if only informally.

8.3.9 Conclusion

In summary, the purpose of this exploration has been to identify a problem and, by analogy with the motion picture industry, a potential answer to it. The discussion has been essentially qualitative and hypothetical, since the objective is not to solve the problem for specific contexts but rather to raise the issue and suggest that there may be appropriate means to do so.

Bibliography

References on Publishing Costs
Association of American University Presses: Directory 1991–1992. New York: Association of American University Presses, 1991.

Bingley, Clive. *Book Publishing Practice.* London: Crosby Lockwood & Son, 1966.

Bowker Annual of Library and Book Trade Information. New York: R.R. Bowker, 1988.

Dessauer, John P. *Book Publishing: What it Is, What it Does.* New York: R.R. Bowker, 1981.

Kerr, Chester. *American University Publishing,* 1955. Ann Arbor, MI: Edwards Bros., 1956.

Kerr, Chester. *American University as Publisher: A Digest of a Report on American University Presses.* Norman: University of Oklahoma Press, 1949.

King, Donald W. and Tenopir, Carol. "Economic Cost Models of Scientific Scholarly Journals," paper presented at the ICSU Press Workshop, Keble College, Oxford, UK, March 31 to April 2, 1998. See website http://www.oxford.bodley.ox.ac.uk/icsu/index.html.

Machlup, Fritz, and Leeson, Kenneth. *Information through the Printed Word: The Dissemination of Scholarly, Scientific, and Intellectual Knowledge.* New York: Praeger, 1978. Volume 1, Book Publishing; Volume 2, Journals; Volume 4, Book, Journals, and Bibliographic Services.

One Book/Five Ways: The Publishing Procedures of Five University Presses. Los Altos, CA: William Kaufmann, 1977.

Underwood, Richard G. *Production and Manufacturing Problems of American University Presses.* New York: Association of American University Presses, 1960.

References on Accounting for Information Investments
American Institute of Certified Public Accountants. Accounting Standards Division. *Statement of*

Position: Accounting Principles and Reporting Practices for Certain Nonprofit Organizations: A Proposed Recommendation to the Financial Accounting Standards Board. Accounting Standards Division, American Institute of Certified Public Accountants. New York, The Institute, 1978.

American Institute of Certified Public Accountants. Committee on the Entertainment Industries. *Accounting for Motion Picture Films: Including Statement of Position Issued by the Accounting Standards Division,* prepared by the Committee on the Entertainment Industries of the American Institute of Certified Public Accountants, 2nd ed. New York: The Institute, 1979.

American Institute of Certified Public Accountants. Subcommittee on Nonprofit Organizations. *Audits of Certain Nonprofit Organizations,* prepared by the Subcommittee on Nonprofit Organizations; including statement of position issued by the Accounting Standards Division. New York, NY (1211 Ave. of the Americas, New York 10036): American Institute of Certified Public Accountants, 1981.

Hayes, Robert M. *Digital Libraries,* University of Sao Paulo.

Hayes, Robert M. *Economics of Digital Libraries,* Dubrovnik, COLIS.

References on Measurement of Information

Belkin, Nicholas J. "Information Concepts for Information Science," *Journal of Documentation* 34, 1 (1978), pp. 55–85.

Blunt, C.R. et al. *An Information Retrieval System Model.* State College, PA: HRB-Singer, 1965.

Boorstin, Daniel J. "Gresham's Law: Knowledge or Information?" Remarks at the White House Conference on Library and Information Services, Washington, DC.

Boyce, Bert R. et al. *Measurement in Information Science.* San Diego, CA: Academic Press, 1994. This, together with Tague-Sutcliffe (q.v.), are two superb textbooks, both individually and as complementary to each other. They are each well organized, well written, and well documented. They are comprehensive and current in coverage of their respective topics. This one is the more general in its objectives and coverage. It consists of five sections, the first of which provides an introduction to the concepts of measurement. The coverage is standard for that objective and could be of value to any context, whether it related to information or any other phenomenon. However, the text is especially valuable in identifying the specific issues in measuring "soft" phenomena, as exemplified by human behavior, in which the data are inherently subject to uncontrollable variables, are unreliable in measurement, and are frequently normative rather than objective. Another valuable contribution is in Chapter 3, on "Accuracy and Reliability of Measures"; again the coverage is standard, but the emphasis is to be praised.

Guiasu, Silviu. *Information Theory with Applications.* New York: McGraw-Hill, 1977.

Hayes, Robert M. The Measurement of Information from a File," in Stevens, Mary E. and others (eds.), *Statistical Association Methods for Mechanized Documentation, Proceedings of the Symposium,* Washington, 1964. Washington, DC: National Bureau of Standards Miscellaneous Publication 269, Dec. 15, 1965, pp. 161–162.

Hayes, Robert M. "A Theory for File Organization," in Karplus, Walter (ed.), *Online Computing: Time-Shared Man-Computer Systems.* New York: McGraw-Hill, pp. 264–289.

Hayes, Robert M. "Measurement of Information," in Vakkari, Pertti and Cronin, Blaise (eds.), *Conceptions of Library and Information Science.* London: Taylor Graham, 1992, pp. 268–285.

Hayes, Robert M. *Measurement of Information and Communication: A Set of Definitions."* Information and Behavior—Volume 4: Relationships between Communication and Information.

Hayes, Robert M. "Measurement of Information," *Information Processing and Management* 29, 1 (1993), pp. 1–11.

Hayes, Robert M. *The Organization of Large Files. Final Report. NSF Contract C-280.* April 30, 1964. Sherman Oaks, CA, 1964.

Hayes, Robert M., and Borko, Harold. *Mathematical models of information system use: the final report on NSF Grant Number IST 79-18497*, March 31, 1982. Los Angeles: Graduate School of Library and Information Science, University of California, 1982.

Hayes, Robert M. *Measurement of File Operation Effectiveness*. Los Angeles: Institute of Library Research, University of California, 1969.

Nitecki, Joseph Z. "The Concept of Information-Knowledge Continuum." *Journal of Library History* 20, 4 (1985), pp. 387–407.

Paisley, William. "Information and Work," in Dervin, Brenda and Voigt, Melvin J. (eds.), *Progress in Communication Sciences*. Vol. 2, pp. 118ff.

Salton, Gerard. *Automatic Information Organization and Retrieval*. New York: McGraw-Hill, 1968.

Salton, Gerard. *Dynamic Information and Library processing*. Englewood Cliffs, NJ: Prentice-Hall, 1975.

Salton, Gerard. *The SMART Retrieval System*. Englewood Cliffs, NJ: Prentice-Hall, 1971.

Shannon, Claude, and Weaver, Warren. *The Mathematical Theory of Communication*. Urbana: University of Illinois Press, 1949.

Tague-Sutcliffe, Jean. *Measuring Information: An Information Services Perspective*. San Diego: Academic Press, 1995. This, together with Boyce (q.v.) are two superb textbooks, both individually and as complementary to each other. They are each well organized, well written, and well documented. Of special value in this book is the review of definitions of "information," provided in Chapter 1, and the discussion of the Shannon measure and, even more important, of various extensions to it such as "weighted entropy," in Chapter 3. The contexts covered in this book include measurement of collections of materials, of the surrogates used for access to them (such as catalogs and indexes), of the processes and results of retrieval, and (of exceptional importance) the forms in which results are presented. Models are presented in more than descriptive form, with analyses provided on which implementation can be based. The central model is presented in Chapter 4. It measures the informativeness of records, providing formalized means for analyzing user preference judgments. The later chapters then build upon it, applying it to evaluation of retrieval operations, services, and collections.

References Related to Publishing Patterns and Policies

"A Response from Gordon & Breach," *American Libraries* (May 1990), p. 405.

"ARL Consultants' Reports, Likely to Widen Serials Rift," *American Libraries* (June 1989), p. 489.

"Gordon & Breach Sues Again," *American Libraries* (April 1990), p. 286.

"Journal Publisher Sues Author of Price Study," *American Libraries* (Sept, 1989), pp. 717–718.

References on Publishing Functions and Costs

Bingley, Clive. *Book Publishing Practice*. London: Crosby Lockwood & Son, 1966.

Bowker Annual of Library and Book Trade Information. New York: R.R. Bowker, 1988.

Brenner Information Group. *Here's What Service Providers Are Charging!* http://www.brenner-books.com/pricetabl.html. This reference book lists typical and average prices currently being charged for every aspect of desktop computer service, including file conversion, writing, keyboarding, editing, proofreading, and typography. Then it covers the input, creative, production and output functions of scanning, graphic design, page layout, printer output, prepress, color proofs, imagesetting, film recording, and CD-ROM archiving. After this comes new media services such as multimedia, 2D and 3D modeling, animation, audio and video services, and website design. Finally it covers postprinting and finishing services such as collating, folding, scoring, binding, mounting, and laminating. And a special section covers other services such as fax service, mailing list services, rush rates, and even rental rates. Based on extensive research including personal interviews. Sold by the region. Regions are New England, Mid Atlantic, South Atlantic, North Central, South Central, Mountain, Pacific, California and Canada. This book is the industry bible on what your competitors are charging. Price $50.00.

Dessauer, John P. *Book Publishing: What it Is, what it Does.* New York: R.R. Bowker, 1981.

Kerr, Chester. *American University as Publisher: A Digest of a Report on American University Presses.* Norman: University of Oklahoma Press, 1949.

Kerr, Chester. *American University Publishing, 1955.* Ann Arbor, MI: Edwards Bros., 1956.

King, Donald W., and Carol Tenopir. "Economic Cost Models of Scientific Scholarly Journals," *ICSU Press Workshop,* Keble College, Oxford, UK, March 31 to April 2, 1998. University of Tennessee School of Information Sciences Center for Information Studies. (See http://www.bodley.ox.ac.uk/icsu/index.html.) This paper summarizes costs of publishing scientific scholarly journals. Activities are described for five publishing components: article processing (e.g., manuscript processing, editing, composition, etc.), non-article processing (i.e., similar activities related to covers, tables-of-content, letters, book reviews, etc.), reproduction (e.g., printing, collating, binding, etc.), distribution (e.g., wrapping, labeling, sorting, mailing, subscription maintenance, etc.). and support (e.g., marketing, administration, finance, etc.). A model is derived for each of these components consisting of cost parameters (e.g., number of issues, pages, subscriptions, etc.) and cost elements (e.g., cost per page of editing, setup cost per issue, postage cost per issue copy mailed, etc.). Total costs of a "typical" journal are presented where cost parameters are estimated from a sample of scientific scholarly journals and cost elements derived from estimates reported in the literature. Costs of electronic publications are also derived.

Machlup, Fritz, and Leeson, Kenneth. *Information Through the Printed Word: The Dissemination of Scholarly, Scientific, and Intellectual Knowledge.* New York: Praeger, 1978. (Volume 1, Book Publishing; Volume 2, Journals; Volume 4, Book, Journals, and Bibliographic Services.)

One Book/Five Ways: The Publishing Procedures of Five University Presses. Los Altos, CA: William Kaufmann, 1977.

Underwood, Richard G. *Production and Manufacturing Problems of American University Presses.* New York: Association of American University Presses, 1960.

http://www.lunis.luc.edu/snm96/publish/cost9601.htm
Contents: Preparation, Storage, and Serving Transmission and Reproduction.

http://members.tripod.it/europeanpress/page2.html
The Future of Academic Publishing
New Perspectives for Academic Publishing, article by Roberto Di Quirico (Ph.D.) founder of European Press Academic Publishing.

http://www-mathdoc.ujf- grenoble.fr/textes/Odlyzko/amo970325/amo970325.html
The Economics of Electronic Journals, Andrew Odlyzko AT&T Labs—Research amo@research.att.com.
Preliminary draft, March 25, 1997.

http://www.gwu.edu/~etlsl20/unit10 journals.htm
Scholarly Publishing and the World Wide Web: The Debate By Kathy Rutkowski

http://www.stir.ac.uk/infoserv/scurl/speakers/question.htm
The Future for Scholarly Publishing
Professor Bryan Coles Questions

http://www.stir.ac.uk/infoserv/scurl/speakers/question.htm
The Future for Scholarly Publishing
Professor Bryan Coles Questions

http://star.arabia.com/960620/TE4.html
The Internet and Economic Theory in Publishing:
Cyberperspectives on Old Paper Cost Issues
By Jawad Abbassi Special to The Star

References Related to CD-ROM Publishing

"CD-ROM Database Sales Should Hit about 2.2 mil by 1996 vs. 1.4 mil in 1991." *Computing World* (March 1992), p. 9.

"Market share of CD-ROM information products, Tabulated by Type of Product for 1988 and 1990," *Computer World* (Jan. 30, 1989), p. 77.

"Sales of Electronic Databases to Grow 20% in 1989 vs. 1988," *New York Times* (Dec. 30, 1988), p. 23.

Case, Donald. *Optical Disk Publication of Databases: A Review of Applications for Academic Libraries.* Los Angeles: GSLIS, Aug. 31, 1986.

Iles. Doug. "CD-ROM Enters Mainstream IS," *Computerworld* (June 5, 1989), pp. 75–80.

Miller, David C. *Special Report: Publishers, Libraries, & CD-ROM.* Benicia, CA: DCM Associates, March 1987. (Prepared for Fred Meyer Charitable Trust.)

Miller, David C. *The New Optical Media in the Library and the Academy Tomorrow* Benicia, CA: DCM Associates, Aug. 1986. (Prepared for Fred Meyer Charitable Trust.)

Miller, David C. *The New Optical Media Mid-1986: A Status Report.* Benicia, CA: DCM Associates, August 1986. (Prepared for Fred Meyer Charitable Trust.)

Paisley, William, and Butler, Matilda. "The First Wave: CD-ROM Adoption in Offices and Libraries," *Microcomputers for Information Management* 4, 2 (June 1987), pp. 109–127.

References Related to Online Publishing

Author's Guide to Electronic Manuscript Preparation and Markup. Version 2.0, rev. ed. Washington, DC: Association of American Publishers, 1989. ("An SGML application conforming to international standard ISO 8879, Standard generalized markup language. This is a companion guide to the American national standard for electronic manuscript preparation and markup ANSI/NISO.")

Castro, Elizabeth. *HTML for the World Wide Web.* Berkeley, CA: Peachpit Press, 1997.

"Making E-Books Easier on the Eyes," *Los Angeles Times,* Monday, March 20, 2000.

Smith, Joan M. *SGML and Related Standards: Document Description and Processing Languages.* New York: Ellis Horwood, 1992.

Technology and Scholarly Communication, edited by Richard Ekman and Richard E. Quandt. Berkeley: University of California Press, 1999. A very recent coverage of the impact of electronic publication.

"U.S. Counting on Web to be Census Source; Bureau Plans to Post Most of its 2000 Enumeration Data on the Internet. Switch from Paper to Hypertext Raises Information Issues," *Los Angeles Times,* Sunday, Nov. 15, 1998, Home Edition, Section A.

9

Libraries Within Larger Structures

Introduction

This chapter moves to the largest frame of reference—large-scale information structures such as national information systems—and explores its implication for library planning. Three structural contexts are discussed: (1) national information structures, (2) interlibrary cooperative structures, and (3) information economy structures.

9.1
Libraries Within National Information Structures

9.1.1 Libraries in Information Publication and Distribution

As was discussed in Chapter 8, libraries play a crucial role in national information structure as one of the primary means for information distribution.

9.1.2 Libraries Within National Social Policy

Among the social policies are two that have specific implications for libraries: (1) equity of access and (2) intellectual property rights (i.e., copyright). The first is a professional commitment of librarianship and has been so from time immemorial. But it is now embedded in *The Federal Telecommunications Act of 1996,* one of the major elements of which is the expanded concept of universal service. As a result of this Act, universal service now includes access, by all Americans, not only to telephones, but also to advanced communications and information services. The Act explicitly identifies "libraries, education, and health care delivery" as the means to assure universal information service.[1]

---

[1] See, for example, *Doorways to Information in the 21st Century,* http://www.nysl.nysed.gov/libdev/edl/thirdpln.htm.

Intellectual property rights are crucial to the development of information resources—to authorship, to investment by companies in the distribution of information, and to the creation of new intellectual products and services. In recognition of the special role played by libraries in our society, *The Copyright Revision Act of 1976* explicitly recognized the principle of "fair use" and provided a variety of special provisions to enable libraries to fulfill their roles in distribution of information.[2] Everything that has happened since then has confirmed both the desirability of those provisions and the ethical manner in which libraries have fulfilled their obligations, both to the copyright holders and to the publics the libraries serve.

However, the onrush of electronic means for distribution poses dramatic problems for the holders of copyright and they are rightly concerned. We cannot here go into the broad range of issues, both legal and technical, that create those problems. We can however, comment on the implications they have for libraries. Specifically, one of the means that the copyright holders have pursued is to place stringent limits on the concept of fair use, as it was formalized in *The Copyright Revision Act of 1976,* at least with respect to information in electronic formats (though much of the rhetoric has the clear intent of abrogating the entire concept of fair use). This would place the entire operation of libraries into an intolerable frame of reference, especially as it relates to library cooperation and the macroeconomic issues with which this chapter is concerned.

9.1.3 Libraries Within Information Economy Structures

Another of the structures with which we will be concerned in this chapter is the national macroeconomic structure. Of concern are policies related to the distribution of the workforce and the means by which they may encourage or support the transition from economies that are based on the relative mix in the labor force of persons devoted to subsistence agriculture (i.e., peasants), organized agriculture, industry, and information. They provide a basis for determining the appropriate allocation of labor to various kinds of activity, given the nature of a national economy.

In this context, then, there is a model of national information economies that has been incorporated into *LPM.* Already that model includes means for estimating the appropriate number of librarians, as a function of the progress toward an information economy within a country.

Its use within *LPM,* though, requires a shifting of the perspective from the point of view of the library, or even of the institution it serves, to that of the

---

[2] Public Law 94-553, revising the Copyright Law of the United States, Title 17, U.S. Code, effective January 1, 1978.

nation. Specifically, the model of the information economy sets the parameters for the range of information activities to reflect the status of national development. Those activities include education and research, so the resulting numbers of persons who are teachers and students represent the numbers of persons to be served by the set of academic libraries in the nation.

With that output from the model of national information economies serving as input to the population matrices of *LPM,* we have the means for deriving the necessary numbers of academic library staff and related budgets. That can be expressed either in terms of totals or as averages across the numbers of universities in the country.

9.2
Libraries Within Cooperative Structures

Among the structures we will examine in this chapter are those to support cooperation among libraries. Of course, libraries have a long history of cooperation, perhaps best exemplified by the system for interlibrary borrowing and lending. It has been a continuing theme for library management for decades. Today, though, there is an expansion of that tradition into a variety of contexts and purposes and into formalized structures.

9.2.1 Library Cooperative Contexts

Today, far beyond the context of interlibrary borrowing and lending, there are several formal contexts within which library cooperation is occurring.

Multiversity Systems

The term "multiversity" was coined by Clark Kerr, onetime President of the University of California (UC), to describe the kind of institution, represented by UC, that is a combination of multiple campuses, multiple disciplines, multiple research institutes, and multiple sources of funding working more or less together within a complex administrative structure. Today, the term is perhaps used in other ways, but taking that definition, it provides one of the most important contexts for library cooperation.

In most of the multiversities, the individual campuses effectively operate as independent institutions, and their libraries as independent libraries. However, typically there will be mechanisms for coordination and they will provide the framework for library cooperation. For example, in the UC system, there is the Library Council which serves formally as advisor to the president of the UC with respect to systemwide library policies.

Statewide Systems

Most of states of the United States have instituted statewide library systems embracing libraries of every type—public, academic, school, and special. The implementation of such systems was fostered by the Library and Construction Act during the 1960s, and development of these cooperative structures occurred at varying paces during the ensuing decades. In most cases, the state library serves as the administrative center.

In these statewide systems, the state library, the university libraries, and the largest public libraries will serve as the primary sources for materials. In some cases, those primary sources will be at least partially funded by the state for their services.

National Systems

There is no formal national system in the United States for library cooperation, except as it may be embodied in some virtual sense in the array of other structures. In contrast, in the United Kingdom, the British Library serves as an organizing focal point for the national system. In countries of Europe, there is a similar degree of centralized formal structure.

Contractual Arrangements

In the United States, there have been several examples of contractual arrangements to formalize library cooperation among a set of institutions. A case in point is the Center for Research Libraries, located in Chicago, which serves for cooperative storage of materials and shared use of those materials.

International Agreements

There are a few examples of international, multinational, and regional cooperative agreements. Some countries of Central and Eastern Europe have cooperated within the framework of such agreements, informal but still real. Another example is given by BIREME, located at the University of Sao Paulo, which serves as a focal point for cooperation among the medical libraries of the Caribbean, Central America, and South America.

9.2.2 Reasons for Library Cooperation

There have been several specific reasons for cooperation among libraries.

Sharing of Resources

This is certainly the starting point for library cooperation. It is explicitly represented by the process for interlibrary borrowing and lending that has been formalized for decades. But it has generated a number of supporting tools in the form of union catalogs, union lists of serials, and other cooperative means for determining where desired materials may be available.

Cooperative Acquisitions

This is a means for cooperation that obviously depends upon the sharing of resources, but it goes further in formalizing agreements in which specific institutions take responsibility for identified areas of acquisition. This implies some degree of sharing of funding as well as responsibility, and some formal arrangements include provision for pooling some portions of the acquisitions budgets of the participants.

Automation

The developments of automated systems has frequently been a focus of cooperation among libraries. The joint contracting for acquisition of a system, the sharing of costs in implementation and in operation, and the sharing of experience and staff expertise—these have been typical ways in which cooperation with respect to automated systems has occurred.

Shared Cataloging

The largest concentrated effort at cooperation among libraries certainly was the development of systems for shared cataloging. That effort is now represented by the international bibliographic databases of OCLC and RLIN. It grew out of the need for cooperation among libraries in the conversion of bibliographic records—catalogs especially—to machine-processible forms. The result, of course, is that now virtually every major library has the catalog for its entire collection in an online public access catalog (OPAC).

Shared Storage

As was identified in Chapter 6, the growth of library collections, whether exponential or linear, leads to the problem of allocating materials to alternative places for storage. The costs of storage facilities, though, are great enough that efficiency requires that they be shared by groups of cooperating libraries. Shared storage has therefore been another of the success stories in library cooperation.

Preservation and Access

Perhaps the most dramatic context for library cooperation has been that of "preservation and access." The underlying problem is the literal disintegration of the paper in books, especially those produced in the years since the introduction of acidic paper that self-destructs. It has been estimated that as much as 25% to 30% of the holdings of major research libraries are at risk.[3] To deal with this problem, the Council on Library Resources established the Commission on Preservation and Access as the focus for management of a major cooperative effort. The objectives were identified in testimony at a March 17 hearing of a

---

[3] Hayes, Robert, *The Magnitude, Costs and Benefits of the Preservation of Brittle Books.* Council on Library Resources, 1987.

Congressional committee: "Commission President Pat Battin proposed a model for a national cooperative microfilming program. A goal of filming 150,000 volumes a year would require 20 institutions to commit to filming 7,500 volumes each. At the 150,000 annual rate, it would take about 20 years to film 3 million volumes—the estimated number of volumes it would be important to save in order to preserve a representative portion of the 10 million or more volumes that will turn to dust by that time.")[4]

9.2.3 Library Network Models

Network Structure Models

Among the most fundamental decisions to be made about a library network is the structure it is to have. Is it to be hierarchical or can every library communicate directly with every other? Although this choice is likely to be based more on political policy than technical considerations, it is desirable to have some means for modeling the effects of the decision. One standard mathematical model is the graph, in which the network is described as a set of nodes with lines connecting them which show the direction of interlibrary communication. In their article in the issue of *Library Quarterly* devoted to the application of operations research to libraries, Korfhage, Bhat, and Nance describe the nature of graphs and illustrate their application to the design of a network of some 49 libraries.[5] A very specific evaluation of network structure alternatives was made in the state of Washington.[6] Three models were defined; estimates were made of the traffic load and processing costs under each; and evaluations were made of their relative cost/effectiveness. One model was the present, highly decentralized system, with each library communicating directly with others (although a few major resources, of course, bear the brunt of the traffic). A second alternative was a hierarchical structure, with libraries organized into both regional and specialized groups which are then combined through a switching center and bibliographic center. The third was a highly centralized system with every library reporting directly to a central switching point.

Communications Traffic Models

In such an evaluation, the volume of traffic to be expected among the libraries is significant since it provides the data on which to estimate the characteristics of the communication system. The data are best presented in the form

---

[4] The Commission on Preservation and Access, *Newsletter* (June 1988), number 1.

[5] Bhat, U. Narayan, Nance, Richard E., and Korfhage, Robert R. Information Networks: A Probabalistic Model for Hierarchical Information Transfer. Dallas, Texas: Southern Methodist University, 1971.

[6] Reynolds, Maryan E. et al. A Study of Library Network Alternatives for the State of Washington. Washington D.C.: U.S. Office of Education, Bureau of Research, 1971.

of a matrix in which the numbers represent the traffic between each pair of nodes in the network configuration being evaluated. Various configurations of switching centers and hierarchical arrangements of transmission among libraries can then be generated by arithmetic processing of this matrix. They can be compared with each other for their relative costs and efficiencies.

Response Time Models

Perhaps the most significant operational issue in network planning is that of response time. Normally, one would expect that material which must be obtained from a remote location, through a network, would be less readily accessible than if it is available at the local library. To explore the significance of this issue, a number of simulation models have been developed. Such models are traditional tools in operations research for exploring the consequences of decisions in exceedingly complex situations. In them, different aspects of a situation are described by equations, which are interrelated with each other. The computer can then carry out the calculations to show the effects of different conditions on the situation or to show changes in the situation over time. One such simulation was developed by HRB-Singer, Inc. to represent the response time from an information retrieval system.[7] The equations define the relations among different types of services, time schedules, work loads, and facilities. The simulation then generates requests for different types of services and shows what the effective response time of the system will be.

User Response Models

The Institute of Library Research designed another simulation model, which includes consideration of the users' response times to be expected from an operating network.[8] The model characterizes the users of a library network in terms of four factors: (a) their sources of information services (both within the library network and external to it); (b) their information requirements, in terms of services needed, subject areas of interest, and most important, the response time needed; (c) their expectations of quality and time of service from the library; and (d) the effects on them of both adequate and inadequate response time from the library. It is the last factor that represents the basic focus of the simulation. It assumes that if the user is disappointed, he or she will be less likely to use the library than before; if he or she is satisfied, more likely. The value of all these models is in their use as a means of exploring the alternative network designs in terms of their effects on cost, performance, or user satisfaction. As such they serve not as a substitute for judgment but as a support to it.

[7] HRB-Singer, Inc. Technical Reports on Information Storage and Retrieval Sysems. State College, Pa: The Company, 1962.

[8] Reilly, Kevin D. "Digital computer simulation model of library-based information retrieval systems," 3rd Annual Computer Science and Statistics Symposium, January 30-31, 1969. Los Angeles: Institute for Library Research, University of California, 1968.

Cost Trade-off Models

The issue of cost is of paramount importance since a major justification for a network is that there will be a cost saving if a group of system libraries can acquire and share a single copy of a book or journal rather than ten copies. Of course, the savings in cost of acquisition, cataloging, and storage of multiple copies must be balanced against the resulting increases in cost due to the need to use some interlibrary loan procedure (mechanized or otherwise). The Center for Research Libraries studied this kind of "trade-off analysis," accumulating data on the costs of both alternatives and determining average number of uses at which one alternative is cheaper than the other.[9]

9.2.4 Utility Functions for Library Cooperation

We turn now to the potential for application of cooperative game theories to library cooperation. As was discussed in Chapter 1, to represent a decision-making problem as a game requires that there be a measure of utility for each participant in the game. What are the elements of such a utility model for library cooperation?

Capital Investments and Operating Costs

We start with the most measurable elements, the capital investments and the operating costs associated with alternative options for solution of the decision-making problem. Normally, they will be measured in dollars, or equivalent, and can be readily accumulated.

Sometimes the context for possible cooperation may affect existing capital investments. For example, an effort to cooperate in the development of a joint automated system may need to recognize that a participant already has a system in place and that cooperation might entail changing that system, losing the existing capital investment and incurring additional capital costs.

Sometimes the context may affect current or future capital investments. Much of the discussion of Chapter 6 is focused specifically on the capital costs for collection. An effort to share acquisitions will usually entail a decision by one of the participants to eliminate the capital investment in acquisition and technical processing of materials in a specific subject area, under the assumption that needs for materials in that subject will be met by another participant. This concept underlay the Farmington Plan, as a national effort in which responsibility for collection development in specific subject areas was to be assigned to specific institutions. The other institutions could then, in principle, count on coverage of the subject fields and concentrate their own budgets on their more specific needs.

---

[9] Williams, Gordon et al. Library Cost Models: Owning versus Borrowing Serial Publications. For the Center for Research Libraries. Bethesda, Md.: Westat Research, Inc., 1968.

Sometime the context may affect operating costs. Much of the discussion in Chapters 4 and 5 focused on the operating costs. As an example, any system for interlibrary borrowing and lending or for document delivery entails substantial costs in both the borrowing and lending institutions. Those operating costs need to be included in any decision concerning shared acquisitions.

A major operating cost in library cooperation is the commitment of the time and energy of the library management and professional staff in negotiation and in governance. Probably the most successful example of library cooperation in the past several decades has been the development of the international bibliographic utilities (as represented by OCLC and RLIN). The impact on both library costs and library effectiveness has been immense. But these efforts have necessitated intense involvement of both directors of libraries, catalogers, and reference staff. The expenditures of time by exceptionally valuable persons have been immense. At some time in the process of evaluating options for library cooperation, those costs need to be considered.

Library Effectiveness

Any utility function for assessing options in library cooperation must consider the effect on users and on the overall productivity of the library. Unfortunately, these effects are not easily quantifiable. Of course, some may be, such as "response time" or "frequency of satisfaction." But others, such as "browseability," are not.

Governance

The utility function will need to recognize issues related to governance. They relate to centralization versus decentralization of decision-making in operation of cooperative enterprises, to the structure for control of policies, and to the relationships of the library to its parent institution. These issues are even less amenable to quantification than those for effectiveness.

Professional Ethics

Underlying all of the contexts of library cooperation is an ethical commitment of librarianship to the very concept itself. It is embedded in the profession and is a commitment evidenced in the long-standing commitment to interlibrary borrowing and lending despite the costs and inequities it entails. The major net lenders periodically will complain about the costs they incur and the adverse impact on services to their primary constituencies, but when the decision finally must be made, invariably it is in favor of cooperation.

In a sense, there is an underlying rationale for that professional commitment in the recognition that no library can be all-encompassing and that sharing is the only way to ensure preserving the record of the past and providing access to that record. But there appears to be something more than simply that pragmatic rationale in the view of librarianship that information indeed is a public good.

The Consequent Utility Function

Would that one could readily identify the utility function that will properly weight and combine this combination of quantitative and qualitative factors. In lieu of that, the utility function for application to library cooperation must be an individual assessment of the relative utility of options and, perhaps, a jointly agreed-upon combination of those individual assessments into a mutually acceptable criterion for the group of libraries participating in library cooperation.

9.2.5 Illustrative Applications of Cooperative Games

Two examples will serve to illustrate the potential for use of cooperative games in decision-making concerning library cooperation. One considers cooperative acquisitions and the other considers library automation.

Cooperative Acquisitions

As a start, for simplicity, let's suppose that there are just two institutions considering an agreement to share acquisitions. If one of them will assume responsibility for acquisition in a subject field, the second will save the costs of acquisition and technical processing for that subject. However, each will incur operating costs in meeting the needs of users in the institution served by the second library who need materials in that subject field from the first. The utility measure to be used will be quantitative and based simply on the total costs represented by any given choice.

In Chapter 1, a numerical example was presented to illustrate the determination of optimal mixtures of choices, and the following repeats the table of values but now interprets them as reflecting the net costs or benefits if the options are interpreted as acceptance of subject responsibility.

Choice	Cost to A	Value to B
Subject 1	−2	4
Subject 2	−2	2
Subject 3	−2	1
Subject 4	−2	2
Subject 5	−4	1

Choice	Value to A	Cost to B
Subject 6	10	−1
Subject 7	4	−1
Subject 8	6	−2
Subject 9	6	−4

The interpretation of this table is that there are nine subject areas being considered for cooperative acquisitions. Library A is renowned in the first five fields, and library B, in the last four. If library A were to accept responsibility for one of the first five fields, there would be estimated costs in fulfilling that obligation. Those costs might consist of increased levels of acquisition to meet the joint needs; they definitely would include costs in providing materials to borrowers from library B. On the other hand, library B would save substantial costs in acquisition and technical processing, though there would be counterbalancing costs in borrowing from library A. The values shown are interpreted as the estimates of those respective costs and benefits.

As was described in Chapter 1, this cooperative game has a solution: Library A accepts responsibility for subject fields 1 through 4 and library B for fields 6 through 8. The remaining fields are left out of the agreement. The net gain both to the individual libraries and in total would be substantially greater than if there were no agreement to cooperate

Now let's complicate the example by including three institutions and ten fields.

Choice Number	A	B	C	Choice Number	A	B	C
1	−2	2	2	6	6	−1	4
2	1	1	−2	7	1	3	−1
3	−2	1	0	8	3	−2	3
4	2	1	−2	9	2	−1	1
5	−4	1	3	10	4	−1	0

This numerical example will be interpreted as follows: There are three libraries (A, B, and C) that are considering a program of cooperative acquisitions. They have identified ten subject fields (choices 1 through 10) as potential candidates. For each choice, if the value for a given library is negative (such as for library A in choice 1), it will be responsible for that subject field. The value is negative for that library because they will now incur, perhaps, additional costs in added acquisitions and, surely, additional costs in providing lending services to users from the other libraries. The values for the other libraries (library B and C in the case of choice 1, for example) are positive because they will now save costs in acquisition in that subject field because they can depend upon the host library (library A for choice 1).

Parenthetically, it should be noted that underlying the choices shown above might be more basic choices reflecting the potential for two-party agreements. For example, choice 1 might be the sum of two more basic choices: $(-2,2,2) = (-1,2,0) + (-1,0,2)$. In this way, if additional libraries were to participate, perhaps without even serving as hosts for subject fields, their impact on costs would be directly represented in a parallel fashion.

But, returning to the example as shown, the options available are essentially the several combinations of the choices, of which there are 1024 (i.e., 2^{10}). The task is to determine the best among those combinations and the resulting distribution of benefits (or costs) among the participants. In general, it would appear that every choice for which the total of values was positive ought to be included, since the group of libraries as a whole would experience a net gain. Whether or not a choice for which there was a total of zero should be included is clearly debatable, but let's see what happens.

For this example, it turns out that the maximum Nash Value occurs if all of the choices are included, including that for which the total of values is negative as well as those for which it is zero. The total individual values are then (11,4,8) with a total for the group of 23 and a Nash Value of 352.

However, the option that excludes choice number 3 has total individual values (13,3,8), with a total for the group of 24 and a Nash Value of 312. It is therefore the option that should be selected if the goal is to maximize the total for the group as a whole.

The Shapley Values are (11.33, 4.33, 8.33), so there would need to be transfers from library A to libraries B and C to provide equity; otherwise, there would be no reason for library B to agree to that option since it would lose in comparison with the Nash Value maximum option (i.e., getting only 3 instead of 4). The Shapley values are calculated as follows:

$$U(A) = (1/3)\star 11 + (1/6)\star 15 + (1/6)\star 19 + (1/3)\star 24 - (1/3)\star 4 - (1/3)\star 8 - (1/6)\star 12 = 11.33$$

$$U(B) = (1/3)\star 4 + (1/6)\star 15 + (1/6)\star 12 + (1/3)\star 24 - (1/3)\star 11 - (1/3)\star 8 - (1/6)\star 19 = 4.33$$

$$U(C) = (1/3)\star 8 + (1/6)\star 19 + (1/6)\star 12 + (1/3)\star 24 - (1/3)\star 11 - (1/3)\star 4 - (1/6)\star 15 = 8.33$$

Cooperation in Automation

Let's suppose that there are several institutions considering an agreement to cooperate in the installation of a common system for automation in their libraries. If they can agree upon a common system, there should be significant benefits in cooperation. For example, as pointed out earlier, there may be savings from joint contracting in acquisition of the common system, savings in costs in implementation and in operation (such as in shared maintenance and replacement parts), efficiencies in sharing of experience and staff expertise, greater effectiveness in adding later improvements, and easier sharing of common data files.

Of course, balancing such benefits from cooperation may be the fact that each institution has a substantial investment in its current system. Part of that investment may be the residual value in amortization of the initial investment in the system. Another part, one likely to weigh even more heavily, is the fact that the existing system is well entrenched in the operating procedures of the library and the usage by its patrons.

All in all, the potential is that the benefits from cooperation will be sufficient enough to warrant at least careful evaluation of alternative systems.

There are thus at least four factors to be considered in the utility function for this application of cooperative game theory: (1) existing capital investments at each institution, (2) the costs for installation of each potential candidate for a replacement system, (3) the net benefits (i.e., difference between benefits and operating costs) to be anticipated from each potential candidate for a replacement system, and (4) the benefits to be anticipated from cooperation (which may vary from system, to system) by selection of a common system.

To apply cooperative game theory, it is assumed that those four factors are commensurate, both across factors and across institutions, so that they can be combined by simple arithmetic operations. It is also assumed that each factor is measured by a linear function of the size of the institution so it is expressible in the form $V(i,j) = A(i,j) + B(i,j) \star \mathrm{Size}(k)$, with the parameters A and B varying by factor (i) and system (j) and the size varying by institution (k). Finally, it is assumed that the parameters for benefits from cooperation are a linear function of the number of institutions selecting a common system so they are expressible in the form $A(4,j) = N(j) \star A'(j)$ and $B(4,j) = N(j) \star B'(j)$, where $N(j)$ is the number of institutions selecting system Sj and the parameters $A'(j)$ and $B'(j)$ are given for each system S_j.

The following numerical example will illustrate the model for just two institutions:

Institution	Size	Existing Investment	Current System	Best Choices	Net for Best	Shapley Values	Needed Transfers
J_1	3	6	1	1	27	24.00	−3.00
J_2	2	3	2	1	10	13.00	3.00

System	Installation Cost		Net Operating Benefit		Cooperation Benefit	
	Fixed	Linear	Fixed	Linear	Fixed	Linear
S_1	2	2	2	5	1	3
S_2	2	1	2	2	1	3
S_3	2	4	2	8	1	3

In this example, the existing investments are, respectively, 6 (for institution J_1 in system S_1) and 3 (for institution J_2 in system S_2). The potential third system, S_3, does not provide sufficient benefits to overcome the loss of the existing capital investment at J_1, but the values in cooperation are sufficient to warrant installation of S_1 at J_2. However, there needs to be compensation for the loss of investment at J_2, and the Shapley values, as shown, provide the basis for such compensation.

If the Net Operating Benefits for J3, are increased from 8 to 10, the results are as follows:

Institution	Size	Existing Investment	Current System	Best Choices	Net for Best	Shapley Values	Needed Transfers
J_1	3	6	1	3	22	23.00	1.00
J_2	2	3	2	3	16	15.00	−1.00

System	Installation Cost		Net Operating Benefit		Cooperation Benefit	
	Fixed	Linear	Fixed	Linear	Fixed	Linear
S_1	2	2	2	5	1	3
S_2	2	1	2	2	1	3
S_3	2	4	2	10	1	3

Note that both institutions lose their existing capital investments, but the benefits both from S_3 and from cooperation more than compensate. The Shapley Values in this case recognize the greater investment loss of institution J_1.

In the implementation of this model in LPM, provision has been made to include up to five institutions and up to six systems. For each institution and each system, the parameters shown in the above illustration need to be entered. That being done, LPM will then determine the optimum selections. In principle, different systems might best be selected by different coalitions, so LPM then determines the Shapley Values for that optimum by assessing the optimum choice for all possible coalitions of institutions and combining them as has been discussed in the definition of the Shapley measure. Specifically, the equitable payoff for each institution J_i is given by:

$$U_i = \Sigma[v(S)\star(s-1)!\star(N-s)!/N!] - \Sigma'[v(S)\star s!\star(N-s-1)!/N!]$$

where $v(S)$ is the total net benefits for coalition S, s is the number of institutions is coalition S, and N is the total number of institutions. The first sum, Σ, is taken over all possible coalitions that include institution i, and the second sum, Σ', is taken over all coalitions that do not include institution i. The sums together include all possible coalitions of institutions.

9.3
Libraries Within Information Economy Structures

9.3.1 Librarians as Components of the Information Economy

Librarians are by definition part of the workforce of the "substance" function and, especially, within the "information distribution" industries. In the United States in 1989, according to Bureau of Labor Statistics data, there were about 212,000 of them including both professional and nonprofessional staff of libraries and library-like agencies. They thus were about 1.3% of the workforce for substantive information staffing.

The librarians are heavily concentrated within distribution industries, though, especially in educational institutions. For example, the major university libraries (those that are members of the Association of Research Libraries) in 1989 employed about 35,000 persons (25% being professionals); higher education as a whole employed about 90,000. Public libraries employed another 90,000. That leaves about 32,000 for the rest of industry, with about half being professionals.

The distribution of professional librarians among the several classes of industry can be derived from statistics for the Special Libraries Association in the United States. The important point is the mismatch between those numbers and the workforce engaged in substantive information work in the low-technology industries. The implication is that there is a substantial need to upgrade the level of library support in those industries. Most particularly, the amount of use made of "published information" (the province of the librarian) is dramatically less in those industries than it is in the high technologies.

9.3.2 Structure of the Model

The starting point for the model is the accumulation of data for the distribution of the national workforce in two ways. First, the 1998 *Statistical Abstract of the United States* provides data on employment by SIC (Standard Industrial Classification) classes which serve as the sources of data for distribution of workforce by type of organization. Second, it provides data on employment by type of function or occupation, independent of the industry of employment (distinguishing between "employed" and "self-employed," though). The model accumulates these data into nine categories of organization and five categories of function.

In passing, it is relevant to note that the SIC will be replaced by the NAICS (North American Industry Classification System) starting in the year 2000. This change is long overdue, since the SIC dates from the mid-1930s and has become inadequate in its representation of national economic structures, especially with respect to the role of information activities.

9.3.3 Process for Determining Row and Column Totals

The Information Economy Model (InfoEcon) within *LPM* starts from data about the distribution of the U.S. workforce in two intersecting perspectives: (1) the distribution by InfoEcon functions, which are the columns of the matrix and (2) the distribution by types of industry, which are the rows of the matrix. In the first version of InfoEcon, presented some ten years ago, those distributions were estimated from a variety of sources. The estimates were, as a result, somewhat uncertain but they served the purpose at the time. Now they need to be more carefully determined and the process for doing so needs to be documented. The Appendix to this chapter provides the details of that process. Here the results will simply be summarized.

Column Totals (Functions)

For Column Totals (i.e., totals by functions in *LPM*'s InfoEcon Model), the primary source of data is Table 672, Employed Civilians, from Chapter 13 of *Statistical Abstract of the United States, 1998* (available at website www.census.gov/statab or on CD-ROM). It provides data for the years 1983 and 1997 showing Total Employment for each category of occupation. The data in it include, in addition to Total Employment, the percentages of the total employment that were Female, Black, or Hispanic, but the only values that will be used here are those for the total employment.

9.3.4 Model of National Information Economies

The following matrix is, with some small changes reflecting prior assessments that should be continued for consistency in the model, derived from those values:

	Category of Function					
	Non/Information	Information Functions				
Category of Organization	Functions	Management	Support	Hardware	Substance	Total
Peasant						0.30
Agriculture						2.70
Noninformation Industries						
Low Tech						62.90
Inform. Facilities						2.40
High Tech						11.30
Information Industries						
Transactions						5.30
Hardware						3.30
Distribution						9.00
Academic						2.80
TOTALS	52.95	10.00	14.58	7.33	15.17	100.00

Note that the 3% of the workforce engaged in Agriculture has been divided into two categories: Peasant and Agriculture. They result from a calculation within the model, as follows:

Peasant = Agriculture⋆ Agriculture/(Agriculture + Industry)

Industrial Agriculture = Agriculture⋆ Industry/(Agriculture + Industry)

The former is intended to represent that portion of the agricultural workforce engaged in "subsistence" agriculture. The latter is intended to represent the portion of the agricultural workforce engaged in "industrial" agriculture. The purpose of this division is to provide means for dealing with those countries that have a significant peasant population. But note that the model projects a peasant population even in so highly industrialized a country as the United States. While that may seem surprising, the facts are that subsistence agriculture is still a reality within the United States in regions such as Appalachia.

Note that the source data do not directly show the values within the body of the matrix. The purpose of the model is to provide means for estimating those values, maintaining the row and column totals as closely as possible, while limiting the number of parameters to as few as possible.

Parameters in the Model of National Information Economies

The model is intended to be a descriptive basis for assessing the fine structure of national information economies, not a predictive one, even though it is expressed numerically. So the numbers used to represent the relevant parameters are deliberately at a low level of precision—just one or two decimal digits. Furthermore, the number of parameters is limited.

The following matrix shows the default values for parameters that relate to the distribution of staff across the several functions for each category of organization.

Distributions of Staff by Function and Category of Organization					
		Category of Function			
Category of Organization	Non/Information Functions	Information Functions			
		Management	Support	Hardware	Substance
Peasant	0.90	0.10	0.00	0.00	0.00
Agriculture	0.65	0.10	0.15	0.03	0.07
Noninformation Industries					
Low Tech	0.65	0.10	0.15	0.03	0.07
Inform. Facilities	0.65	0.10	0.15	0.03	0.07
High Tech	0.25	0.10	0.15	0.15	0.35
Information Industries					
Transactions	0.25	0.10	0.15	0.15	0.35
Hardware	0.25	0.10	0.15	0.15	0.35
Distribution	0.25	0.10	0.15	0.15	0.35
Academic	0.25	0.10	0.15	0.15	0.35

The values for "management" and for "support" are taken uniformly, over all categories of organization (except peasant agriculture), at 10% and 15%, respectively, based on the reported data for employment in the United States. The other values for distribution of staff reflect the relative levels for use of staff by function in the different categories of organization. Note that the values used as defaults are minimal in number and reflect simple, repeated ratios. Note also that the values in each row must total 1.00, so the values for noninformation functions are taken as the difference between 1.00 and the sum of the other values in the row.

The resulting estimate for distribution of the workforce is then derived by multiplying the values in corresponding cells of these two matrices with the respective row totals. The result is as follows:

Percentage Distribution of U.S. Workforce in 1990					
		Category of Function			
Category of Organization	Non/Information Functions	Information Functions			
		Management	Support	Hardware	Substance	TOTAL
Peasant	0.27	0.03	0.00	0.00	0.00	0.30
Agriculture Noninformation Industries	1.76	0.27	0.41	0.08	0.19	2.70
Low Tech	40.89	6.29	9.44	1.89	4.40	62.90
Inform. Facilities	1.56	0.24	0.36	0.07	0.17	2.40
High Tech Information Industries	2.83	1.13	1.70	1.70	3.96	11.30
Transactions	1.33	0.53	0.80	0.80	1.86	5.30
Hardware	0.83	0.33	0.50	0.50	1.16	3.30
Distribution	2.25	0.90	1.35	1.35	3.15	9.00
Academic	0.70	0.28	0.42	0.42	0.98	2.80
Totals	52.40	10.00	14.96	6.80	15.86	100.00

Despite the limited number of parameters and the low precision in the related values, the column totals are remarkably close to those from the original data:

Original	52.95	10.00	14.58	7.33	15.17	100.00
Model	52.40	10.00	14.96	6.80	15.86	100.00

A second set of parameters represents the ratio of "outsource" to "in-house" and allows the model to represent the fact that there is essential equivalence between doing work in-house and purchasing it from an outside vendor, but the former results in a need for staff. Multiplying that ratio on the level of in-house staff provides the basis for estimating externally contracted staff or the materials or services they provide.

The values used for "Outsource/In-House" reflect published data on that ratio for different specific functions. In particular, they are uniformly taken at 3/4 for noninformation functions and at 1/3 for most information functions. However, for information functions, there is evidence of a strong "diagonal dominance," with transaction industries purchasing heavily from transaction industries, information hardware and software from hardware and software industries, and distribution from distribution industries. For example, banking as a transaction industry depends heavily upon accounting services and telecom-munications, which are other transaction industries. For those diagonal ele-ments, therefore, the ratio is taken at 2/3.

Distributions of Outsource/In-House Ratio by Function and Category of Organization					
		Category of Function			
Category of Organization	Non/Information Functions	Information Functions			
		Management	Support	Hardware	Substance
Peasant	0.75	0.10	0.10	0.10	0.10
Agriculture	0.75	0.33	0.33	0.33	0.33
Noninformation Industries					
Low Tech	0.75	0.33	0.33	0.33	0.33
Inform. Facilities	0.75	0.33	0.33	0.33	0.33
High Tech	0.75	0.33	0.33	0.33	0.33
Information Industries					
Transactions	0.75	0.33	0.66	0.33	0.33
Hardware	0.75	0.33	0.33	0.66	0.33
Distribution	0.75	0.33	0.33	0.33	0.66
Academic	0.75	0.33	0.33	0.33	0.66

9.3.5 National Policy Planning in Other Countries

To this point, the model has been derived as a representation of the infor-mation economy of the United States. If that were the end of it, there would be at most descriptive value. The intent in developing the model is to provide a basis for assessment of other contexts, especially those in countries in transi-tion through the stages from subsistence agriculture to industry into the infor-mation age.

To that end, one more parameter is needed—one that represents the stage or level in that development. The underlying assumption is that the level of development is exhibited in the extent to which various kinds of information resources are used within the economy. That parameter (shown by X) enters into the model as a multiplier on the percentage values for the distributions in the United States in 1990, as shown above, in the following fashion:

		Application of Level of Information Economy Development			

		Category of Function			
			Information Functions		
Category of Organization	Non/Information Functions	Management	Support	Hardware	Substance
Peasant	1	1	0	0	0
Agriculture Noninformation Industries	1	1	X	X	X
Low Tech	1	1	X	X	X
Inform. Facilities	1	1	X	X	X
High Tech Information Industries	1	1	X	X	X
Transactions	1	1	1	X	X
Hardware	1	1	X	1	X
Distribution	1	1	X	X	1
Academic	1	1	X	X	1

The model determines the level of development by the following calculation:

Let A = Percent of Workforce in Industrial Agriculture (i.e., nonsubsistence agriculture)
B = Percent of Workforce in Industry
C = Percent of Workforce in Services

$$X = 1.6 \star (C - 0.2 \star (A + B + C))$$

The rationale underlying this calculation is the assumption that there is a basic component of services that is really "personal services" and that is taken at 20% of the non-peasant population. The remainder of the Services workforce is then assumed to be information related. The factor of 1.6 is so that X is normalized to the United States in 1990.

A second calculation is made in the model to estimate the allocation of non-information industry staff totals between low-technology industries and high-technology industry. It is based on the assumption that high-technology industry depends heavily upon the information infrastructure of the country. The calculation is as follows:

$$Y = 115 \star X / (B + X)$$

The factor of 115 again serves to normalize to the United States in 1990. The value of Y is multiplied onto B, the percent of the workforce in industry, to estimate the percentage in high technology. The value $(1 - Y)$ is multiplied onto B to estimate the percentage in low technology.

9.3.6 The Effects of Digital Libraries

Online services overall represent only about 5% of the total of $20B for organizations engaged in information distribution, though they are totally concentrated on digital information while the other agencies (book distributors and retail outlets, academic and public libraries) cover the full range of information media. In academic libraries, for example, computer data files in 1996 represented only 5% of total acquisitions.[10] Assuming that a similar proportion applies to the other Distribution agencies and that staff are roughly in the same proportion, that would imply another $1B (i.e., 5% of $20B) in digital library distribution. Hence, the total commitment of manpower in digital library distribution—Internet and CD-ROM—would be about 260K with 87K in non-information industries and 173K in Distribution agencies. The total of 173K represents about 3% of the total substantive staffing within Distribution industries.

Now, the evidence is clear that digital libraries are increasing exponentially. CD-ROM publication has been doubling every two to three years for several years, and the Internet overall has been doubling every six months to one year. If a doubling at say every two years were to continue for the coming five-year period, the number of persons in total would increase by a factor of about 6 to nearly 1.5M persons. That is not a dramatic proportion of the substantive information workers, amounting to just 10% of the 15M total.

Is that rational? Well, just consider one expected effect of digital libraries—the conversion of library acquisitions of scholarly journals from print formats to digital formats. It is possible that within the coming five-year period, 20% of scholarly journals might experience such a change and within the coming ten-year period, perhaps 50%. Beyond that, libraries themselves are increasingly becoming involved in the production of digital libraries. This would imply a shifting of staff in both the producers of them and in the libraries that acquire them and provide services from them from a focus on print to one on digital libraries.

An even more important phenomenon is the extent to which companies in the noninformation sector are using the Internet as means for distributing digital libraries related to their business. In effect, they are becoming a part of the information sector. In the macroeconomic context, the result is a significant increase in the percentage of the nation's workforce in substantive information work, all with a focus on digital libraries.

---

[10] Stubbs, Kenyon L. and Molyneux, Robert E., *Research Library Statistics*. Washington, DC: Association of Research Libraries. Data for 1995/96 and 1996/97 downloaded from http://viva.lib.virginia.edu/socsci/arl/data.html.

Another fascinating phenomenon is the growth of personal websites. Many of them are highly professional both in appearance and in content. In effect, the consumers are becoming producers of information products, and the result again is a significant increase in the percentage of the nation's workforce in substantive information work. Note that the FTE involved in maintenance of a service provider website is really minuscule—perhaps 1% of an FTE (as calculated above in the discussion of service providers) This makes it completely feasible for a person to produce and maintain a site simply as a hobby. This is a growth in the number of persons focused on digital libraries that is a net increase, not simply a shifting of focus. All of this makes the projected growth not only rational but likely.

Of course, everything said to this point has been in the context of a highly developed information economy such as is found in the United States. What is the picture for countries at other stages in development?

The data for Internet sites includes a row for "Other Countries." The following expands that into four subgroups, essentially reflecting levels of development of information economies. To arrive at these values, the totals for each country, as reported in the *Internet Domain Survey*,[11] were divided by the country's population: the entire set of some 250 countries was sequenced in descending order by the values for Hosts/Population.[12] The countries were divided into four groups (of 30, 30, 30, and 160); totals were calculated for each column and then divided by the total population for the group.

		Population (in millions)	Hosts per Population	Level 2 per Population	Level 3 per Population	Level 4 per Population
\multicolumn{7}{l}{**Internet Hosts in Groups of Countries**}						
1998						
Group 1	30 Countries	917	31,309	838	11,099	19,366
Group 2	30 Countries	736	1,025	14	235	776
Group 3	30 Countries	667	205	1	24	180
Group 4	160 Countries	4,691	10	0	1	9
1999						
Group 1	30 Countries	916	45,497	1,395	15,904	28,244
Group 2	30 Countries	849	1,543	23	343	1,177
Group 3	30 Countries	548	249	1	27	222
Group 4	160 Countries	4,699	16	0	2	14
2000						
Group 1	30 Countries	917	75,871	2,167	23,235	50,509
Group 2	30 Countries	920	2,607	31	523	2,052
Group 3	30 Countries	323	529	3	68	458
Group 4	160 Countries	4,851	38	0	3	35

[11] Op cit *(Internet Domain Survey)*.

[12] It is fascinating to find Finland, with a population 1/60th that of the United States, 25% greater in the number of Internet hosts per person (at least, in January 1998)!

Note that the mix of countries in each group changed slightly from year to year, as shown in the population data (which was held constant for each country). The countries in Group 1 are quite similar to the United States in their general economic development; those in the other three groups, successively less developed. There are four levels of development that are parallels to these four groups of countries. Those in Group 1 would be similar to the picture for the United States; those in Group 2 are other industrialized countries; those in Group 3 are less industrialized, and those in Group 4 are essentially peasant economies.

Bibliography

References on Library Networks

"ARL and RLG to Study ILL Costs," *Library Hotline* 21, 17 (April 17, 1992), p. 102.

"Research Library Directors Evaluate OCLC's Future at Conference," *Research Libraries in OCLC: A Quarterly* 309 (Spring 1989).

"RLG in 1992: Setting the Stage for Change," *Research Library Group News* 26 (Fall 1991), pp. 3–4.

ARL/RLG Interlibrary Loan Cost Study: Worksheet. Washington, DC: ARL, 1992.

Currier, Lura Gibbons. *Sharing Resources in the Pacific Northwest.* Olympia: Washington State Library, 1969.

Hayes, Robert M. "The Benefits and Costs of Inter-institutional Cooperation," in Woodsworth, Anne, *Managing the Economics of Owning, Leasing, and Contracting Out Information Services.* Anne Woodsworth and James F. Williams, II. Aldershot, England, Gower, Brookfield. VT: Ashgate, 1994.

Hayes, Robert M. "Distributed Library Networks: Programs and Problems," *The Responsibility of the University Library Collection in Meeting the Needs of its Campus and Local Community.* La Jolla: Friends of the UCSD Library, 1976.

Lowry, Charles B. "Resource Sharing or Cost Shifting? The unequal Burden of Cooperative Cataloging and ILL in Network," *College and Research Libraries,* (January 1990), pp. 11–19. Press Release: RLG Board Sets Organization's Course for the 1990s" (March 8, 1991).

Reynolds, Maryan E., et al. *A Study of Library Network Alternatives for the State of Washington.* Olympia: Washington State Library, January 1971.

Reynolds, Maryan E., et al. *Construction of a Decision-Making Model for Library Network Implementation in Washington State.* Olympia: Washington State Library, June 1970.

Rouse, William B. *Management of Library Networks: Policy Analysis, Implementation, and Control.* New York: Wiley, 1980.

Shurkin, Joel. "The Rise and Fall and Rise of RLG," *American Libraries* (July/August 1982), pp. 450–455.

The Structure and Governance of Library Networks: Proceedings of the 1978 Conference in Pittsburgh, Pennsylvania. Co-sponsored by National Commission on Libraries and Information Science and University of Pittsburgh; edited by Allen Kent, Thomas J. Galvin. New York: Dekker, 1979.

Stubbs, Kenyon. "Introduction." *ARL Statistics, 1990–91.* Washington, DC: ARL, 1992. (Shows increase in ILL borrowing of 47% from 1985/86 through 1990/91, a compounded rate of 8%. However, OCLC data showed a *doubling* of ILL borrowing from 1985/86 through 1990/91, a compounded rate of 15%!)

References on Intellectual Property Rights and Fair Use

"Intellectual Property Rights and Fair Use: Strengthening Scholarly Communication in the 1990s," *Proceedings of the 9th Annual Conference of Research Library Directors.* Dublin, OH: OCLC, 1991.

191 US Congress, Senate Committee on the Judiciary. *Moral Rights in Our Copyright Laws:* Hearings before the Subcommittee: June 20, September 20, and October 24, 1989. Washington: U.S. GPO, 1990.

Avram, Henriette D. "Copyright in the Electronic Environment," *Educom Review,* 24, 3 Fall 1989, pp. 31–33.

Copyright Policies in ARL Libraries. Washington, DC: Association of Research Libraries, Office of Management Studies, Systems and Procedures Exchange Center, 1984. SPEC Kit 102.

Crews, Donald Kenneth. *Copyright Policies at American Research Universities: Balancing Information Needs and Legal Limits.* Los Angeles: UCLA doctoral dissertation, 1990.

Crews, Kenneth D. *Copyright at the Research University: A Select Bibliography of Secondary Literature, 1967–1986.* Los Angeles: GSLIS, October 31, 1986.

Griffiths, Jose-Marie, and Donald W. King. *Intellectual Property Rights in an Age of Electronics and Information.* Washington, DC: Office of Technology Assessment, U.S. Congress, 1986.

Nimmer, David. *The Berne Convention Implementation Act of 1988.* New York: Bender, 1989.

Ricketson, Sam. *The Berne Convention for the Protection of Literary and Artistic Works: 1886–1986.* London: Centre for Commercial Law Studies, Queen Mary College, Kluwer, 1987.

S2370 and HR 4263, to amend the Copyright Act to clarify applicability of fair use standards to both published and unpublished works

S521-34 Fair Use and Unpublished Works. Washington, DC: GPO, July 11, 1990.

United States Code, 1988 Edition. Title 17, Section 107 defines fair use. Section 107 defines the rights of libraries to make copies under specific conditions.

University Copyright Policies in ARL Libraries. Washington, DC: Association of Research Libraries, Office of Management Studies, 1987. SPEC kit 138.

U.S. Congress, House Committee on the Judiciary *Berne Convention Implementation Act of 1987. Hearings Before the Subcommittee:* June 17, July 23, September 16 and 30, 1987, February 9 and 10, 1988. Washington, DC: U.S. GPO, 1988.

U.S. Congress, Senate Committee on the Judiciary. *The Berne Convention: Hearings Before the Subcommittee:* February 18 and March 3, 1988. Washington, DC: U.S. GPO, 1988.

References Related to National Information Policies

"Federal Data Go Private: Vendors Repackage Public Information—At a Price that Limits Access," *Christian Science Monitor* 82, 209 (Monday, Sep. 24, 1990), p. 15.

A Proposal to Establish the Library of Congress Fee Services Fund. Washington, DC: Library of Congress, June 12, 1990.

Crowe, Beryl. "The Tragedy of the Commons Revisited," *Science* 166, 3909 (Nov. 28, 1969), pp. 1103–1107.

Freeman, Harry L. "Blame Statistics for Trade Deficit," *Wall Street Journal,* (July 1989).

Fuerbringer, Jonathan. "Accuracy in Short Supply in Flood of U.S. Statistics," *New York Times* 139, 48039 (Oct. 30, 1989), pp. A1, D4.

Hardin, G. "The Tragedy of the Commons," *Science,* 162, 3859 (Dec. 13, 1968), pp. 1243–1248.

Hayes, Robert M. "A Commentary on the NCLIS Public Sector/Private Sector Task Force and its Report," *Minutes of the Ninety-Ninth Annual Meeting, The Association of Research Libraries.* Washington, DC: ARL, 1982, pp. 12–41.

Hayes, Robert M. "Politics and Publishing in Washington," *Special Libraries* 74, 4 (Oct. 1983), pp. 322–331.

Hayes, Robert M. "Pricing Policies of the National Library of Medicine," editorial, *Annals of Internal medicine* 100, 4 (April 1984), pp. 601–604.

Hayes, Robert M. *Pricing of Products and Services of the National Library of Medicine and Competition with the Private Sector: A Review of Relevant Reports. A Report to the U.S. Department of Health and Human Services,* August 1983. The NLM repeatedly was attacked by Excerpta Medica and accused of unfair competition because of NLM's pricing policies. I was asked by DHEW to review the reports that related to this issue.

Hayes, Robert M. "The President's Private Sector Survey on Cost Control: An Opinion Essay on the Grace Commission Report," *Government Information Quarterly* 3, 1 (Jan. 1986), pp. 73–81; and Hayes, Robert M. "Response to J.P. Grace," *Government Information Quarterly* 3, 3 (1986), pp. 307–312. The "Grace Commission Report" was really the statement of the agenda of the Reagan administration. I was asked to review it for *Government Information Quarterly,* but my review was sufficiently controversial that they decided to publish it not as a review as such but as an "opinion essay" (that being their term). J. Peter Grace wrote a letter to *Government Information Quarterly* attacking what I had said and I responded to his letter. It was an interesting exercise in mathematical modeling.

North American Industry Classification System. Prepared by the Office of Management and Budget's Economic Classification Policy. See http://www.naics.com/. The NAICS has replaced the SIC (Standard Industry Classification) that has been the basis for U.S. economic statistics for the past many decades. The changes are not cosmetic but are quite substantive and reflect, in particular, the "information economy." This site makes reference to the "official" NAICS manual which includes: 350 new industries, more than 300 pages of detailed industry definitions, tables showing correspondence between 1997 NAICS and 1987 SICs codes and vice versa, and alphabetic lists of more than 18,000 types of business activities and their corresponding NAICS code. It also provides access to a History of SIC/NAICS, discussion of the Principles of NAICS Development, the NAICS Structure and Implementation Schedule, and Key Government Contacts.

Public Sector/Private Sector Interaction in Providing Information Services: Report to the NCLIS from the Public Sector/Private Sector Task Force. Washington, DC: NCLIS, 1982. I served as Chairman of this Task Force and was largely responsible for its Report. This reference is included because of the issues related to government information policy.

Reagan, Ronald. *The President's Decision Memorandum: Transfer of the Civil Space Remote Sensing Systems to the Private Sector.* The White House, Feb. 28, 1983.

Rich, Spencer. "Drawing the Line on Poverty: Census Bureau Measurement Sparks Criticism from Many Quarters," *Washington Post* (Oct. 30, 1989), p. A13.

References on Information Economy

Hayes, Robert M. "Economics of Information," in Feather, John and Sturges, Paul, *International Encyclopedia of Information and Library Science.* London: Routledge, 1997, pp. 116–129.

Hayes, Robert M. "Libraries as a Component of the Information Economy," *Proceedings, 2nd Pacific Conference on New Information Economies,* Singapore, May 29–31, 1989, pp. 141–158.

Hayes, Robert M. "A Simplified Model for the Fine Structure of National Information Economies," Chen, Ching-chih. *Proceedings of NIT'92, 5th International Conference on New Information Technology.* West Newton, MA: MicroUse Information, 1992.

Hayes, Robert M. "Added Value as a Function of Purchases of Information Services," (with Timothy Erickson), *The Information Society* 1, 4 (Dec. 1982), pp. 307–338.

Hayes, Robert M. "Information and Productivity," *Proceedings of the Conference on Universities in World Network of Information and Communication III,* Dubrovnik, Yugoslavia, May 20–23, 1980. *IRICHE Bulletin,* vol. 6, nos. 1/2, 1980, pp. 21–35. Zagreb: Inter-University.

Hayes, Robert M. "Libraries as a Component of the Information Economy," *Proceedings, 2nd Pacific Conference on New Information Economies,* Singapore, 29-1 May 1989, pp. 141–158.

Hayes, Robert M. "Productivity, Libraries, and Information Services: A Quantitative Approach," *Mathematical Social Sciences* 7 (Feb. 1984), pp. 112–114.

Hayes, Robert M. *Strategic Management for Academic Libraries.* Westport, CT: Greenwood Press, 1993 (in press).

Hayes, Robert M. *Strategic Management for Public Libraries.* Westport, CT: Greenwood Press, 1996.

Hayes, Robert M. "The Fine Structure of Community Information Economies," *Proceedings, Collogue International Economie fr L Information.* May 18–20, 1995.

Hayes, Robert M. "The Management of Library Resources: The Balance Between Capital and Staff in Providing Services," *Library Research* 1, 2 (Summer 1979), pp. 119–142.

Hayes, Robert M. (ed.). *Libraries and the Information Economy of California.* Los Angeles: UCLA/GSLIS, 1987.

Hayes, Robert M., and Erickson, Timothy. "Added Value as a Function of Purchases of Information Services," *The Information Society* 1, 4 (Dec. 1982), pp. 307–338.

Hayes, Robert M., Pollock, Ann M., and Nordhaus, Shirley. "An Application of the Cobb-Douglas Model to the Association of Research Libraries," *Library and Information Science Research* 5, 3 (Fall 1983), pp. 291–325.

Porat, Marc Uri. *The Information Economy: Definition and Measurement.* Washington, DC: U.S. Department of Commerce, Office of Telecommunications, May 1977.

Appendix

The Information Economy Model within *LPM* starts from data about the distribution of the U.S. workforce in two intersecting perspectives: (1) the distribution by information economy functions, which are the columns of the matrix and (2) the distribution by types of industry, which are the rows of the matrix. In the first version of this information economy model, presented some ten years ago, those distributions were estimated from a variety of sources. The estimates were, as a result, somewhat uncertain but they served the purpose at the time. Now they need to be more carefully determined and the process for doing so needs to be documented.

This Appendix to Chapter 9 provides the details of that process.

Column Totals (Types of Occupation)

The following table presents the data on which the column totals are calculated, together with an assignment of each occupation to a function in the information economy model. The codes are shown in the first column and represent the following assignments.

(1) Noninformation functions
(2) Management functions
(3) Support functions
(4) Information Hardware functions
(5) Information Substantive functions

(Blank) Represented either in the preceding total or in the following detailed entries

A double entry (like "5 2") means that the data needs to be recorded under the first code ("5" in the example) but subtracted from the second code

("2" in the example). The subtraction from the second code is because the entry was included in a larger entry under that code.

Unfortunately, it is by no means self-evident or easy to make those assignments. For several of the occupations there are suboccupations, but for some of those (as indicated by a "2" at the end of the name) the suboccupations do not include all of those in the main occupation. Beyond that, it is difficult from the title to identify the major function involved. As a result, the assignments shown here are somewhat arbitrary, so you should feel free to make other assignments and test them for their effect on the InfoEcon Model.

	OCCUPATION	1983	1997		OCCUPATION	1983	1997
		Total (1,000)	Total (1,000)			Total (1,000)	Total (1,000)
	Total	100,834	129,558	3	......Information clerks	1,174	1,993
	Managerial and professional specialty	23,592	37,686	3	......Records process, less financial 2	866	935
2	...Executive, managerial 2	10,772	18,440	3	......Financial records processing 2	2,457	2,196
5 2	......Administrators, education s	415	733	4	......Duplicating, office machine ops	68	77
5 2	......Managers, medicine and health	91	701	4	......Commun equipment operators	256	185
5 2	......Managers, properties, real estate	305	535	1	......Mail and message distributing	799	977
3 2	......Management-related occup 2	2,966	4,604	1	......Material record, schedule, distrib 2	1,562	1,953
5	...Professional specialty 2	12,820	19,245	5	......Adjusters and investigators	675	1,701
4	...Technicians and related support	3,053	4,214	3	......Misc admin support 2	2,397	3,576
2	......Supervisors and proprietors	2,958	4,635	1	Service occupations	13,857	17,537
5	......Sales reps, finance services 2	1,853	2,613	1	......Mechanicss, not supervisors 2	3,906	4,428
5	......Sales reprs, commod, except retail	1,442	1,507	4 1	......Electric, electronic repair 2	674	726
1	......Sales, retail, personal services	5,511	6,887	1	...Construction trades	4,289	5,378
1	......Sales-related occupations	54	91	1	...Extractive occup	196	145
3	......Supervisors	676	685	4	...Precision production occup	3,685	3,926
4	......Computer equipment operators	605	392	1	Operators, fabricators, and laborers	16,091	18,399
3	......Secretaries, stenograph, typists 2	4,861	3,692	1	Farming & Forestry	3,648	4,143

But employees is not the whole story. We must also consider Table 661, Self-Employed Persons.

Item	1970	1980	1990	1993	1994	1995	1996	1997
Total self-employed	7,031	8,642	10,097	10,280	10,648	10,482	10,490	10,513
Industry:								
Agriculture	1,810	1,642	1,378	1,320	1,645	1,580	1,518	1,457
Nonagriculture	5,221	7,000	8,719	8,960	9,003	8,902	8,971	9,056
Mining	14	28	24	17	13	16	15	14
Construction	687	1,173	1,457	1,549	1,506	1,460	1,496	1,492
Manufacturing	264	358	427	439	426	433	406	422
Transportation	196	282	301	372	385	396	432	438
Trade	1,667	1,899	1,851	1,886	1,906	1,772	1,760	1,761
Finance, etc	254	458	630	655	625	660	674	629
Services	2,140	2,804	4,030	4,041	4,142	4,166	4,189	4,300
Occupation:								
5 Managerial professional	(NA)	(NA)	3,050	3,078	3,106	3,147	3,288	3,432
5 Technical, sales, and adminis support.	(NA)	(NA)	2,240	2,319	2,380	2,341	2,304	2,219
1 Service occupations	(NA)	(NA)	1,207	1,044	1,178	1,190	1,198	1,179
4 Precision product, craft, and repair	(NA)	(NA)	1,675	1,888	1,740	1,618	1,595	1,651
1 Operators, fabricators, laborers	(NA)	(NA)	567	631	639	631	634	629
1 Farming, forestry, and fishing	(NA)	(NA)	1,358	1,320	1,605	1,556	1,471	1,403

The data are even more uncertain since they are totally agglomerated into just the few major categories. Given no other data, the distributions for each occupation category for the self-employed will be taken as in the same ratios as those for the employed (as shown above). The values from this table for 1997 will be added to those for 1997 in the table above, as shown below:

	Managerial and professional specialty	3,432
2	Managerial and professional specialty	1,018
3	Managerial and professional specialty	431
5	Managerial and professional specialty	1980
	Technical, sales, and administrative support.	2,219
1	Technical, sales, and administrative support.	563
2	Technical, sales, and administrative support.	210
3	Technical, sales, and administrative support.	345
4	Technical, sales, and administrative support.	420
5	Technical, sales, and administrative support.	282
1	Service occupations	1,179
	Precision production, craft, and repair	1,651
1	Precision production, craft, and repair	1,067
4	Precision production, craft, and repair	584
1	Operators, fabricators, and laborers	629
	Farming, forestry, and fishing	1,403
1	Farming, forestry, and fishing	1,263
2	Farming, forestry, and fishing	140

The following shows the final results as percentages for comparison with default values as used in *LPM* and with the results from applying *LPM* to development at 110% of U.S. 1980. Note that the 1983 data do not include consideration of self-employment, since occupation distribution data for that year were "not available" in Table 661.

Code	LPM Column	1983 Percent	1997 Percent	LPM Orig	LPM @ 110
1	Non-Information Functions	49	45	49.51	44.04
2	Management Functions	10	13	10.00	10.00
3	Support Functions	15	13	14.83	16.42
4	Information Hardware Functions	8	8	7.69	8.97
5	Information Substantive Functions	17	21	17.97	20.57
		100	100	100.00	100.00

The *LPM* original values were largely based on pre-1980 data. It would appear that there has been a substantial increase in development of the U.S. information economy.

Row Totals (Types of Industry)

The following will be used as the sources for data for the row totals:

Note that the time periods for these tables vary greatly. This is obviously a complication in bringing the several sources together into a coherent total picture.

The starting point for estimation of the row totals in the InfoEcon Model is Table 675, also from Chapter 13 of *Statistical Abstract of the United States, 1999*. It provides data for the employment by industry for the years 1970, 1980, 1990, 1995, and 1997. The total shown for 1997 is the same as that from Table 661, so it also does not include the self-employed. In the first column, each row has been coded to reflect the assumed assignment to the *LPM* type of industry, with the following codes:

(R1) Agriculture
(R2) Low-Technology Industries (including Information Facilities)
(R3) High-Technology Industries
(R4) Information Hardware and Software Industries
(R5) Information Transaction Industries
(R6) Information Distribution Industries

Table 675

Employment, by Industry: 1970 to 1997

	Industry	1970	1980	1990	1995	1997
	Total employed	78,678	99,303	118,793	124,900	129,558
R1	Agriculture	3,463	3,364	3,223	3,440	3,399
R2	Mining	516	979	724	627	634
R2	Construction	4,818	6,215	7,764	7,668	8,302
	Manufacturing	20,746	21,942	21,346	20,493	20,835
	Transport, Communication	5,320	6,525	8,168	8,709	9,182
	Trade (Retail and Wholesale)	15,008	20,191	24,622	26,071	26,777
R5	Finance, etc	3,945	5,993	8,051	7,983	8,297
	Services 3	20,385	28,752	39,267	43,953	46,393

To these again must be added the data from Table 661 for self-employed, this time for the distribution by type of industry:

	Item	1970	1980	1990	1995	1997
	Total self-employed	7,031	8,642	10,097	10,482	10,513
R1	Agriculture	1,810	1,642	1,378	1,580	1,457
	Nonagriculture	5,221	7,000	8,719	8,902	9,056
R2	Mining	14	28	24	16	14
R2	Construction	687	1,173	1,457	1,460	1,492
	Manufacturing	264	358	427	433	422
	Transportation	196	282	301	396	438
	Trade	1,667	1,899	1,851	1,772	1,761
R5	Finance, etc	254	458	630	660	629
	Services	2,140	2,804	4,030	4,166	4,300

Note, though, that there needs to be a deeper analysis in order to subdivide four of the rows—for Manufacturing, Transportation and Communication, Wholesale and Retail Trade, and Services.

Unfortunately, this is complicated in several respects. First, the time periods for the available data differ from table to table so it is difficult to combine them. Second, there continue to be small be significant anomalies in the data because of unreported subdivisions.

First, let's examine the Manufacturing sector more carefully. The source of data to do so is from Table 1233 of Chapter 26, Manufactures. It provides data for each SIC class for the years 1992 and 1996. For each of those years, it shows employees, payroll, values added, and values shipped. The task is to assign SIC classes to the six *LPM* categories.

Table No. 1233

Manufactures—Summary by Industry: 1992 and 1996 [Data based on various editions of the Standard Industrial Classification (SIC) Manual, published by the Office of Management and Budget; see text, Section 26. nec= Not elsewhere classified]

			1992		1996
Industry	SIC	Number (1,000)	Payroll mil.dol.	Number 1 (1,000)	Total mil. dol.
All manufacturing establishments	(X)	16,949	494,109	18,665.6	645,032
R2 Food and kindred products	20	1,503	36,772	1,516.6	40,380
R2 Tobacco products	21	38	1,524	31.4	1,522
R2 Textile mill products	22	616	12,398	576.4	13,215
R2 Apparel and other textile products	23	985	15,325	864.9	14,920
R2 Lumber and wood products	24	656	13,882	739	17,314

R2	Furniture and fixtures 2	25	471	10,227	515	12,414
R2	Paper and allied products	26	626	20,492	631	22,947
R6	Printing and publishing (distribution)	271–4	724	20271	729	22,588
R2	Printing (commercial)	275–9	769	20865	786	23,586
R3	Chemicals and allied products	28	849	32,502	824	36,331
R3	Petroleum and coal products	29	114	4,967	106	5,238
R2	Rubber and misc plastics products	30	907	23,156	1,018	28,436
R2	Leather and leather products	31	101	1,806	77	1,600
R2	Stone, clay, and glass products	32	469	13,113	520	15,857
R2	Primary metal industries 2	33	662	22,202	687	25,644
R2	Fabricated metal products	34	1,362	38,962	1,483	46,130
R2	Engines and turbines	351	83	3,135	79	3,186
R2	Farm and garden machinery	352	86	2,354	94	2,918
R2	Construction and related machinery	353	176	5,664	205	7,157
R2	Metalworking machinery	354	255	8,571	295	10,985
R3	Special industry machinery	355	162	5,515	192	7,311
R2	General industrial machinery	356	244	7,742	265	9,130
R4	Computer and office equipment	357	251	10,143	259	11,211
R2	Refrigeration and service machinery	358	179	5,264	201	6,493
R2	Industrial machinery, nec	359	304	8,843	392	12,340
R3	Electric distribution equipment	361	68	1,946	74	2,499
R3	Electrical industrial apparatus	362	157	4,387	171	5,373
R2	Household appliances	363	103	2,571	108	3,072
R2	Electric lighting and wiring equipment	364	148	3,974	157	4,617
R4	Household audio and video equipment	365	47	1,123	49	1,333
R4	Communications equipment	366	239	9,111	258	11,522
R4	Electronic components and accessories	367	530	16,752	588	20,830
R2	Misc electrical equipment and supplies	369	147	4,332	151	5,067
R2	Motor vehicles and equipment	371	703	26,213	772	32,867
R3	Aircraft and parts	372	548	22,647	377	18,733
R2	Ship and boat building and repairing	373	163	4,634	141	4,353
R2	Railroad equipment	374	28	900	31	1,141
R2	Motorcycles, bicycles, and parts	375	13	343	18	565
R3	Guided missiles, space vehicles, parts	376	146	6,780	81	4,632
R2	Miscellaneous transportation equipment	379	46	1,218	47	1,241
R4	Instruments and related products	38	907	33,067	821	33,783
R2	Misc manufacturing industries	39	366	8,417	397	10,042
			16,951	494,110	17,327	560,523

Note that, while the totals of the separate entries for 1992 are the same as the reported total (except for a small roundoff error), that for 1996 is over 1300 less than the reported total. There is no evident reason for that difference, since the values shown are exactly as reported in Table 1233.

Second, turning to Retail and Wholesale Trade, Tables 1276 and 1293 provide the relevant data:

No 1276

Retail Trade—Establishments, Employees, and Payroll: 1990 and 1995 [Covers establishments with payroll. Employees are for the week including March 12. Most government employees are excluded. For statement on methodology, see Appendix III

			1990		1995	
			Employees	Payroll	Employees	Payroll
	Kind of Business	SIC	(1,000)	(bil dol)	(1,000)	(bil dol)
	Retail trade, total	(G)	19,815	241.7	21,085	300
R2	Building materials and garden supplies2	52	703	11.9	740	14.5
R2	General merchandise stores 2	53	2,135	22.9	2,291	29.1
R2	Food stores 2	54	3,124	35.8	3,188	41.5
R2	Automotive dealers and service stations 2	55	2,104	40.0	2,190	51.2
R2	Apparel and accessory stores 2	56	1,193	12.2	1,148	12.9
R2	Home furnishings (not including 573)	57	504	8.4	541	10.2
R4	Radio, television, and computer stores 2	573	245	3.9	318	5.5
R2	Eating and drinking places 2	58	6,461	49.6	7,208	64.7
R2	Miscellaneous retail (not including 5942)	59	2,401	32.4	2,500	39.4
R6	Book stores	5,942	86	0.8	111	1.3
R2	Administrative and auxiliary	(X)	860	23.7	850	29.8
			19,816	241.6	21,085	300.1

X Not applicable.
1 Based on 1987 Standard Industrial Classification; see text, Section 13
2 Includes kinds of business not shown separately
3 Includes government employees.
Source: U.S. Bureau of the Census, County Business Patterns, annual.

Note again that there are small roundoff errors:

No. 1293

Wholesale Trade—by Kind of Business: 1987 and 1992
[Based on 1987 Standard Industrial Classification (SIC) code; see text, Section 13]

		1987		1992	
	Kind of Business	Employ	Payroll mil.dol	Employ2	Payroll mil.dol
R2	Wholesale trade	5,596	133,357	5,791	173,272

Third, turning to services, Tables 1296 and 1300 provide the relevant data, but there is a fundamental problem with the data from these tables, which is crucial in the analysis. There are data only for 1992. How do we estimate the distribution of Services in 1996? Simplest would be to take the distribution as that for 1992 but project the amounts as proportional to the totals. The problem is that the data are not consistent with what is reported in Table 672. Specifically, Table 675 shows the following:

Industry	1970	1980	1990	1995	1997
Services 3	20,385	28,752	39,267	43,953	46,393

But the total from Tables 1296 and 1300, for 1992, is only 23,399. For the moment, I will take the values for 1995 as those for 1992 times 1.07. That is, I will estimate the total for 1992 from Table 672 as linear between 1990 and the values in 1995 as proportional to those in 1992:

No. 1296
Service Industries Summary of Taxable Firms: 1992

				Estimated
		1992		1995
	SIC	Employ	Payroll	Employ
Kind of Business	code	(1,000)	(mil.dol.)	(1,000)
Firms subject to Federal income tax 4	(X)	19,290	452,697	20,447
R2 Hotels and other lodging places 4 5	70	1,489	19,633	1,593
R2 Personal services 4	72	1,218	14,379	1,303
R2 Business services (less 731, 732, 737, 7375)	73	43,626	63,217	46,679
R6 Advertising	731	196	7,223	209
R6 Credit Reporting, Collection	732	98	2,163	104
R4 Computer and data process services (less 7375)	737	854	35,598	913
R6 Information retrieval services	7,375	32	1,098	34
R2 Auto repair, services, and parking 4	75	864	15,550	924
R2 Miscellaneous repair services 4	76	428	9,695	457
R6 Amusement and recreation services 4 6	787,984	1,382	25,357	1,478
R3 Health services 4	80	4,453	129,093	4,764
R6 Legal services	81	924	39,328	988
R6 Selected educational services	82,349	133	2,457	142
R2 Social services 4	83	505	5,466	540
R3 Engineering and architectural services 4	871	825	32,745	882
R3 Accounting, auditing, and bookkeeping	872	521	14,001	557
R3 Research and testing services 8	873	282	9,227	301
R3 Management and public relations 4	874	644	23,371	689

NA Not available, X Not applicable
1 Based on 1987 Standard Industrial Classification; see text, Section 13
2 Represents the number of establishments in business at any time during year
3 For pay period including March 12
4 Includes other kinds of business, not shown separately
5 Excludes membership lodging
6 Includes motion pictures and museums
7 Excludes motion picture producers
8 Excludes noncommercial research organizations.

No. 1300

Service Industries—Summary of Tax-Exempt Firms: 1992 [Covers establishments with payroll]

Kind of Business	1987 SIC code 1	Paid employees 3 (1000)	Annual payroll (mil.dol.)
Firms exempt from Federal income tax 4	(X)	8,109	186,672
R2 Nursing and personal care facilities	805	498	7,591
R3 Hospitals	806	4,566	126,202
Hospitals, excluding government	806	3,252	87,062
R2 Social services 4	83	1,407	19,331
Individual and family social services	832	434	6,381
Residential care	836	319	4,830
R6 Business associations	861	102	3,157
Civic, social, and fraternal associations	864	355	3,657
R4 Research and testing services	873	126	4,511

X Not applicable. 1 Based on 1987 Standard Industrial Classification; see text, Section 13.2 Represents the number of establishments in business at any time during year.
3 For pay period including March 12.
4 Includes other kinds of business, not shown separately, Source: U.S. Bureau of the Census, 1992 Census of Service Industries, SC92-A-52 and SC92-N-1.

Financial and related services is a special category that must be separately considered. Table 693 provides the data:

No. 793

Finance, Insurance, and Real Estate Establishments, Employees, and Payroll: 1990 and 1995 [Covers establishments with payroll. Employees are for the week including March 12. Most government employees are excluded. For statement on methodology, see Appendix III]

Kind of business	SIC	Establishment TS (1,000) 1990	1995	Employees (1,000) 1990	1995	Payroll (bil. dol.) 1990	1995
R5 Finance, insurance, real estate	(H)	544.7	628.5	6,957	6,998	197.4	256.2
Depository institutions 2 3	60	81.2	104.7	2,033	2,079	48.4	62.5
Central reserve depositories	601	0.1	0.1	31	25	0.9	1.0
Commercial banks	602	52.3	66.9	1,472	1,532	35.6	45.7
Savings institutions	603	21.7	16.6	417	268	8.8	7.4
Credit unions	606	3.6	15.1	51	158	1.0	3.5
Functions closely related to banking	609	2.8	5.3	44	61	1.4	2.1
Nondepository institutions 2 3	61	42.0	45.4	506	490	14.0	18.4
Federal and fed.-sponsored credit	611	0.6	1.3	14	24	0.4	1.1
Personal credit institutions	614	25.0	17.9	236	161	5.5	5.4

Kind of business	SIC	Establishment TS (1,000)		Employees (1,000)		Payroll (bil. dol.)	
		1990	1995	1990	1995	1990	1995
Business credit institutions	615	3.7	4.8	88	101	3.1	4.4
Mortgage bankers and brokers	616	10.9	20.5	153	202	4.6	7.5
Security and commodity brokers 2	62	25.2	41.0	411	523	26.6	45.5
Security brokers and dealers	621	15.9	24.3	308	382	20.8	34.4
Commodity contracts brokers, dealers	622	1.2	1.5	15	13	0.7	0.7
Security and commodity exchanges	623	0.2	0.1	9	8	0.5	0.4
Security and commodity services	628	7.1	14.8	76	120	4.5	9.9
Insurance carriers 2	63	43.3	41.3	1,407	1,503	41.5	56.6
Life insurance	631	14.1	11.8	572	557	16.3	19.7
Medical service and health insurance 2	632	2.1	3.0	188	271	5.1	9.6
Accident and health insurance	6321	1.1	1.1	48	52	1.3	1.7
Hospital and medical service plans	6324	1.0	1.9	139	219	3.8	8.0
Fire, marine, and casualty insurance	633	18.3	20.8	533	588	17.0	24.2
Surety insurance	635	0.6	0.6	15	11	0.5	0.5
Title insurance	636	3.2	2.5	57	39	1.6	1.4
Pension, health and welfare funds	637	3.8	2.3	25	35	0.6	1.0
Insurance agents, brokers, and service	64	110.8	125.4	712	677	20.3	22.8
Real estate 2	65	217.0	246.1	1,374	1,403	28.5	32.9
Real estate operators and lessors	651	95.7	100.2	509	492	8.7	9.6
Real estate agents and managers	653	72.2	115.4	585	743	13.3	18.8
Title abstract offices	654	3.1	4.8	24	34	0.5	0.9
Subdividers and developers 2	655	19.6	17.6	140	119	3.4	3.2
Subdividers and developers, n.e.c. 4	6552	10.8	10.3	88	69	2.3	2.2
Cemetery subdividers and developers	6553	4.4	6.1	35	46	0.6	0.9
Holding and other investment offices 2	67	22.6	23.2	263	255	10.0	13.8
Holding offices	671	6.2	8.5	124	137	5.4	8.2
Investment offices	672	1.0	0.9	16	23	1.0	1.7
Trusts	673	7.8	5.2	65	35	1.4	1.0
Educational, religious, etc. trusts	6732	3.6	2.5	42	21	0.9	0.6
Miscellaneous investing	679	5.0	7.5	44	50	1.5	2.7
Patent owners and lessors	6794	0.9	1.4	15	16	0.4	0.7
Administrative and auxiliary	(X)	2.6	1.5	251	69	8.2	3.6

X Not applicable. 1 Standard Industrial Classification; see text, Section 13.2
Includes industries not shown separately. 3 Includes government employees. 4
N.e.c.=Not elsewhere classified.
Source: U.S. Bureau of the Census, County Business Patterns, annual.

Turning to Table 531, government employment:

No. 531

All Governments, Employment and Payroll—by Function: 1995 [For October. Covers both full-time and part-time employees. Local government amounts are estimates subject to sampling variation; see Appendix III and source]

	Function	Employees (1,000)					October Payroll	
				State and Local				
		Total	Federal	Total	State	Local	Total	Federal
	Total	19,521	2,895	16,626	4,719	11,906	(NA)	(NA)
R2	National defense 2	831	831	(X)	(X)	(X)	(NA)	(NA)
R5	Postal Service	849	849	(X)	(X)	(X)	(NA)	(NA)
R3	Space research and technology	22	22	(X)	(X)	(X)	(NA)	(NA)
R6	Elem and secondary educ	6,252	(X)	6,252	50	6,202	13,939	(NA)
R7	Higher education	2,414	(X)	2,414	1,954	461	4,591	(NA)
R6	Other education	129	12	117	117	(X)	260	(NA)
R3	Health	544	141	403	166	238	(NA)	(NA)
R3	Hospitals	1,303	174	1,129	522	608	(NA)	(NA)
R2	Public welfare	526	10	516	230	286	(NA)	(NA)
R5	Social insurance administration	167	68	98	98	–	(NA)	(NA)
R2	Police protection	926	86	840	91	749	(NA)	(NA)
R2	Fire protection	360	(X)	360	(X)	360	950	(NA)
R2	Correction	655	28	627	413	213	(NA)	(NA)
R2	Streets & highways	564	4	560	257	303	(NA)	(NA)
R3	Air transportation	86	49	37	3	35	(NA)	(NA)
R2	Water transport/ Terminals	27	15	12	5	7	(NA)	(NA)
R2	Solid waste management	115	(X)	115	2	114	263	(NA)
R2	Sewerage	130	(X)	130	1	128	345	(NA)
R2	Parks & recreation	387	26	361	47	314	(NA)	(NA)
R2	Natural resources	421	210	211	168	43	(NA)	(NA)
R2	Housing & community dev.	151	20	131	(X)	131	(NA)	(NA)
R2	Water supply	165	–	165	1	164	410	(NA)
R2	Electric power	82	–	82	6	76	296	(NA)
R2	Gas supply	11	–	11	(X)	11	28	(NA)
R2	Transit	210	(X)	210	20	190	676	(NA)
R6	Libraries	152	5	147	1	147	(NA)	(NA)
R2	State liquor stores	10	(X)	10	10	(X)	18	(NA)
R5	Financial administration	520	131	388	168	220	(NA)	(NA)

	Function	Employees (1,000)					October Payrol	
				State and Local				
		Total	Federal	Total	State	Local	Total	Federal
R5	Other government administration	436	24	413	53	359	(NA)	(NA)
R6	Judicial and legal	401	53	349	130	219	(NA)	(NA)
R2	Other & Allocable	673	138	535	206	329	(NA)	(NA)

– Represents zero. NA Not available. X Not applicable. 1 Includes employees/outside the United States. 2 Includes international relations.
Source: U.S. Bureau of the Census;
http://www.census.gov/pub/govs/www/apes.html>; (accessed 8 July 1998).

Strangely, Table 1300 for tax-exempt organizations did not include private education. We therefore need to turn to Table 315:

No. 315

Employees in Higher Education Institutions—by Sex and Occupation: 1976 to 1995 [In thousands, as of fall. Based on survey and subject to sampling error; see source]

Years Status	Total	Professional Staff Total	Managerial Male	Managerial Female	Faculty 1 Male	Faculty 1 Female	Assistants Male	Assistants Female	Other Male	Other Female	Nonprof
1976	1,863.8	1,073.1	74.6	26.6	460.6	172.7	106.5	53.6	87.5	91.0	790.7
Full	1,339.9	709.4	72.0	25.0	326.8	107.2	18.6	9.4	76.2	74.1	630.5
Part	523.9	363.7	2.6	1.7	133.7	65.4	87.9	44.2	11.3	16.9	160.2
1991	2,545.2	1,595.5	85.4	59.3	525.6	300.7	119.1	78.6	165.4	261.3	949.8
Full	1,812.9	1,031.8	82.9	56.2	366.2	169.4	(NA)	(NA)	142.2	214.8	781.1
Part	732.3	563.7	2.5	3.1	159.4	131.2	119.1	78.6	23.2	46.4	168.7
1993	2,602.6	1,687.3	82.7	60.9	561.1	354.4	120.4	82.4	166.7	258.6	915.3
Full	1,783.5	1,039.1	80.1	57.7	363.4	182.3	(NA)	(NA)	142.7	212.9	744.4
Part	819.1	648.2	2.7	3.2	197.7	172.1	120.4	82.4	24.0	45.8	170.9
1995	2,662.1	1,744.9	82.1	65.3	562.9	368.8	124.0	91.9	177.2	272.7	917.2
Full	1,801.4	1,066.5	79.2	61.8	360.2	190.7	(NA)	(NA)	151.5	223.2	734.9
Part	860.7	678.4	2.9	3.6	202.7	178.1	124.0	91.9	25.6	49.5	182.3

NA Not available.
1 Instruction and research. Source: U.S. Center for Education Statistics, Fall Staff in Postsecondary Institutions, 1995, March 1998.

The remaining piece that needs to be considered is obtained from Table 912 of Chapter 18.

No. 912
Information Technologies (IT)—Employment and Wages: 1985 to 1996

Industry	SIC code	Employment (1,000)			Annual wages and earnings (dol.)		
		1985	1990	1996	1985	1990	1996
Total private	(X)	80,992	91,098	100,076	18,843	23,209	28,352
Total IT-producing industries	(X)	4,056	4,134	4,638	27,768	36,248	48,488
R4 Hardware	(X)	1,666	1,574	1,550	28,098	37,598	48,494
R4 Software services 3	(X)	558	790	1,228	27,683	38,764	55,760
R4 Communications equipment 3	(X)	514	461	522	23,919	30,195	37,398
R5 Communication services (less 4832,33,41)	48	973	948	924	28,885	35,239	46,136
R6 Radio broadcasting	4,832	113	119	115	18,244	22,088	28,964
R6 Television broadcasting	4,833	115	115	128	30,880	41,726	50,732
R6 Cable & other pay TV services	4,841	118	126	171	21,633	25,994	35,238

Combining these pieces is by no means easy since they are for different time periods. To simplify, I will take values from Retail and Information Technology for 1990 as though they were for 1992 and values from Retail, Education, and Government for 1995 as though they were for 1996. The result is the following table:

	1992		1996	
	Employees	Percentage	Employees	Percentage
Agriculture	4,500	0.03	4,601	0.03
Low Technology	87,520	0.65	99,144	0.65
High Technology	15,115	0.11	15,861	0.11
Information Transactions	9,655	0.07	9,894	0.07
Information Hardware	6,024	0.04	6,641	0.04
Information Distribution	10,617	0.08	11,255	0.08
Higher Education	2,580	0.02	2,662	0.02
	135,631	1.00	149,811	1.00

The totals from Tables 675 and 661 are estimated to be 134,127 for 1992 and 137,726 for 1996, so there seems to be some double counting, at least in 1996. However, the percentages are quite consistent (which is not a surprise given that some values needed to be estimated and were made proportional), so, for the moment, they will be used as shown:

	1992	1995
Agriculture	0.03	0.03
Low Technology	0.65	0.65
High Technology	0.11	0.11
Information Transactions	0.07	0.07
Information Hardware	0.04	0.04
Information Distribution	0.08	0.08
Higher Education	0.02	0.02
Total	1.00	1.00

Index

269

Library and Information Science

(Continued from page ii)

Lois Swan Jones and Sarah Scott Gibson
Art Libraries and Information Services

Nancy Jones Pruett
Scientific and Technical Libraries: Functions and Management
Volume 1 and Volume 2

Peter Judge and Brenda Gerrie
Small Bibliographic Databases

Dorothy B. Lilley and Ronald W. Trice
A History of Information Sciences 1945–1985

Elaine Svenonius
The Conceptual Foundations of Descriptive Cataloging

Robert M. Losee, Jr.
The Science of Information: Measurement and Applications

Irene P. Godden
Library Technical Services: Operations and Management, Second
Edition

Donald H. Kraft and Bert R. Boyce
Operations Research for Libraries and Information Agencies:
Techniques for the Evaluation of Management Decision Alternatives

James Cabeceiras
The Multimedia Library: Materials Selection and Use, Second Edition

Charles T. Meadow
Text Information Retrieval Systems, First Edition

Robert M. Losee, Jr., and Karen A. Worley
Research and Evaluation for Information Professionals

Carmel Maguire, Edward J. Kazlauskas, and Anthony D. Weir
Information Services for Innovative Organizations

Karen Markey Drabenstott and Diane Vizine-Goetz
Using Subject Headings for Online Retrieval

277

278

DATE DUE
